Bible Study Sourcebook

Bible Study Sourcebook
Old Testament

Edited by Robert C. Walton

John Knox Press
ATLANTA

Library of Congress Cataloging in Publication Data
Main entry under title:

Bible study sourcebook.

    First published in Britain in 1970 as parts 1, 3,
and 4 of A source book of the Bible for teachers.
    CONTENTS: v. 1. Old Testament.—v. 2. New Testament.
ment.
    Bibliography: p.
    Includes index.
    1.   Bible—Study—Addresses, essays, lectures.
2.   Bible—Introductions—Addresses, essays, lectures.
I.   Walton, Robert Clifford.
BS600.2.S652   1981   220′.07   80-26358
ISBN 0-8042-0008-4 (v. 1)
ISBN 0-8042-0009-2 (v. 2)

10 9 8 7 6 5 4 3 2 1
First published in Britain in 1970 as Parts One and Three of *A Source Book of
the Bible for Teachers;* first published in this edition in 1980.
Published in the United States of America in 1981
by John Knox Press
Atlanta, Georgia 30365
Printed in the United States of America

CONTENTS

Introduction   11

Illustrations   12

1   What is the Bible ?   *Robert C. Walton*   13
    The arrangement of the Bible   15
    The truth of the Bible   15

2   The Biblical Scholar and his Tools   *John Bowden*   17
    The beginnings of modern biblical scholarship   18
    What is 'criticism' ?   18
    Asking the right questions   19
    Can we trust the text that we read ?   20
      1.   The New Testament   20
        (i) Manuscripts   20
        (ii) Making a decision   21
      2.   The Old Testament   22
        (i) The Massoretic text   22
        (ii) Other texts   22
    Who wrote the books?   22
      1.   External evidence   22
      2.   Internal evidence   23
    How were the books written ?   24
    Before writing   25
      1.   The Old Testament   25
      2.   The New Testament   26
    Archaeology and the world of the Bible   26
    Technological tools   27
    Assured results ?   27

3   The Land and the People   *J.R. Bartlett*   29
    Geology   30
    Geography   31
      1.   Mesopotamia   31
      2.   The Levant   32

	Climate	36
	Near Eastern ways of life	37
1.	Nomadic	37
2.	Agricultural	37
3.	Urban	38

4 How Israel Became a Nation *Ernest Nicholson*   41

	The origins of the Pentateuch	42
	The salvation-history in the Pentateuchal documents	46
1.	The 'J' document	46
2.	The 'E' document	49
3.	The 'D' document	51
4.	The 'P' document	54
	The historicity of the Pentateuch tradition	56

5 In the Beginning *Robert Davidson*   59

	The background	60
	The nature of the material	60
	Content and meaning	61
1.	The hymn of creation	61
2.	The enigma of man	62
3.	Cain and Abel	63
4.	The descendants of Cain	64
5.	The beginning of the worship of Yahweh	64
6.	The first Priestly genealogy	64
7.	The prologue to the flood story	64
8.	The flood	64
9.	The covenant with Noah	65
10.	The family of Noah	65
11.	The table of the nations	66
12.	The tower of Babel	66
13.	The genealogy of the sons of Shem	66

6 The Patriarchs *Robert Davidson*   67

	The historical question	68
	The character of the traditions	69
	The theology of the narratives	71
1.	Call or election	71
2.	Promise	71
3.	Covenant	72
4.	The presence of God	73

7   Moses   *Robert Davidson*   **75**

The historical problem	76
Extra-biblical evidence	77
The significance of Moses	78
1. The revelation of the character and name of God	78
2. The exodus	79
3. The covenant	81
4. The Decalogue	82
The legacy of Moses	84

8   Joshua and the Judges   *J. R. Porter*   **85**

The evidence	86
1. Biblical material	86
2. Archaeological evidence	86
A reconstruction of events	86
Canaanite religion	87
A gradual conquest	88
Judges and the Deuteronomic history	90
The people of Israel	91
The tribal league	92
The central sanctuary and the ark of the covenant	93
The holy war	94

9   The United Monarchy   *R. N. Whybray*   **95**

The evidence	96
1. Biblical sources	96
2. Archaeological evidence	96
Becoming a nation	96
Saul: the first king	97
Saul and David	98
The reign of David	99
Jerusalem: capital of the kingdom	100
The organization of the state	101
The accession of Solomon	102

10   The Divided Kingdoms   *R. N. Whybray*   **105**

The evidence	106
1. Biblical sources	106
2. Archaeological evidence	106
The revolt of the northern tribes	106

The threat from Assyria   108
The end of Israel   111
The kingdom of Judah   112
The threat of Babylon   113

11 Prophecy in Israel   *R. E. Clements*   115
The nature of early prophecy   116
The nature of developed prophecy   118
   1. Amos   118
   2. Hosea   120
   3. Isaiah   123
   4. Micah   126
   5. Jeremiah   127
The prophetic interpretation of history   130

12 Worship in Israel   *J. H. Eaton*   133
Places of worship   134
Seasons of worship   136
Leaders of worship   139
Sacrifices in worship   140
Glimpses of worship   141
The psalms   144
   1. The journey to the festival 145
   2. Acts of penitence and purification 146
   3. The resanctification of the temple 147
   4. God's battle   148
   5. God's procession of victory 149
   6. The proclamation of God's kingship 150
   7. The speech of God   151
   8. The new year of growth   151
   9. God confirms the dynasty of David 152
Epilogue   154

13 Wisdom in Israel   *William McKane*   155
Wisdom in Israel and the ancient Near East   156
Statesmen versus prophets   158
The book of Proverbs   158
   1. The character of wisdom   159
   2. Proverbial maxims   160
The book of Job   161

1.	The speeches of Elihu		162
2.	The three friends		162
3.	The majesty of God		163
4.	Is God just ?		163
	The book of Ecclesiastes		165
	'Vanity of vanities?		166
	Job and Ecclesiastes		169

14 The Exile   *Henry McKeating*   171

The evidence		172
1. Biblical references		172
2. Archaeological evidence		172
Why this period is important		173
The Neo-Babylonians		173
The life and thought of the Jews		174
1. In Babylon		174
2. In Egypt		175
3. In Palestine		175
The coming of the Persians and the Babylonian defeat		176
Developments in prophecy		177
1. Ezekiel		177
2. Deutero-Isaiah		180
3. Obadiah		183

15 The Return   *Henry McKeating*   185

The evidence		186
1. Biblical references		186
2. Non-biblical literature		186
3. Archaeological evidence		187
The Persian achievement		187
Persian religion		188
The rebuilding of the temple		188
The work of Ezra and Nehemiah		190
Judaism in the post-exilic age		192
The literature		193
1. The final shaping of the Pentateuch		193
2. The book of Ruth		193
3. The work of the Chronicler		194
4. The Song of Songs		195
5. Trito-Isaiah		195

6. The book of Joel 195
7. The book of Jonah 196
8. Haggai and Zechariah 1–8 196
9. The book of Malachi 197

16 The Seleucids and the Maccabees *J. R. Bartlett* 199
   The evidence 200
     1. Biblical references 200
     2. Extra-biblical references 200
   The coming of the Seleucid rulers 200
   The Greek way of life: 'Hellenization' 200
   Jewish resistance to Hellenization 203
   Independence 204
   The literature 205
     1. The book of Daniel 205
     2. The Apocrypha 207

For Further Reading 209

Index of Biblical References 211

INTRODUCTION

Straightforward, matter-of-fact information about the Bible is not always easy to come by. On closer inspection, books with promising titles often prove too superficial or too complex, presuppose specialist knowledge or engage in special pleading.

This *Basic Introduction to the Old Testament*, and its companion volume on the New Testament, set out to present enough information to make the reader feel at home in the way modern scholars understand the Bible and to provide a basis for exploring the results of their work further without losing sight of the main contours of the landscape. After short discussions of the nature of the Bible and the way in which modern scholars approach it, a series of articles sets the scene for the emergence of the people Israel and outlines the main developments in its history and religion; there are also outline accounts of the main books of the Old Testament and detailed discussions of some of the most important passages in them. A list of books for further reading gives some guidance as to where more detailed information can be found.

The articles were originally commissioned for *A Source Book of the Bible for Teachers*, first published by SCM Press in 1970 and still available. Because the *Source Book* contains a good deal of material relevant only to teachers it seemed worth while to reissue separately the sections specifically on the Bible so that they could be used by students (who will find these books particularly useful in studying or revising for examinations), clergy and any other interested readers.

ILLUSTRATIONS

Page

13   The computer-set Bible. *(The Bible Society)*

17   Detail from a page of the Codex Babylonicus.

29   The Negev desert. *(Aerofilms Ltd)*

40-41 Symbols of the twelve tribes of Israel.

59   A reconstruction of the Ziggurat at Ur. *(Reproduced by Courtesy of the Trustees of the British Museum)*

67   Tomb painting from Beni-Hassan.

75   Jebel Mûsa, often identified with Mount Sinai. *(Matson Photo Service, Los Angeles)*

85   Excavation at Jericho. *(J. Allan Cash Ltd)*

95   The Blind Harper. *(Rijksmuseum von Oudheden, Leiden, Holland)*

105   Detail of an Assyrian relief in the palace of Ashurbanapal at Nineveh. *(Reproduced by Courtesy of the Trustees of the British Museum)*

115   Isaiah and Daniel. Sculptures by Claus Sluter in the Charterhouse of Champmol, Dijon. *(Jean Roubier)*

133   The Howland Garber Reconstruction of Solomon's Temple. *(Available through South-eastern Films, 22 7th St. N.E., Atlanta, Georgia 30308)*

155   An Egyptian scribe. *(Rijksmuseum von Oudheden, Leiden, Holland)*

171   Babylonian wall decoration. *(The Mansell Collection)*

184-5 The Cyrus Cylinder, which describes Cyrus' liberal policy over worship. *(Reproduced by Courtesy of the Trustees of the British Museum)*

198-9 The fortress of Masada. *(Ronald Sheridan Ltd)*

1 What is the Bible?

'The book of books, the storehouse and magazine of life and comfort, the holy scriptures.' This is George Herbert's answer to the question which is the title of this article. He was a seventeenth-century parson and poet, a man of deep and sensitive faith, a Christian of mature understanding. Such an answer, however, is not enough for the twentieth-century. In a secular age, to say that the Bible is 'the word of God' or that it enshrines 'divine revelation' is to use phrases which have lost their meaning. They are vague and imprecise and belong to a different world from that of a present-day audience.

What, then, is the Bible? It is not, from a literary point of view, a book, though it is normally bound between two covers, often of funereal black. Between these covers are two Testaments, the Old and the New. The Old Testament is a selection of the literature of the Israelite people over a thousand years of their history, roughly comparable to the English literature which has survived from the Anglo-Saxon Chronicle to the writings of Sir Winston Churchill. The comparison is, of course, inexact. There is a far greater volume of English literature, partly because the English suffered no foreign invasion since the Norman Conquest; still more, because since the fifteenth century books have been printed, not inscribed by hand. The New Testament is a selection of the literature of a new religion – Christianity – in the first hundred years of its existence. These selections are to some extent arbitrary, depending partly upon what chanced to escape destruction, but also upon the needs of the communities which preserved the writings. There was the wastage of the years but also deliberate acceptance and rejection.

This literature is not all 'religious' in the narrow sense of that word. In the Old Testament there are tales of long ago which, like the Norse sagas or the story of King Arthur and the Knights of the Round Table, tell of the nation's origins and reveal the inward, intuitive interpretation which the people of Israel put upon the realities of their national life. There are many historical narratives, and like any shelf of history books these vary both in accuracy and in literary quality. There are codes of law; reporting of events which today we should call 'current affairs'; protests against social injustice; poetry and songs both sacred and secular and a special kind of literature which has preserved the spoken and written message of the prophets. The New Testament begins with four brief records of the life of Jesus and the first three of these – the Gospels of Mark, Matthew and Luke – are linked together in a particular literary relationship. Some events in the early history of the Christian church are recorded in the Acts of the Apostles, and there is a selection of letters written by Paul of Tarsus and by others to warn, encourage and instruct individuals or the members of young churches, in places like Corinth, Ephesus, Philippi or Rome.

In the varied literature of the Old Testament we can read about the fluctuating fortunes of the people of Israel. They began as nomadic tribesmen, some of whom had escaped from slavery in Egypt, who slowly infiltrated into the land of Canaan until at last they possessed it. Then they changed their way of life, ceasing to be 'wandering Arameans' and settling down in fortified villages and walled towns. About 1000 BC they were welded into a single nation by a remarkable king named David, under whose leadership, and that of his son Solomon, Israel became an empire with influence and prestige in Middle-East politics. After Solomon's death the nation split into two separate kingdoms; Israel in the north and Judah in the south. The dreams of empire and world power declined and both nations were overwhelmed by more powerful neighbours. When the Old Testament ends and the New Testament begins, Israel is an unimportant outpost of the Roman empire. The ministry of Jesus was exercised, the Christian church took root, in a world dominated by Roman power.

The arrangement of the Bible

By modern standards, the books of the Bible are arranged in a most arbitrary and confusing way. The thirty-nine books of the Old Testament are not printed in the order in which they were written, which would enable us to trace more easily the development of Israelite thought and experience. Moreover, many of the books consist of different strands of writing by different authors which, at a later stage, have been woven together by an editor. Two examples may be given. The book of Genesis, which is printed first in the Bible, consists of at least three separate strands of writing by different authors which, at a later time, were amalgamated by someone else. The earliest of these strands was probably written down about the time of David (c.1000 BC), though it tells of events which belong to a much earlier period. Another strand of tradition was later woven in with this, and Genesis was finally edited in its present form by members of the priestly class round about 400 BC.

The second example is the book of Isaiah. It consists of three separate collections of writings. Chapters 1–39 refer mostly to events which occurred in the lifetime of the prophet Isaiah (c.740–701 BC), though there are insertions of a later date. Chapters 40–55 consist of prophecies by an unknown author living towards the end of the exile (c.542–538 BC), while chapters 55–66 contain oracles by unknown men living in Palestine about 450 BC.

The truth of the Bible

The Bible is more than 'a slab of ancient history in archaic language'. It contains many different kinds of truth. It is, in part, a source book for the history and social life of Israel, and without this information the nation's religion cannot be understood. It reflects the nation's way of life, reveals its developing standards and values, and bears witness to the head waters which nourished and sustained its soul. It is also the record of the spiritual wrestlings, questionings and affirmations of a deeply religious people, and traces their progress and their decline in thought and action towards a deeper understanding of God's purpose. It contains, in the New Testament, documents which preserve in rather fragmentary form recollections of the life and ministry, the death and resurrection of Jesus of Nazareth, interpretations of those events, and information about the early formative years of the Christian church.

At first sight it may seem that there is little of

religious value in narratives which tell of kings crowned and buried or deposed and assassinated, and of armies defending frontiers or extending a nation's territory by conquest; little to stimulate man's spiritual quest in the enunciation of laws which one finds in the books of Exodus and Deuteronomy; little to help a man to worship in the often unbridled denunciations of the prophets. Let us be honest and admit that there is nickel among the gold. Yet – and it is this which makes the Bible relevant in every age and gives it unity – all these activities by which a nation lives are declared to be the direct concern of God. When a historian or chronicler records victory or defeat in battle, he sees behind the event the overruling purposes of God. When a lawyer codifies a set of laws, and includes one about safety precautions for houses with flat roofs (Deut.22.8), he is writing down 'the commandments, the statutes and the judgments of the Lord'. When a prophet denounces greed and exploitation he prefaces his stern warning with the phrase, 'Thus saith the Lord', and when he speaks of people abiding 'in a peaceful habitation, in secure dwellings and in quiet resting places' (Isa.32.18), he is transmitting to sorely battered men and women a promise of God. This unity is the reason why the biblical library may properly be bound up as one book. Every part of this corpus of literature, whether poetry, law, or prophecy; whether recollections of the deeds and words of Jesus, or letters to young churches, speaks of the will of God, the acts of God, the purpose of God.

ROBERT C. WALTON

2 The Biblical Scholar and his Tools

What is the Bible? The previous section compared a seventeenth-century answer with one which might be given today. But for the same contrast, we might choose a period even nearer home. In the Bible, 'every scientific statement is infallibly accurate, all its history and narrations of every kind are without any inaccuracy'. That verdict comes from mid-Victorian England, from a popular manual much used by potential clergy, at a time when the church had a virtual monopoly on education. Doubts might be stirring, particularly as science began to raise serious problems, but a similar view was shared by the vast majority of Christians. To challenge it publicly in England was to invite personal abuse, dismissal, even legal action. *Essays and Reviews*, a collection of essays by Oxford scholars, was condemned after a petition signed by 11,000 clergy and over 150,000 laity, when its most provocative essay merely urged that the Bible should be approached like any other book.

The change to a more modest assessment of the Bible has happened in just over a century, not a long time alongside its whole history. It came about because questions were asked quite unlike any others in the past. These questions were prompted by a revolution which has affected not only the Bible, but the entire modern world.

The beginnings of modern biblical scholarship

At the end of the eighteenth century, an old world was showing signs of strain. A political and social revolution was under way, and with it came another in the realm of ideas, with new philosophical questioning and the slow development of the scientific method. Its consequence was that nothing was accepted any more simply because it was old, honoured, accepted; it all had to be tested, for the new principle was 'begin from doubt and build up knowledge on well-established foundations'. Even the Bible was not exempt.

The traditional claim was that the Bible was the word of God. The question now was: if that is so, how is it so? Is the Bible really different from other books? Is it true? Is it an accurate record? The only way to find out was to look and see, and so modern scholarship began. The chief questioners were not outsiders, but were themselves Christians, who did not hesitate to apply the strictest tests to their beliefs. This is not always recognized, but it is a tribute to the integrity of the first pioneers.

What is 'criticism'?

Professional study of the Bible by scholars is usually called 'criticism'. What is meant by the word, however, is not always clear, and it can give a misleading impression, because it has two different senses. In everyday talk, we use 'criticism' in an unfavourable sense, to mean passing a negative judgment on, finding fault with. But 'criticism' also has a more specialist sense, as when we talk about artistic, literary or musical criticism. Here the word describes a method of interpretation which draws out the qualities of a work in a systematic way, and it need have no unfavourable overtones. After all, critics often write good reviews.

Now, because of the way in which biblical criticism had to begin, challenging accepted and often dearly cherished views, and because of the sometimes unwelcome conclusions that it had to come to, it was taken very much as criticism in the unfavourable sense, and this association still clings to it. But the aim and ideal of scholarly investigation is criticism in the second sense: a systematic attempt at *understanding*, by examining and explaining the form, content and background of the Bible in the light of all available and relevant knowledge.

If he is going to understand, the critic needs to ask the right questions, those that will help him to express his subject in an undistorted way. With the Bible, finding the right questions was not easy at first, and there were some false starts before the proper approach was found.

Asking the right questions

As we saw, the first kind of question to appear concerned the Bible as authoritative and holy Scripture: 'Is this true ?', 'Did that happen ?', 'Is there a possible explanation for this ?' There were great arguments about whether Genesis could be reconciled with science or whether the Israelites could have crossed the Red Sea with dry feet, or whether Moses could have written the books which bear his name, or whether Jesus could have turned water into wine. Each of these questions was discussed as though the whole fate of the Bible depended on the answer.

At the same time, however, such discussions came in the way of seeing what the Bible might be if it were allowed to speak for itself. They showed too much eagerness to make the Bible measure up to a particular set of standards. They tended to involve only a few incidents in the Bible at the expense of the rest. They were often about a principle rather than what the Bible actually contained. Above all, they ignored one all-important fact: the writers of the books of the Bible were different from us in many ways. Their world was different, their way of thinking was different, the questions they asked were different. Another approach was needed.

As they gained experience, scholars learnt to match their own questioning to that of the *world* they were investigating. They learnt that they had to do more than look at a book by itself; they had to recreate its world. It might be Palestine in the tenth century BC or Babylon in the sixth or Corinth in the first century AD; only when there was better knowledge of how people in these places and times lived and thought and spoke would the relevant parts of the Bible take their place in the new picture.

A useful illustration of this development has been given by Dr Leonard Hodgson; he comments that:

modern zoology began when, instead of relying on Aristotelian and heraldic representations of animals in traditional bestiaries, men based their research on the observation of the actual nature and behaviour of living creatures . . . As a result of this last century's biblical studies, we are at a similar turning point in the history of Christian theology . . . A hundred years ago our forefathers looked to the Bible in the same way that mediaeval zoologists looked to Aristotle and heraldic bestiaries. To their successors' substituting of observation of actual animals corresponds our attention to the historical provenance of the biblical writings.

This meant cultivating a historical sense. That, too, has been developed only over the last century. But now it affects almost any arts subject, from music to languages, and even some of the sciences. We begin to understand a thing by looking at its origins and discovering how it came to be so.

Biblical criticism had been in progress some time before this point became clear. And in any case, it was originally in no position to reconstruct past worlds. It did not have sufficient material to do so. But this does not mean that useful and lasting work could not be done on more limited, though still important matters. Even before archaeology made its impressive contribution towards understanding the Bible, a great deal was learnt about the text of the Old and New Testaments and the literary character of the various books.

Can we trust the text that we read ?

Editions of the Bible can be bought today in many languages; the Bible is probably the easiest book in the world to get. But there is a gap of more than 1800 years between the time when its last book was finished and the present. What has happened to the Bible down the ages ? How can we be sure that what we read now corresponds to what was originally written ? Printing by movable type was only invented in the fifteenth century; for a thousand and more years before that manuscripts had to be laboriously copied by hand, either through one scribe making a single copy from a manuscript in front of him, or through a scriptorium, where a lector dictated a manuscript to a small group. Ancient manuscripts were written with no space between words and with abbreviations for many common words; unintentional mistakes must have been easy. In addition, manuscripts must often have been altered deliberately, perhaps by scribes who thought that they were correcting mistakes (and whose insight was not always as good as their intentions).

The task of reaching a text as close as possible to the original and of explaining how this text was handed down is known as *textual criticism*. It is a highly complicated business and applies not only to the Bible but also to any ancient manuscript.

1. *The New Testament*

To see how strong the textual evidence for the New Testament is, it is only necessary to compare it with what the classical textual critic often has to work on. The 'bible' of the ancient Greeks, Homer's *Iliad*, is preserved in about 650 manuscripts of various kinds; the best-attested Greek tragedian, Euripides, in about 330; at the other end of the scale, the first six books of the *Annals* of Tacitus, the late first-century Roman historian, survive in only one manuscript, dating from the ninth century. On the other hand, there are over 5000 extant manuscripts of the New Testament, though many of these contain only part of it, and their age varies.

(i) *Manuscripts*

(a) *Dating*. Dating manuscripts is done by examining closely the context in which they were found, their format, the material used and the style of writing. The palaeographer, as the specialist in this kind of work is called, develops a 'feel' for dating, in the same way as the expert in antiques, but he has one independent test to help him. This is a scientific test known as the Carbon 14 process (for more details, see below). When classified, manuscripts are assigned a letter or number for easy reference.

(b) *Papyri.* The earliest text of any passage from the New Testament that we have is a papyrus fragment from the Fourth Gospel, probably dating from early in the second century. This fragment contains only a few verses, but there are more extensive papyri, covering the greater part of the New Testament, from the third century to the seventh. These are about eighty in number.

(c) *Uncials.* Parchment manuscripts are much more numerous, because they are more durable. Pride of place among them goes to the great 'uncial' manuscripts dating from the fourth century to about the tenth. They are named after the type of letters in which they are written, rather like our capitals. The two most famous of these, Codex Vaticanus and Codex Sinaiticus, only became available for detailed study in the late nineteenth century, in quite dramatic circumstances. Originally they contained all the Old Testament as well. There are 250 uncial manuscripts now extant.

(d) *Minuscules.* In the ninth century, a new style of writing was invented, of smaller letters in a running (cursive) hand, which enabled books to be written more quickly and more cheaply. This writing is called 'minuscule'. From this time onwards we have a wealth of material: over 2500 manuscripts in all.

(e) *Other sources.* In addition, there are almost 2000 Greek New Testament lectionaries, selections to be read on particular days of the year. Translations of the New Testament made at an early date into Syriac, Coptic, Latin, Georgian, Armenian, Gothic, Ethiopic and Old Slavonic can be used for comparison. Finally, there are New Testament quotations in the writings of Christian theologians from the second century onwards which indicate something of the text they knew.

In view of the complex variety of evidence which goes back almost to the beginning, it is unlikely that any large-scale interference with the text has gone undetected. But the complicated manuscript tradition has produced a mass of minor variants which need to be resolved. Furthermore, there may have been slight changes between the time of the originals and the dates of the earliest manuscripts we possess.

(ii) *Making a decision*

It has been said that 'to teach another how to become a textual critic is like teaching another how to become a poet'. A full account is impossible, but here are some indications of how decisions are made.

First, manuscripts can be organized into groups or 'families', i.e., the critic can see which manuscript was copied from which. This becomes evident if, for example, an obvious error occurs at the same point in the text of two different manuscripts. Assuming that each was copied from only one manuscript, a common descent can be assumed. (The process is similar to that used in detecting forms of cheating in schools!) Later manuscripts in families, great-great-grandchildren and the like, can often be disregarded completely. This clears the air.

After this classification, further decisions are still necessary. Mistakes are possible in the best manuscripts, and generally inferior ones sometimes preserve the truth. So decisions have to be made on individual readings, drawing on past experience of possible causes of error, and knowledge of the author and subject-matter of the writing in question. Two obvious examples are:

(a) The more difficult reading is to be preferred. The tendency among scribes was to make a text more understandable, and unless an obvious error has been made, the reading which is harder to make sense of is usually more likely to be original.

(b) Assimilation. Where, as in the first three Gospels, passages are similar, the scribe might alter, e.g., a less familiar wording in Luke to one he knew well from Matthew. Here the divergent reading is more likely to be original.

In this way, grounds for a decision are gradually built up. Time has given rise to a large and sophisticated literature about textual criticism which takes experts years to master; but it has also brought us to a position when we can be more certain about the text of the New Testament we use than ever before.

2. The Old Testament

The Old Testament can be discussed much more briefly, as the basic principles are the same. Language, background and manuscript tradition, though, are different.

(i) *The Massoretic text.* When a move towards the purification and consolidation of Judaism began at the end of the first century AD, attempts were made to obtain a normative text of the Hebrew Old Testament. The scholars responsible for this work took great care in transmitting their chosen text, which was accompanied by a commentary (*Massorah*). The commentary was first oral and then written in the margins; it contained statistical details about the text and notes for interpretation. These scholars were called Massoretes, and so the standard text of the Hebrew Old Testament is known as the Massoretic text. Uniformity was not complete, as there were differences over principles between rival groups of Massoretes, but basically their work was most successful, as unexpected evidence shows.

(ii) *Other texts.* Before the rise of the Massoretic text a variety of text-forms existed, some of which have only recently come to light. Scrolls were discovered, not only at Qumran but also in a *genizah* (a storehouse for manuscripts no longer usable in worship, which were considered too sacred to be thrown away) in Cairo. Between them they may take us back as far as the second century BC. Together with ancient translations like the Greek version (Septuagint), the Samaritan version of the Law and the Syriac version (Peshitta), they show forms of the texts prior to the Massoretic process of standardization. But interesting as this new evidence is, it does not compel any far-reaching new conclusions about the reliability of the Old Testament text.

Who wrote the books ?

Having established that he has a reasonably accurate text to work from, the critic's next concern is with the origin and background of the books of the Bible. Who wrote them, where and when? He has two ways of answering his questions. First he can see what information has been handed down about authorship and circumstances by earlier authors: this is known as *external evidence*. Secondly, he can examine the books carefully and see what their content suggests: this is known as *internal evidence*. Unfortunately the two often disagree.

1. External evidence

Numerous remarks about authorship, etc.,

can be found in Jewish and Christian commentators. They vary from the plausible (that the Gospel of Mark was written by John Mark and contains reminiscences of the apostle Peter) to the implausible (that the text of the 'Five Books of Moses' was dictated by Ezra, through inspiration, when they had been lost at the Fall of Jerusalem). Often apparent fact and apparent fancy are combined, as when, for example, at one moment the second-century theologian Irenaeus remarks that Luke was a follower of Paul and wrote down the gospel he preached, and at the next that there must be no more and no less than four Gospels because there are four zones of the world, four winds, and four faces to the cherubim.

In particular, we have to remember the temptation there was to embellish claims about the Bible to show what a marvellous book it was, and the pressure in the case of the New Testament to demonstrate that a book was written by, or had connections with, an apostle, to qualify it for inclusion in the church's official collection (canon). If all this sounds dangerously near to forgery, we must remember the historical background; ancient literary conventions were rather different from ours.

In any case, the ancients were often quite in the dark about the origin of books which after all were not first written to be Holy Scripture. Sometimes they seem to have made their own guesses from internal evidence. In that case their external evidence is internal evidence in disguise. (Irenaeus seems to have come to his conclusion about Luke and Acts on internal evidence.) Because of this, the critic approaches external evidence suspiciously; he checks each argument carefully, and because he has better facilities for investigation than the ancients, he usually prefers to trust what he can discover from a book itself.

2. *Internal evidence*

As he studies some of the biblical books, the critic may begin to doubt what tradition says about them. The 'Five Books of Moses' do not in fact seem to have come from him. Not only do they record his death, but they contain material apparently from a much later time. The German scholar Wellhausen described how difficult it was to read the 'historical books' of the Old Testament on the assumption that, say, Saul and David knew Leviticus; everything fell into place when he tried the theory that the Law, rather than coming from Moses, belongs to a period later than that of I Samuel–II Kings. His approach is typical of the modern scholar: he tries to construct the kind of sequence which fits the known facts and shows how one thing grows out of another.

Some conclusions from internal evidence are:

(a) Careful reading of the book attributed to Isaiah shows that it seems to come from three different periods spread over more than two hundred years. Of course, there are loose ends, but the assignment of material to two writers in addition to Isaiah makes better sense.

(b) All the letters attributed to Paul do not come from his hand. The headings of the Authorized Version assign him fourteen letters, but some are problematical. The Epistle to the Hebrews has a very different style and subject-matter from the rest (and even the external evidence is doubtful). The Epistles to Timothy and Titus also suggest a different historical setting, later than Paul's time. These are therefore usually attributed to other authors. Over Ephesians, Colossians and II Thessalonians the debate is fiercer. Some claim that these were written by disciples or imitators of Paul, others that Paul himself wrote them. Here, however, the differences are less important precisely because they are slighter; a decision either way makes little difference to our reconstruction of first-century Christianity.

Usually, however, dating and finding an appropriate background are vitally important. The way in which the biblical literature is arranged will make all the difference to our picture of the world of the Bible. And as we saw earlier, this is the critic's final aim.

How were the books written ?

When he has reached the probable circumstances in which a book was written, the critic tries to go further back, for it is only rarely that an author wrote as it were 'out of his head'. This happens, for example, with some of the letters of Paul, but even they refer to or draw on other material. I Corinthians is a reply to an earlier letter written to Paul from Corinth, and before that came a still earlier letter from him which is now lost. Clearly I Corinthians will mean much more if something of the file of earlier correspondence can be reconstructed. Other biblical books incorporate chunks of earlier material. Where this happens is not always easy to detect; just as the ancient world had different conventions about authorship, so too it had different conventions about quotation. Borrowings were not documented and acknowledged in footnotes as they are today; in fact, imitation was thought to be a form of flattery.

One vivid illustration of this comes from the book of Proverbs. When a document from ancient Egypt, the *Sayings of Amenemopet*, came to light in 1922, it became clear that this was the source for several chapters of Proverbs, which reproduced it almost word for word.

Investigating the sources on which authors drew is one way of finding out more about their works. The process is known as *source criticism*.

Source criticism is easier in some places than in others. As soon as the first three Gospels are set out in parallel columns it is plain that they are in some way related. Exactly what this relationship is may be more difficult to define, but the material for a solution which explains which Gospel came first and how the others made use of it is there to hand. Similarly, I and II Chronicles draws on much of I Samuel–II Kings; what the Chronicler leaves out of the latter can be seen by a careful comparison and sheds much light on his views. In these instances, as with Proverbs and *Amenemopet*, both the 'source' and the book in which it is used still survive.

Where a book uses sources without too much alteration, it is possible to detect them even if they do not survive in their original form. In the first five books of the Bible, the Pentateuch, for example, an analysis of style and vocabulary makes it possible to detect different strands of material, each of which can be followed for some length. Within the prophetic books, it is often possible to distinguish sayings which go back to the prophet himself from the comments and additions made at later times, and even to see alternative ways in which his prophecies were first combined.

The difficulty arises when the final book is a more polished literary work in which earlier sources have been worked over and given a new form. Did the evangelist John know the Synoptic Gospels, or only a form of the tradition on which they also drew ? Did he make use of other sources ? It is very hard to tell. What sources did the author of Acts have ? There must have been some, but his style is so good and his literary skill so great that discovering the material on which he drew is about as easy as returning a well-baked cake to its original ingredients !

Source criticism can penetrate behind a book to an earlier stage. But its aim is not just to get back as far as possible. It seeks to illuminate the whole process of the literary composition of a book: the middle and end as well as the beginning. Later material added to the original can tell us much, say, about the way in which the prophets were regarded by their followers, just as insertions discovered by textual critics can tell us a bit about what earlier generations thought as they read the Bible. Here, too, is one way of discovering the personality of a writer, as well as the tradition on which he drew.

Before writing

Source criticism is essentially a literary process. It deals with the relationship of one document to another. But there are more ways of handing on tradition than by writing it down. Literature is usually preceded and accompanied by an oral stage in which stories, poems, hymns, proverbs, even laws, are passed on by word of mouth. Even modern civilization has its oral tradition, e.g., anecdotes and sayings, which only occasionally find their way into writing. Biblical literature begins from an oral tradition and is fed by it at numerous stages on the way.

As with the transmission of books by copying, so too with oral tradition some general principles can be established, this time by comparison with similar cultures and parallel situations. In this way the critic can see what is likely to happen to oral material.

At the oral stage, the individual is a much less prominent figure (for how many, e.g., 'shaggy dog stories' do you know an author ?). Much more influential is the life of the community and the activities in which it engages. These shape spoken material and produce distinctive forms. Hence study of the oral stage of tradition has come to be known as *form criticism*.

What a 'form' is can be illustrated from the modern world; we can recognize the difference between a joke and a limerick, a hymn and a ballad, a testimonial and a legal charge. All these are forms. Form, content and purpose even now are closely connected; a testimonial will not normally be written as a limerick nor a legal charge as a ballad (though see Gilbert and Sullivan's *Trial by Jury* !). But our society is a complex and relatively sophisticated one and so few conclusions can be drawn from forms. In a less highly developed, more structured community it is a different matter.

In the ancient Near East, forms are closely related to the life of the community. Once it is accepted that a particular form will have been determined by its place in the life of the community, we can argue back from the form (which we have) to the community life (which has passed away). This method is not an abstract one, as a check on conclusions reached is often possible from relevant archaeological evidence.

Here are some illustrations:

1. The Old Testament

(a) *The Pentateuch*. Here it is possible to identify by their forms riddles, work-songs, hymns, legends, prescriptions for worship and codes of law of various kinds (e.g., 'apodeictic law': 'Thou shalt (not) . . .' has a different form from 'casuistic law': 'If a man . . . then'). Like all forms, these are usually fairly brief. This helps us to see something of earliest Israelite interests and concerns.

(b) *The Prophetic Books*. Prophetic oracles assumed particular forms, and when we have recognized these it is possible to use the knowledge to distinguish what the prophet originally said from what has been added later.

(c) *The Psalms*. These differ in form: compare a hymn like Ps. 100 with a lament (Ps. 44) or a thanksgiving (Ps. 124). This helps us to reconstruct the pattern of Israelite worship.

(d) *Proverbs*. Even the collections of proverbs can be analysed by forms, which help to indicate their background and origin.

2. *The New Testament*

(a) *The Gospels*. The stories about Jesus assumed different forms depending on their use in the early church. Compare, for example, the shape of the 'controversy stories' in Mark 2.1–3.6 with that of the 'miracle stories' in 4.35–5.43. Here, too, we can argue from the form to the use of these stories in the church.

(b) *The Epistles*. An epistle is itself a form, and by recognizing the characteristics of an epistle it is possible to distinguish real epistles (e.g., of Paul) from books like Hebrews or I John, which though named epistles are much more like sermons. Were they ever sent as letters ? Within the epistles, early Christian confessions, hymns, etc, may be detected (perhaps Phil.2.5–11; I Cor.15.3 ff.).

Form criticism is inevitably a less precise approach than source criticism, but its uses have been proved.

It can also help in clarifying the character and purpose of the writers in whose work the 'forms' are included. Arrangements of individual units may be the only way in which a writer who is faithful to the tradition he has received may make his point. For example, is the order in the Gospel of Mark purely historical, or are units sometimes arranged on a different principle to put over a theological point ?

When the method of form criticism is extended in an attempt to discover the intentions of the final author or editor, it is known as *redaction criticism*. (This rather ugly name comes from the term used for the author/editor, 'redactor', which indicates that he is half-way between the one and the other.) As an approach, it tends to be very subjective, because of the complicated questions it has to ask, but it, too, is a promising development.

Archaeology and the world of the Bible

The methods we have looked at help the critic to understand the *Bible*; they are used hand in hand with his more general work, as a historian, in understanding the biblical *world*. Here archaeology is his chief tool.

The amazing discoveries at Qumran are the most publicized achievements of modern archaeology, but there are many more besides. Specific details will be found in the sections which follow. Numerous important sites have produced material of various kinds, bringing to life a whole new world of Palestinian, Egyptian and Mesopotamian culture. New Testament studies have been helped, too. Discoveries of second-century writings by Gnostics (a deviant form of Christianity) have been made at Nag Hammadi, in Egypt; these help us to see what happened in the obscure period between the end of the New Testament and the first 'Fathers'.

The amount of new information provided by archaeology is enormous, but it is important to see just what its limitations are. Here, too, mistakes were made at the start because this had not been realized. A comparison will show the right way and the wrong way:

1. In his excavations at Ur in the 1920s, Sir Leonard Woolley found a stratum of mud some ten feet thick and on the basis of this confidently concluded that here was evidence of Noah's flood. He was not slow to publicize this. But why should the mud be a relic of *Noah's* flood ? It has no label to say so, and other explanations are far more likely. This is a hangover of the mistake mentioned earlier, the concern to *prove* the Bible right. (Werner Keller's book, *The Bible as History*, is a thorough-going representative of this concern.) But the Bible is not there to be vindicated; it and its world are to be understood.

2. A better illustration of the uses of archaeology is the study of Megiddo, a vital fortress in Lower Galilee from Canaanite times to the days of the Maccabees, which has been described as the most important archaeological site in Palestine. No sensational conclusions can be drawn from here to particular biblical events, but simply trying to understand what Megiddo was like at various periods deepens our knowledge of the biblical world.

Responsible archaeologists are only too anxious to point out the limitations of their work. Its contribution is usually of this latter general and indirect kind: to bring to life past cultures and their conditions. Discoveries need to be interpreted, and there is as much room for disagreement and alternative explanations here as with any complex study. Exaggerated claims ought therefore to be treated with care. Even when new written documents are found, the chances that they relate directly to the biblical narrative are slight. But once this has been said,

there is much that archaeology can do and has done.

Technological tools

From what has been said so far, it will have become clear that the critic's most important tools are his own acuteness, sympathy, imagination and insight. Like the historian and the literary critic, he must have many of the qualities of the artist. But the scientist, too, has produced aids which he can gratefully use.

Photography has transformed the study of texts. Not only is it easy to copy precious manuscripts, but photographic techniques can make difficult manuscripts more legible and even detect what lay under erasures. The Carbon 14 Process, mentioned earlier, can date accurately the age of materials by measuring the rate of emission of the rare isotope whose name it bears. Impressive resources can be marshalled for a particular project, e.g., opening the great Copper Scroll of Qumran.

Computers can be used in problems that require analysis of statistics, as in classifying manuscripts or enumerating characteristics of style. Striking conclusions have already been published, but it should be emphasized that this kind of work is very much in its infancy, and that in any case the amount of material available for the computer to work on is often small to be significant.

Assured results ?

All these critical activities are still being actively carried on. Of course, no individual scholar would consider that he has mastered more than a very limited aspect of them; he is conscious how much the drawing of a wider picture is a co-operative effort. Unfortunately, however, there is a problem here. When individual results are put together there are often considerable disagreements. Indeed, the first thing that strikes and dismays many students is the extent to which authorities disagree. Where two scholars differ radically in their conclusions, each producing a mass of individual facts, which is the non-specialist to choose?

First, it should be remembered that the openness of biblical scholarship, the way in which it follows the same pattern as other studies, is an important guarantee of its genuineness. There is little room for biased argument and special pleading. Biblical criticism is not a 'closed shop'. In other subjects, history, philosophy, languages, even science, similar disagreements are not uncommon. So biblical scholarship does not stand entirely apart.

Where it differs is in the importance attached to its conclusions. So much has in the past been based on the Bible that changes in understanding are felt to have very far-reaching significance. But if, as is so often the case, there is just not enough evidence to come to any definite conclusion, then living with questions is the only answer. And we shall have to get used to it.

But in that case, can we be sure of anything?

It might be misleading to single out a set of assured results and present them by saying 'of this much, at least, we may be certain'. All results are only probable, though some are more probable than others, and many 'assured results' of the past have since been overturned. The reader has to make up his mind for himself; first, perhaps, as a result of the impression made by this book. Many different writers have contributed to it, by no means all of the same background or viewpoint. Is their approach convincing? Does the book as a whole add up to the beginnings of a picture which seems capable of being developed into a coherent shape? Or is it a ramshackle assemblage of doubtful ideas with little to support them?

A good deal of tension will go out of the question 'Of what can we be sure?' once the distinction drawn earlier between 'understanding' and 'proving' has been made. The Bible bears witness to God through the whole life of a particular people and the way in which it looked at the world – and life has many aspects. Begin to see that, and a great deal will fall into place of its own accord.

JOHN BOWDEN

3 The Land and the People

If Abraham as a person seems remote, his story can at least be brought to life by the use of geography. Abraham starts in Ur of the Chaldees and travels round the Fertile Crescent as far as Egypt, and one of the undoubted attractions of the Bible is that it is set in such a fascinating land. 'Mesopotamia' and 'Canaan' are not names found in the political atlases, but they are part of the deep-seated mental picture which every Christian and perhaps nearly every western European has of the Near East. They are names which arouse feeling. It will help our understanding considerably, however, if we can see how 'Mesopotamia' and 'Canaan' by their very geographical peculiarities helped to shape the history of Abraham and his descendants, and so acquired for us a more than merely geographical meaning.

Geology

Geography begins with geology. At the heart of this whole area – sometimes called the 'Near' East, sometimes the 'Middle' East, and sometimes more accurately 'South-west Asia' – lies the plateau of Arabia. This was once part of a large block called by the geologists 'Gondwanaland'. To the north and west of this block lay a sea which we call Tethys, of which the present Mediterranean Sea is a remnant. The coast-line of this sea fluctuated, sometimes extending far into what is now the land east and south-east of the Dead Sea, and leaving behind on top of the sandstone layers of the Primary and Secondary geological ages a layer of limestone. The

sandstone can be seen round Petra, south-east of the Dead Sea, and the limestone in the hills round Jerusalem. Another layer of much softer limestone ('Senonian chalk') followed, and this has worn away to leave some of the mountain passes of the modern Israel. On top of this came a third, harder layer of limestone, now seen, for example, between Mt Carmel and Samaria, or in the mountains east of the Jordan.

However, in the Tertiary period the seabed of Tethys, which was based on less resistant rock than Gondwanaland, was forced up by pressure acting from the north, and was pushed and folded into mountain chains against the unyielding edge of Gondwanaland. At the same time the Gondwanaland platform itself fractured in several places, dividing roughly into what is now Africa, Arabia, India and western Australia. At its edges, the platform warped and sometimes actually 'faulted', or broke, and the sedimentary limestone deposits on top folded upwards. In this way the present shape of 'Canaan' was produced, the faults being clearly seen, for example, in the Jordan valley, or the division of Upper and Lower Galilee, or the canyons of the trans-Jordan region. Later, volcanic activity east of the Jordan and the Red Sea, and sediment building up the coast-line and the Jordan valley contributed to the shaping of the land.

Further east, the basic platform did not get overlaid by deposits from the sea. When the platform fractured, the part which became Arabia tilted slightly, so that its western edge was higher than its eastern, and a trough was formed at the base of the Iranian mountains which the Euphrates and Tigris rivers have slowly filled with alluvium.

It can be seen, then, that Mesopotamia and Canaan belong together to one geologically related area. The frontier between eastern and western powers has crossed this region many times in the course of history; and on either side of this region the flora and fauna of Africa and Asia show many similarities (e.g., the African and Asian elephant). This, too, is an area of routes and backwaters; thus such communities as the Maronites in Lebanon, the Druses in Gilead, and the Samaritans in the central hills west of the Jordan have retreated for security to the heights, by-passed by the main routes of the 'Fertile Crescent'. The Mediterranean coast of this region is famous as a bridge between Asia and Africa, and this feature of south-west Asia has clearly helped the rise of its civilizations.

Geography

1. *Mesopotamia*

When Abraham travelled from Ur to Haran, he passed from one distinct geographical region to another. For 'Mesopotamia' (strictly, the land between the Tigris and the Euphrates, but often used of a wider area) is composed of two regions. The northern region is the 'island' between the two great rivers, beginning where they, deriving the bulk of their waters from the snows of Armenia and Kurdistan, cut through the Kurdish scarp to the basic plateau of the Arabian massif. The plateau slopes southwards, dropping from about 1300 feet above sea level at the base of the scarp to about 200 feet at the edge of the southern, Delta, region a little north of Baghdad. On the plateau the two rivers flow across hard limestone, often between cliffs, and the riverbeds have moved very little in the course of time, so that the mounds of ancient cities still lie close to the river banks. The Zagros hills, whose waters feed the Tigris, receive more rain than areas further west, and so the Tigris, though shorter than the Euphrates, is a faster flowing stream, bringing down nearly fifty per cent more alluvium than the Euphrates. The plain between the Zagros hills and the Tigris was the home of the Assyrians, and the rainfall, rising from twelve inches per annum in the plain to thirty inches in the foothills, made for rich harvests of grain and orchard fruit (and nowadays, tobacco), even without artificial irrigation. Further west, between the two great rivers, the valley plains are narrow and the soil often barren or eroded. Cultivation therefore tends to be restricted (as in the case of the Nile valley) largely to river banks. In ancient times there was a certain amount of artificial irrigation here, and recently there have been attempts to store the river flood waters, and irrigate large tracts of land, especially in the upper valleys of the Balik and Khabur, tributaries of the Euphrates. But this steppe area between the two rivers was important in antiquity; Haran lay on the Balik (Gen.11.31 f.; 12.4 f.), Gozan on the Khabur (II Kings 17.6; 18.11), Carchemish on the upper Euphrates (Isa.10.9; Jer.46.2), commanding an important ford for traffic between the Mediterranean and the East, Pitru (perhaps Pethor of Num.22.5; Deut.23.4) a little lower down, and Mari just below the confluence of the Khabur and Euphrates. In the fifteenth and fourteenth centuries BC this was the region of the Hurrian kingdom of Mitanni, later taken over by the Aramaeans; hence the land was called

Paddan-Aram (Gen.28.2: *padanu* in Assyrian denoted a measure of land) or Aram-naharaim ('Aram of the two rivers', i.e., perhaps the Euphrates and the Khabur; Ps.60, title).

The Delta region of the south – ancient Sumer and Akkad, Babylon, biblical Shinar, with Elam away to the east – was quite a distinct area. It was formed by river silt being deposited on the slowly sinking bedrock of the plateau. Here the rivers have frequently changed their courses, and the ruins of ancient cities past which the Euphrates once flowed, such as Babylon, Nippur, Shuruppak, Uruk, Larsa, Ur, now lie in the desert well away from the river. The southern end of this region is swamp land, inhabited by the Marsh Arabs who use the reeds to built their huts and boats, and hunt the wild boar and wild fowl.

In this Delta region agriculture has always depended on irrigation, for there is a mere three to eight inches of rain each winter, and the main water supply comes from the flood waters of the rivers between March and May. But the floods have always been unpredictable in quantity, badly timed for agriculture (too late for winter crops and too early for summer crops), and irrigation has been complicated by the silting up of the canals and salination. The latter is Mesopotamia's greatest agricultural problem: the land becomes saline from evaporation of water spread out over the fields, or from salt in the ground water brought to the surface by capillary action. There is not enough rainfall to wash the salt away, and drainage is hampered by the impermeability of the soil. A recent study of the Diyala river area has shown that between 2400 and 1700 BC the wheat harvest fell to nothing and the barley yield fell from twenty-eight bushels per acre to ten. A temple archive from Lagash (*c*.2400 BC) states

that salt had made part of the temple's territory unfit for agriculture, and we are reminded of Judg.9.45 where Abimelech 'razed the city and sowed it with salt' to end settlement at that place. However, until the land became too saline, the yield of barley and wheat is said to have been as good as in modern Canadian fields, and in *c*.2000 BC measures of barley were used as measures of value in Mesopotamia. In this southern area grew the highly nutritious date palm, as it did not north of Baghdad, and thus the staple foods of the area were flour and dates; a variety of vegetables and fruits can also be grown here – for example, onions, cucumbers, marrows, beans, figs, apricots, and nowadays tobacco and various narcotics.

2. The Levant

West of Haran, perhaps at Carchemish (modern Jerablus, a mere hundred miles from the Mediterranean *via* the oasis of Aleppo), Abraham would reach the Euphrates. Crossing this, he would enter the Levant, the 400 miles long by sixty miles broad coastal strip of mountains stretching down to Gaza and the southern end of the Dead Sea. The area is divided from west to east into four zones, each traceable the whole length of the area – a coastal plain, the central mountain range, the rift valley, and a second chain of hills east of the rift. From north to south the land is divided by several crossrifts into separate blocks, and the only zone which has a continuous north-south route is that east of the rift, where one can use the 'Haj' (pilgrim) route (perhaps described in Gen.14.5 ff.) along the desert edge of the mountains. We can best picture the area in three main sections.

(i) In the northern section, the Orontes river flows north down the rift valley and then turns south-west through Antakya (Antioch of the New Testament) to meet the sea. (The ancient port of Seleucia, from which Paul sailed, was seven miles further north.) West of the Orontes lies the main mountain range, consisting here of Jebel Akra (5500 feet; the Old Testament Mt Zaphon, the mountain of the north, cf. Isa.14.13 ff; Ezek.28.14, 16; Pss.48.2; 68.15 f.; 89.12; and the home of the Canaanite pantheon headed by the god El and worshipped at Ugarit nearby) and Jebel Ansariya (4500 feet). Though these mountains are high, the interior is easily reached from the sea, and the nearness of the Eurphrates has ensured the importance of the region as a land bridge between the Mediterranean and the east. The climatic influence of the Mediterranean, too, penetrates deeply here, bringing ten inches of rain per annum to Aleppo and upper Mesopotamia, making the cultivation of cereals possible.

(ii) The Lebanon ('white mountain') and anti-Lebanon range rise immediately south of the west-east gap between Tripoli and Homs, and from here until we reach Galilee there is no easy east-west communication. From north to south communication is little easier, for the rift valley offers only a difficult passage southwards into the upper Jordan valley, and a route south down the Litani is blocked by deep gorges at the elbow of this river. But this is a fertile region, well forested, and rich in grain and fruit in the valleys, because it takes all the rain moving east from the Mediterranean. The lands around Damascus, too, are well watered from the rains, dews and snows of the mountains, and produce a large amount of fruit – walnuts, apricots, apples, vines, olives and also wheat.

(iii) South of this Lebanon region we reach the land we have come to know variously as Palestine (after the Philistines who settled mainly in its south-west corner), Canaan (after the purple dye and the pre-Israelite merchants of the coastal cities who traded it), and Israel (after the Jewish people). Christians think of it as the 'Holy Land', and geographers think of it in terms of Cis-jordan (i.e.,'this side of Jordan') and Trans-jordan. Like the rest of the Levant, it can be divided into four zones from west to east, broken by various cross-rifts.

(a) East of the Jordan the mountains rise steeply out of the rift valley and fall away gently to the desert. In the north, east of the Sea of Galilee, rise the volcanic Jebel ed-Druz and Jebel Hauran, with large lava fields to their west, the Old Testament area of Bashan, famous for its oaks and cattle. South across the River Yarmuk is the well forested Ajlun, among whose trees David's son Absalom was killed (II Sam.18.6 ff.). This area became known as Gilead, but the term perhaps originally referred to a mountain just south of the Nahr ez-Zerka (Old Testament, Jabbok), the valley in which Jacob made his covenant with Laban, met Esau, and wrestled with God (Gen.31–32). South of Gilead we come to the fertile plain called *ham-mishor* (Josh.13.9; 20.8), whose possession was a matter of dispute between Israel and Moab (cf.Judg.11.12ff.), the slopes of Pisgah of which Mt Nebo was part (Num.21.20; Deut.34.1), the sheep country of Moab with its city Kir-hareseth (II Kings 3), and the mountains of Edom to its south. The Israelite part of this Trans-jordan territory could be summed up (Josh.20.8) by the three areas of the table-land (*mishor*), Gilead, and Bashan. The country of Ammon lay on the east of the area between the Arnon and the Jabbok. The whole length of this Trans-jordan country from Syria to Edom was traversed by the 'King's Highway' (Num.21.22), which is still an important route.

(b) The rift valley now descends about 3000 feet to reach its lowest point in the Dead Sea, whose surface is 1292 feet below sea level, and whose bed at the northern end is 1300 feet lower still. This section of the rift, about 100 miles long, is drained by the Jordan (the name probably means 'the descender'), which rises on the south-west slopes of Mr Hermon and descends rapidly into Lake Huleh, seven feet above sea level (perhaps 'the waters of Merom', Josh.11.5,7), slowly piling silt against the basalt dam which forms the southern edge of the lake, and creating round it papyrus filled marshes. The river then drops steeply for a distance of ten and a half miles to the Sea of Galilee, or Tiberias, 682 feet below sea level. It was also called 'the sea of Chinnereth' (Num.34.11) or 'the waters of Gennesaret' (from Gennasar on its western side, I Macc.11.67). A large non-Jewish population lived here in such towns as Tiberias (built by Herod Antipas in honour of the Roman emperor) and the towns of the Decapolis (Mark 5.20; 7.31). The Decapolis was a league of ten Graeco-Roman cities south-east of the Sea of Galilee, formed in the first century BC for reasons of commerce and mutual defence against their Jewish neighbours. The Jordan now falls 600 feet in about sixty-five miles (as the crow flies; the actual course of the river is about 200 miles) through tropical thickets (the 'pride' of the Jordan, Jer.12.5; 49.19) where boar are still hunted. On either side of this lie desolate badlands of ash-grey marl, and beyond that, on the higher slopes of the valley, fields and pastures. The whole valley floor is called in the Old Testament the 'Arabah' (i.e., the desert; cf. II Sam.4.7). The valley widens at Beisan (biblical Bethshan), where the Jezreel valley runs into it, narrows to a width of two miles just north of the conflu-

ence of the Jabbok, and slowly widens to twelve miles' width towards the north end of the Dead Sea. Here the valley plain was called 'the round' (Gen.13.10 ff.; II Sam.18.23). To the west were the plains of Jericho, and to the east the plains of Moab. To the south was the Sea of Arabah, or the Sea of Salt; the name 'Dead Sea' was coined or popularized by Jerome, and the modern Arabic name is 'the sea of Lot'. On its north-western shore on the edge of the barren hills of the wilderness of Judaea lay the settlement of the now famous community of Qumran. South of the Sea the rift valley continued, dividing biblical Edom from Judah, and reaching the Red Sea at Ezion-geber, Solomon's port (I Kings 9.26).

(c) West of the Jordan, the mountains are higher towards the south, and get more rain on the western slopes than on the east – geographical facts with economic consequences which have often affected political boundaries. In the north, Upper Galilee did not play much part in Old Testament history, though it was settled by the tribe of Naphtali. The important city hereabouts was Hazor, destroyed in the thirteenth century BC and re-settled by the Israelites, and later destroyed by Syrians and Assyrians; it commanded the route south between upper Galilee and the Jordan. Lower Galilee, the land of the tribes of Zebulun and Issachar, was a much more populous area, consisting of hills under 2000 feet high, broken in every direction by faults, well watered and productive except in the south-west and south-east corners. In southern Lower Galilee Mt Tabor is prominent, from which Barak's forces swept down to destroy Sisera's army (Judg.4.6 ff.), and where Gideon destroyed the Midianites (Judg.7.1; 8.18). 'Galilee' means 'ring', though whether this refers to cities or the physical features of the area is not clear; its large non-Israelite population earned it the name from early times of 'Galilee of the Gentiles' (Isa.9.1).

Immediately south of Galilee is one of the most important features of the land – the plain of Esdraelon, through which the Kishon (Judg.5.21) flows north-west to the sea between Galilee and Carmel, and the plain of Jezreel, through which the Jalud flows east to the Jordan, rising from the spring of Harod (Judg.7.1). The watershed is only about 300 feet above sea level, and thus the two plains make a unique pass between the Mediterranean and the Jordan. On the southern edge a low ridge runs north-west from the hills of Samaria to Mt Carmel, crossed by the main Egypt-Damascus road. At Megiddo this road meets the road running along the plains, so Megiddo has been a key point in many campaigns (cf.Judg.5.19; II Kings 23.29 ff.). The Armageddon of Rev.16.16 ('mount Megiddo') was thus an appropriate symbolic name for the final battle between the forces of good and evil.

To the south of Esdraelon rise the hills of Israel. The northern half of these hills, settled by Manasseh, is lower than the southern half, settled by Ephraim, and has no clearly recognizable frontiers. Samaria became its chief city (I Kings 16.24). The area is a basin, with Mt Carmel and Mt Gilboa and the higher mountains of Ephraim and Judah forming the edges on the north-west, north-east and south, with limestone hills like Mts Ebal and Gerizim pushed up in the middle, between which lie Jacob's well (John 4.6) and Old Testament Shechem. The towns here were in valleys, not on the heights. South of Shechem the road rises steeply up the watershed into the highlands of Ephraim ('Mt Ephraim'), which top 3000 feet

and contained such important places as Shiloh (I Sam.1) and Bethel. The road through these places from Megiddo *via* Dothan and Shechem is mentioned in Judg.20.31 f.; 21.19; it went south along the watershed through Jerusalem to Hebron and Beersheba, and so on to Egypt.

It is not always appreciated that Jerusalem lies on the very northern border of the Judaean hill country, which stretched fifty miles 'from Geba to Beersheba' (II Kings 23.8). Indeed, Jerusalem only became attached to Judah when David captured it and ruled both Judah and Israel from a centrally situated capital. Before this time, 'Bethlehem in Judah' was perhaps the northernmost Judaean town (Judg.19.1ff.). The central and highest point of the region lies at Hebron, and Beersheba, at the foot of the mountains to the south-west of Hebron, marks the transition to the desert of the Negeb. To the west, the Judaean hills drop steeply, with deep valleys cut by erosion into the fault-line; west of this a sunken mountain plateau forms rolling foothills about 1000 feet high, increasing in breadth as they get further south. To the east, the hills drop through a barren wilderness towards the Dead Sea, in sharp contrast to the more fertile land west of the main watershed. These southern regions are well portrayed in the story of David's years as a raiding bedouin chief, enemy of Saul and dubious ally of Achish of Gath in I Sam.20–II Sam.2, until his coronation at Hebron as king of Judah.

(d) Lastly, we come to the zone of the coastal plains. North of Mt Carmel, this was the territory of the tribe of Asher. South of Carmel, the plain widened southwards, and was originally occupied by Philistines and other kindred 'Sea-peoples', probably being incorporated into the kingdom of Judah after David's defeat of the Philistines (see the province list of I Kings

4.7ff.). Between the Philistine plain and the mountains is the low limestone plateau known as the 'Shephelah' (from a word meaning 'to make low'), where the tribe of Dan, to which Samson belonged, first settled, a richly fertile, well wooded buffer zone, crossed by the valley of Aijalon, down which the Philistines fled after their defeat at Michmash (I Sam.14.31), and the valley of Sorek, the scene of some of Samson's exploits (Judg.13 ff.), and the valley of Elah, where Goliath was killed (I Sam.17). The coast itself is flat, without natural harbours; at Caesarea and Joppa reefs running out into the sea were used to built up artificial harbours, but not by the Israelites, who found access to the sea difficult from their mountains, and were no great sailors. Jonah had to take a foreign ship from Joppa.

Climate

Near Eastern and European ways of life differ largely because their climates differ. In winter, from October to May, masses of humid air move into the Near East *via* the Mediterranean from the Atlantic. These winter cyclones bring rain; the Mediterranean seaboard is well watered, north Mesopotamia and the foothills north-east of the Tigris receive some rain, but beyond Mecca there is no rain. This westerly airstream is responsible for the 'former rains' (Deut.11.14; Jer.5.24, etc.) of early winter; but this airstream draws in behind it cold air from the north which heats up as it meets the Near East and becomes unstable, producing showers and even snow in mountain areas. This begins about Christmas time, and culminates in the 'latter rains' of March and April, which are a result of the turbulence from the heating-up in spring of the cold winter air. Without the former rains, the farmer could not plough and sow his ground, and without the latter rains the crops would not ripen. In the spring, north Africa and the southern desert areas of the Near East heat up, and the resulting air pressure causes hot, sand-laden winds to blow (cf.Jer.4.11; Isa.27.8; Jonah 4.8; Luke 12.55), which can scorch and destroy the grass and crops if it comes too soon. The summer climate depends on air from the monsoons of the Indian Ocean, which gets steadily drier as it moves north-west across the land-mass. Thus from May to October is a dry season throughout most of south-west Asia, and the water supply comes from whatever has been stored in wells or cisterns (Deut.6.11; II Kings 18.31; Jer.38.6), or from the rivers. In some parts, snow is stored in caves, and carried down to the towns later in the year.

All this naturally affects the region's vegetation, which has either to adapt itself to the summer season (like the vine, whose roots spread just below the surface to get the dew, or the bulbs of the anemones, the iris and lily which lie dormant for the summer), or to complete its growth season in the winter. Thus cereals are sown in autumn, harvested from April to June, and their seeds survive to germinate the following year. Different areas, however, have different types of vegetation; by the rivers grow the date palm, willow and poplar trees; in the mountains the evergreen, coniferous and deciduous trees; in the desert the thorn bushes and various grasses; in the steppe a variety of shrubs and grasses, especially the broom (I Kings 19.5); but it is in the Mediterranean climate of the Levant that the richest variety of fruits and cereals, trees and grasses may be found. But in this region considerable damage has been done over the centuries by the cutting down of the trees for fuel, and by the ceaseless cropping of the grass by goats. Woods of oak and beech, cedar and pine have been replaced by scrub; the soil has been eroded, thus lowering the water-table, making the water run-off easier, and making renewed growth more difficult. Over the last five or six thousand years these and other factors of human mismanagement such as misrule and war, rather than any noticeable change of climate, have been responsible for the visible decay of once thriving Near Eastern civilizations.

Near Eastern ways of life

In the ancient Near East as elsewhere, the main forms of life, in general order of development, were nomadic, agricultural, and urban, all much influenced by the geographic and climatic conditions. The bedouin shepherd, the country farmer and the town trader have flourished side by side in the Near East, only recently joined by the cosmopolitan cities and their business men, brought to the Near East by the discovery of oil.

1. Nomadic

Social conditions create the modern gypsies and wandering tinkers, but the desert creates the bedouin nomad of the Near East. This people derived its living by hunting, by grazing flocks of sheep, goats and cattle, or camels, on the sparse herbage (and thus constantly seeking new pastures), and by raiding both fellow-nomads and settled farmers. In Jerusalem to this day the shopkeeper will despise his bedouin customer as uncouth, and the bedouin will despise the shopkeeper as effete, and in ancient Israel there seems to have been something of both attitudes. There were Jews (including the Rechabite sect) who looked back with respect and nostalgia to Israel's wilderness days or to the period of the patriarchs as the formative period of Israel's great tradition (cf., e.g., Jer.35.6 ff.; Josh.24.2 ff.), perhaps fearing the effect of the Canaanite way of life with its agricultural deities and fertility cults on Israel's loyalty to Yahweh (see Hos.2). On the other hand, there were Jews for whom the desert was a place to avoid, the haunt of demons, where the sin-laden scapegoat was sent to wander (Lev.16.22). But Israel's ancestors may not have been true desert nomads. The patriarchs were perhaps ass-nomads, moving backwards and forwards with their flocks to the desert fringes in winter and the hill country in summer. A famous tomb-painting from *c*.1900 BC shows a group of ass-nomads entering Egypt (always the nomad's refuge in hard times), wearing gaily coloured clothing and carrying bows, spears, a sort of lyre, and what are perhaps bellows, indicating that this group were wandering tinkers by trade. But the Bible illustrates most clearly one basic feature of nomad life – family solidarity. In the desert the family is the natural community, and even when Israel settled in towns she never entirely forgot this, as the long genealogies of the Bible and many of the laws (e.g., of blood revenge; cf. Num.35.19, 24) show.

2. Agricultural

The laws of the Old Testament 'Book of the Covenant' (Ex.21–23) reflect largely agricultural societies. In ancient Israel, the earliest calendars known to us are given in terms of the agricultural year. A tenth-century BC verse inscription from Gezer describes the farmer's annual programme, beginning in late autumn:

His two months are (olive) harvest,
His two months are planting (grain),
His two months are late planting;
His month is hoeing up of flax,
His month is harvest of barley,
His month is harvest and feasting;
His two months are vine-tending,
His month is summer fruit.

The Book of the Covenant mentions as the three important seasons of the year the feast of Unleavened Bread (the barley harvest in April), the feast of First-fruits (or of Weeks, i.e. seven weeks later; the wheat harvest in May/June), and the feast of Ingathering at the end of the year (or Tabernacles, the autumn vintage feast, cf. Judg.21.19 ff.). These feasts have had a long history of re-interpretation, and are now celebrated by the church as Easter, Whitsun and Harvest Festival.

In both Mesopotamia and Israel, sheep, goats, oxen and asses played a large part in agriculture, being bred for meat, milk, and wool and for labour. In Gen.31.38 ff. Jacob describes the perils of minding the flocks; Deut.22.10 legislates against maltreatment of ox and ass at threshing time. Moab, east of the Dead Sea (II Kings 3.4), was famous for sheep and wool, and Bashan (Ps.22.12) for cattle.

In theory, the land of Israel was Yahweh's, and could not be sold in perpetuity (Lev.25.23); it was also said that God gave Israel the land as an inheritance, and each tribe, clan and family had its portion of the inheritance. Under the monarchy, the increase of trade led to the growth of rich land-owners who bought out the poorer farmers when forced to sell in time of need. But when Ahab tried to buy Naboth's vineyard, Naboth refused because it was the inheritance of his fathers (I Kings 21.3). Micah denounced the wealthy who coveted fields, and stole a man's inheritance (Micah 2.2). The land was, and is, of religious significance to Israel.

3. *Urban*

Neither in Mesopotamia nor in Israel was there a sharp distinction between city and country, for the city was an agricultural centre, a large part of whose population worked in the fields, and whose surrounding villages were known as 'her daughters' (e.g., Josh.15.32; Num.21.25). The oldest settlement yet discovered in the Near East is Jericho, where *c.*7800 BC Mesolithic hunters built near a stream what may have been a sanctuary. By 7000 BC a stone wall and a tower defended the site. But it is not until the fourth millennium BC that we find such walled cities in Mesopotamia, and in the third millennium the city-state, with its wall, its temple built on a platform, and its irrigation system, was the basis of Sumerian society. Mud-brick buildings may be seen today in the Jordan valley, but up in the hills of Israel cities could be built of the limestone – easily cut, and gleaming white in the sun – and records written on potsherds (*ostraca*). But both Mesopotamia and Israel used stone for more important records and monuments.

The site of an ancient city was largely determined by the needs of defence, the availability of water, and the importance of the place on a route or at a crossroads or as a control point for the surrounding agricultural land. Cities could be small, like David's Jerusalem (eleven acres), or large, like Hazor (175 acres), but all would have their temple or sanctuary ('high place', cf. I Sam.9.13 ff.), and their gate, a space just inside the main gate where people met for gossip, business or judicial purposes (cf. Ruth 4.1; II Sam.15.2; Job 29.7, etc.). The king would have his palace, often an acropolis or tower close to the temple (cf. Judg.9.46; I Kings 7.1–12; Ezek.43.8); the people's houses would cluster round without real plan or streets (until the Hellenistic period). They had flat roofs of beams, covered with brushwood or laths, topped with clay, often needing renewal, on which flax could be dried (Josh.2.6), or even an upper chamber built (cf. II Kings 4.10: this one had a bed, table, chair and lamp).

The city, then as now, was the natural centre for trade, industry, and cultural activities. I Kings 20.34 refers to trading quarters set up by diplomatic agreement in Samaria and Damascus. At biblical Debir archaeological evidence of a dye-works and textile industry has been found. Ezion-geber on the Gulf of Aqabah (I Kings 9.26) was important for both trade and its copper industry. The court at Jerusalem seems to have been a centre of literary activity, especially in the time of Solomon (cf. I Kings 4.29 ff.), and Jerusalem's cultural centrality was naturally bound up with the prime importance for Israel of the temple, especially after the exile.

Geology, geography and climate, forming and influencing desert, field and city, provide the background of the Old Testament, which shows us men and women reacting and responding with varying degrees of faith to that background and the events which came from it. A feeling for that background makes the men and their message real to us. Perhaps the greatest student of this background was George Adam Smith, who wrote in the introduction to *The Historical Geography of the Holy Land* the following words:

What is needed by the reader or teacher of the Bible is some idea of the outlines of Palestine – its shape and disposition; its plains, passes and mountains; its rains, winds and temperatures; its colours, lights and shades. Students of the Bible desire to see a background and to feel an atmosphere; to discover from 'the lie of the land' why the history took certain lines and the prophecy and the gospel were expressed in certain styles; to learn what geography has to contribute to questions of biblical criticism; above all, to discern between what physical nature contributed to the religious development of Israel, and what was the product of moral and spiritual forces. On this last point the geography of the Holy Land reaches its highest interest.

J.R. BARTLETT

4 How Israel Became a Nation

The Old Testament record of how Israel became a nation is contained in the first five books of the Bible, the Pentateuch. The composition of these books is traditionally ascribed to Moses who stands out in them as the central figure involved in the crucial events of exodus and the covenant ceremony on Mt Sinai, which Israel looked back upon as having called her into existence as the people of God. The investigation of these books in modern scholarship, however, has made it clear that this traditional view of their authorship cannot be sustained. On the contrary, it is now widely agreed that the Pentateuch comprises several originally separate documents which were composed in considerably differing periods of Israel's history and only gradually woven together into the corpus of literature which they now constitute. The Pentateuch can thus no longer be regarded as offering an eye-witness account of such events as the exodus, the covenant on Mt Sinai, the wilderness wandering and the preparation for the conquest of the land of Canaan; indeed, it has emerged that even the earliest of the documents which it comprises was composed at a time several centuries removed from these events.

This does not mean that these documents are of little use for the task of reconstructing the history of the origins of Israel. On the contrary, in each instance they contain many traditions and much material which are of great antiquity and of considerable relevance for the modern historian of early Israel. The point is, however, that the authors of the documents in question were not merely concerned with recording the facts of history; they were not mere chroniclers. Rather, they sought to present an interpretation of the events of Israel's origins for the generation in which they lived. In this way they must be regarded as historians even though the history which they wrote differs in many important respects from modern historiography. The main difference is that for them the course of history was directed by God, not just in the sense that he was believed to be the ultimate reality behind history, but that he actively intervened in the affairs of men and nations in order to fulfil his divine purposes. The history which they wrote was thus salvation-history, that is, the history of God's saving acts on behalf of his people Israel.

The origins of the Pentateuch

One of the most permanent contributions of scholars of the nineteenth century to biblical studies was their isolation of four main documents in the Pentateuch and the chronological order in which they arranged them. The four main documents thus isolated are designated by the letters J, E, D and P. The simplest to isolate is 'D' since it consists for the most part of the book of Deuteronomy with its very distinctive style and theological point of view. The Priestly document ('P') is also relatively easy to discern and there has been widespread agreement on its contents. It also has an easily recognizable style and displays many characteristic features such as its fondness for genealogies. It also contains an elaborate description of Israel's sacral institutions, the origins of which are traced back to creation and primaeval history but chiefly to the work of Moses at Sinai. When these two documents have been removed what remains is a general narrative which is composite. The most important document in this general narrative is known as 'J' since it regards the divine name Yahweh (=Jehovah) as having been known since primaeval times and in addition shows a keen interest in the southern tribe Judah. The author of this document is accordingly usually referred to as the Yahwist. The 'J' strand in this general narrative is extensive and in many places can be isolated from the surrounding material with reasonable certainty. Thus, for example, the creation story complex in Gen.1–3 can be divided into a 'P' story (Gen.1–2.4a) and a 'J' narrative (Gen.2.4b–3). But it is not always so easy to isolate 'J', for it has been closely interwoven with a second document in this general narrative, a document known as 'E' because it uses the name *Elohim* for God up to the revelation of the divine name Yahweh to Moses, and in addition shows an interest in northern Israel (Ephraim). The presence of these two sources in this general narrative in the Pentateuch is perhaps best illustrated by the story of the maltreatment of Joseph by his brothers in Gen.37. In part of the story Joseph is cast into a pit and left to die but is then found by a band of passing Midianites who bring him to Egypt and sell him into slavery. The strand of the narrative which relates this is 'E'. On the other hand, the same chapter relates that he was actually sold by his brothers to some passing Ishmaelites and this derives from the 'J' source. Furthermore, the 'E' source describes the

patriarch Reuben (the ancestor who gave his name to one of the future northern Israelite tribes) as the one who saved Joseph from death while the 'J' source with its southern, Judaean orientation depicts the patriarch Judah as having done so. By postulating the presence of two originally separate documents, which have been closely interwoven in this narrative, some sense can be made of what is otherwise a story producing not a little confusion for the modern reader. We may note, however, that such a separation of 'J' from 'E' is not always possible and for this reason scholars often refer to the material in the Pentateuch apart from 'D' and 'P' as 'JE'.

The date of the documents was determined largely with reference to 'D', for at an early stage in the scholarly investigation of the Pentateuch, Deuteronomy (in its original form) was identified with the book of the law found in the temple in 621 BC and made the basis of a reformation by Josiah (II Kings 22–23). On the basis of this and other arguments it was concluded that Deuteronomy was composed in the seventh century BC. It was then concluded by comparing the documents that 'D' represented an advancement upon 'JE', one of the main considerations being that Deuteronomy demands the centralization of the cult to one sanctuary while 'JE' still thinks in terms of a multiplicity of sanctuaries where Israel worships God. On the other hand it was very widely agreed that the Priestly document simply presupposes such centralization of worship and belongs to a later period than 'D' in which centralization still appears to be a major concern to be set forth as forcibly as possible. Accordingly, on these and other grounds it was established that 'JE' preceded 'D' and that 'P' followed it so that the chronological order of the documents is 'J', 'E', 'D' and 'P'.

In spite of various attempts to discredit it, this theory still commands the assent of the majority of Old Testament scholars. At the same time some of the grounds on which it was arrived at, as well as the assessment of the documents by older scholars for the understanding of the origins and emergence of Israel as the people of God, have been rejected or considerably modified during the past generation. In particular it has become increasingly clear that the documents are not to be regarded as largely the *ad hoc* creations of their individual authors in which they have reflected for the most part the views on the faith of Israel peculiar to their own particular age. On the contrary, it is now widely accepted that underlying the documents are traditions and material of great antiquity and this has brought with it a great deal of interest and research into the pre-literary stage of the documents and the various literary units which they contain. Thus, for example, Deuteronomy can now no longer be regarded as the work of an author who sought to set out in a programmatic form the implications for Israel's religion of the ethical teaching of the great eighth-century prophets. It is seen rather as the literary formulation at a relatively late period of traditions and legal material which point for their origins to very varied periods in Israel's history, in some instances the earliest period. Similarly, the Priestly document, though providing us with much information about Israel's religion as it developed in the exilic and post-exilic period, contains traditions and material of great age and value for our understanding of Israel's history and religion in much earlier periods.

While, however, increasing attention has been devoted to the pre-literary history of individual units of material and traditions in the Pentateuch in recent years, most significant of all has been the investigation of the emergence of what may be referred to as the Pentateuch tradition. By this is meant the basic schema of the Pentateuch as a whole comprising a number of themes which the various documents present or at least presuppose wholly or partly. This schema is as follows: (1) God who created the world and man (2) called Israel's ancestors and promised them the land of Canaan, (3) delivered their descendants from bondage in Egypt and (4) entered into covenant with them on the sacred mountain of Sinai, after which (5) he led them in the wilderness for forty years and finally (6) brought them into the promised land. The last of these themes is not actually recorded in the Pentateuch but is contained in the book of Joshua and Judg.1. It seems clear, however, that the book of Joshua is to be related to the book of Deuteronomy as the continuation of the latter while it is probable that Judg.1 contains at least partially the 'J' conquest narrative. Furthermore, 'J' and 'E' both point forward to the entry into the land as the fulfilment of a promise made by God to Israel's ancestors and for this reason also the conquest theme must be regarded as belonging to the basic Pentateuch tradition. These themes taken together constitute the framework of the Pentateuch and present a summary of Israel's salvation-history of which the Pentateuch as a whole presents an elaborate record.

The question which now arises is the origin of this schema. The earliest of the Pentateuchal sources, 'J', follows it step by step and most probably it is to the author of this document that it owes its present form. Nevertheless, there are strong grounds for believing that he was not responsible for its creation *in toto* and that this schema represents only an expansion, albeit a significant expansion, of a schema which had already taken shape and developed at an earlier time.

In attempting to ascertain the form of this earlier schema attention has been directed above all to a short passage in Deut.26.5–10 which, with the exception of a few secondarily inserted phrases, is regarded by many scholars as an old *credo* which briefly summarizes the history of salvation which Israel regarded as having called her into existence as God's people. In this chapter in Deuteronomy we are told that when a worshipper came to the shrine to offer to Yahweh a basket of the first fruits of the harvest he made the following confession:

A wandering Aramaean was my father; and he went down into Egypt and sojourned there, few in number; and there he became a nation, great, mighty, and populous. And the Egyptians treated us harshly, and afflicted us, and laid upon us hard bondage. Then we cried to the Lord, the God of our fathers, and the Lord heard our voice, and saw our affliction, our toil, and our oppression; and the Lord brought us out of Egypt with a mighty hand and an outstretched arm, with great terror, with signs and wonders; and he brought us into this place and gave us this land flowing with milk and honey. And behold, now I bring the first of the fruit of the ground, which thou, O Lord, hast given me.

It is clear that already this old creed presents an outline of the salvation-history and for this reason it has often been referred to as the Pentateuch or Hexateuch in miniature. There are, however, two striking omissions. First of all, the saving history as here recited contains no reference to the creation or primaeval history; it begins with the patriarchs. Secondly, there is no mention of the momentous events at Mt Sinai where the making of the covenant, so central to Israel's faith, took place. How are we to account for these omissions ?

The absence of the creation theme with its related primaeval history may be explained quite simply on the grounds that it was not brought into the framework of the salvation-history until a relatively late stage in the development of Israel's faith. In fact while there is no need to doubt that creation stories circulated in Israel at a very early time it is very probable that it was the Yahwist who first linked this theme with the salvation-history as it is outlined in the old *credo*. This finds some further support in the fact that this theme is not contained in the second oldest of the Pentateuchal documents, 'E', which otherwise follows closely the same schema as the 'J' document. That is to say, the schema of the salvation-history which both 'J' and 'E' presuppose began not with creation and the primaeval history but with the patriarchs.

But what of the Sinai covenant then ? Is it possible that it was also the Yahwist who first linked this theme with the *credo* themes ? This suggestion has been made, but it is much more likely that in this instance the *credo* themes and the Sinai theme were already united in the basic schema which the Yahwist employed in writing his epic. The absence of the Sinai theme from the old creed is possibly due to the manner in which the themes were used liturgically; the recitation of God's mighty deeds on Israel's behalf may have formed the introduction to a Sinai covenant festival held annually in early Israel. Indeed such festivals may well have provided the occasion for recalling the events

45

which were believed to have made the covenant possible or which at least witnessed to that covenant as forming the unique relationship between God and his people Israel. In this way Israel's cult would have lent itself to the creation of a national epic which not only would have united the basic themes of the salvation-history – the call of the patriarchs, bondage and exodus, the covenant on Sinai, the traditions about the wandering in the wilderness, and the gift of the promised land – but would also have included a not inconsiderable filling out of these themes with other relevant material.

Something approaching this view has been argued by the German scholar Martin Noth who believes that during the period of the 'judges', when the tribes of Israel constituted a tribal league, a national epic designated by him as 'G' (=*Grundlage*), containing a history of the saving acts of Yahweh on behalf of Israel, was created. It is argued that it was this source – whether oral or written cannot be decided – which the authors of 'J' and 'E' separately employed in writing their own histories of how Israel became a nation and that this explains the well-known similarity between these two documents both in the basic schema which they follow and the traditions and sagas which they share.

This means that there is a much longer history behind the Pentateuch than scholars formerly believed. More important still, it indicates that in the earliest period of her existence Israel already confessed her faith in her God Yahweh as a God who had acted mightily on her behalf, calling her into existence and making her his people. And it is this confession which forms the very heart of the Pentateuch and which each of the documents in its own individual manner is concerned to describe and proclaim. The story of how Israel became a nation is, as far as the Pentateuch is concerned, the history of salvation. We must now turn to an examination of each of the four main documents to see just how each one of them in its own age interpreted and presented this salvation-history.

The salvation-history in the Pentateuchal documents

1. The 'J' document

The earliest literary strand in the Pentateuch is, as we have noted, the 'J' document. There are a number of indications that this document originated in Judah such as, for example, the interest it shows in the old southern sanctuary of Hebron with which the patriarch Abraham is closely associated (cf. Gen.13.18 and 18.1) and the prominence of the patriarch Judah in the cycle of Joseph stories in Gen.37. In addition, the saying concerning Judah in the 'Blessing of Jacob' (Gen.49.8 ff.) seems to presuppose the place of supremacy attained by the house of Judah under David. This in turn affords an indication of the period in which 'J' was composed, for although it has sometimes been dated as late as 850 BC it is much more probable that it was written during the David-Solomonic period. It reflects a spirit of national confidence and fulfilment which can be fully understood against the background of national ascendancy achieved under David and Solomon, rather than against the background of the period after the disruption of the state in 922 BC. Probably, therefore, the 'J' document was composed about 950 BC.

We have seen that the author of 'J' in composing his work was dependent upon an earlier Israelite national epic ('G') which already contained the main themes of the salvation-history from the call of the patriarchs to the entry into the land of Canaan, together with much old material which had been assembled during the period of the judges and fitted within the framework of that epic. But the Yahwist did not simply reproduce this early Israelite epic; on the contrary, he expanded its framework by including the primaeval history and at the same time employed the material which it and other sources placed at his disposal in such a manner as to set forth his own theological interpretation of the salvation-history.

The Yahwist's narrative of the primaeval history begins with creation (Gen.2.4b–25) and the fall of man (Gen.3), and continues with the story of Cain and Abel (Gen.4), the stories of Noah and the flood and the rebirth of civilization after the flood (Gen.5–10 where 'J' and 'P' are blended), and the episode of the tower of Babel which brings the primaeval history to its dismal end (Gen.11.1–9). In prefacing his epic of Israel's salvation-history with the primaeval history the Yahwist sought to achieve several theological objectives. In the first place he affirmed that Yahweh was not only the God of Israel but Creator of the world and Lord of all the peoples of the earth. He also placed the history of his own people within the context of world history in general from the beginning and, more important still, asserted that Israel's election and redemption by God was not merely of national significance but of universal significance, since it was through Abraham and his descendants that God wished to bring salvation 'to all the families of the earth' (cf. Gen.12.3).

Throughout his narrative of the primaeval history, however, the Yahwist describes in bold colours man's sinfulness and persistent and increasing rebellion against God. At the same time, while at every stage God's judgment upon man is fully narrated, the Yahwist stresses throughout God's tender care for his creature and his will to save: Yahweh perceives man's loneliness and creates woman as ' helper fit for him' (Gen.2.18); having pronounced judgment upon Adam and Eve for their rebellion against him, he makes them garments to conceal their nakedness (Gen.3.21); Cain is cursed for murdering his brother Abel but is graciously given a protective mark by Yahweh (Gen.4.15); man's sin becomes such that Yahweh destroys the world but even then acts to save by preserving Noah through whom a new beginning can be achieved (Gen.6.5–8; 7.1–5); and when, even after this, things once more go from bad to worse and man's sinfulness once again asserts itself (Gen.11), here again Yahweh's judgment is accompanied by a new act of grace through which he purposes to save, for though the primaeval history comes to an end in dismal failure it is immediately followed by the call of Abraham through whom Yahweh's saving activity acquires a new direction (Gen.12).

Genesis 12–50, which includes also much material from 'E' and 'P', presents the history of the patriarchs and as such marks the beginning of Israel's salvation-history proper. It is probable that stories about the patriarchs were already contained in the early Israelite epic 'G'; their importance as recipients of divine promises of land would have assured them a firm place in the salvation-history at an early stage. Nevertheless, the Yahwist has skilfully emphasized the element of promise throughout his work in which it becomes one of the two poles, promise and fulfilment, around which the epic as a whole is composed.

Thus Abraham receives the promise (Gen.12 and 15) which is in turn renewed to his son Isaac (Gen.26) and then his grandson Jacob (Gen.28.10 ff.), who becomes the father of the twelve patriarchs whose descendants constitute the tribes of Israel. The Yahwist stresses the tenacity of the promise and God's will to fulfil his word by describing throughout the work a series of crises in which the promise was placed in jeopardy and preserved only through the gracious intervention of Yahweh. Thus having received the promise Abraham is forced immediately to leave the land in which it is to be fulfilled to go to Egypt in a time of famine (Gen.12.10 ff.). In Egypt Sarah, who is to be the mother of Abraham's 'seed', is taken into Pharaoh's harem. But Yahweh intervenes and the patriarch returns with his wife to the land of Canaan (Gen.12.17 ff.). Here, however, yet another crisis arises, for the strife between the herdsmen of Abraham and Lot raises the possibility that Abraham will again have to leave the promised land. But Lot chooses the land to the east and Abraham remains in Canaan (Gen.13.3 ff.). The future of the promise is likewise challenged in the case of Isaac, Abraham's son and the heir to the divine promise. In this instance the crisis arises because Isaac cannot have a wife from the Canaanites among whom he lives. But again Yahweh graciously intervenes and one of his own kindred from Aram, Rebekah, becomes his wife (Gen.24). Rebekah's barrenness, which presents yet another challenge to the promise, is overcome by Yahweh and she bears two sons, Esau and Jacob (Gen.25.21 ff.). Jacob, who by cunning strategy robs his brother of his birthright and becomes heir to the promise of blessing (Gen.25.27 ff.; 27.1 ff.), is forced to leave the promised land but while in exile acquires two wives, Leah and Rachel, and is eventually led back to the promised land, having regained Esau's favour (Gen.29 ff.). And this pattern of crisis and deliverance continues with the eventual bondage of Jacob's descendants in Egypt when as never before the promise is reactivated by Yahweh who calls Moses and delivers his people from slavery. During the period in the wilderness Israel's own sin (cf. Num.14) jeopardizes the promise, but after some years of wandering, inflicted in judgment upon Israel for her rebellion, Yahweh is able to let his people enter the promised land.

A brief sketch such as this cannot hope to do justice to the Yahwist's achievement. But perhaps enough has been said to provide at least the outlines of the breadth of vision and dimension of his theology. Two aspects of the history of salvation which he wrote are particularly worthy of emphasis. In the first place he transcended the older and narrower presentation of the salvation-history by seeing it and describing it as having been orientated not merely towards Israel but as being part of God's universal plan to bring salvation to all the peoples of the world. Israel was indeed Yahweh's peculiar people, but as such the agent through which he purposed to gather all men to himself. As we have seen, it was mainly by composing the primaeval history that the Yahwist succeeded in adding this dimension to the salvation-history. And secondly, from beginning to end the Yahwist's epic asserts that no matter what obstacles human weakness and sinfulness may create, God's will to save emerges triumphantly; through all the vicissitudes of time and the persistent attempts of men and nations to frustrate his purposes, Yahweh's word is established.

The Yahwist's achievement is further illuminated when the period in which he composed his epic is recalled, for he wrote at a time when the old tribal system of early Israel had all but disappeared and Israel was established as a national state under David and Solomon to play a role in the international affairs of the world in which it existed. Israel was not exposed to ideas and cultural movements from far beyond the borders of the little land in which she had settled, and the international atmosphere in which she now found herself, especially during the reign of Solomon, must have threatened to render the old faith inadequate if not altogether irrelevant. It was the noblest achievement of the Yahwist that he presented an interpretation of Israel's history and her divine election so as to make them relevant to the new situation in which she now found herself; there was a larger world around Israel now, and that, as the Yahwist saw it, was itself all part of the unfolding drama of salvation. This means that the Yahwist was not just narrating what was long past; he was not looking backwards. Rather, his work pointed forward. God had called the fathers and given their descendants the land. There was indeed fulfilment in this. But the process of salvation goes on so that the element of promise and expectation is still there. The Yahwist's epic thus points forward to the full realization of God's blessing upon the world.

2. The 'E' document

The second oldest document in the Pentateuch is the 'E' or Elohistic strand, so designated because it employs the word *Elohim* for God in the period before Moses to whom the divine name Yahweh was first revealed (Ex.3). It is generally agreed that the 'E' document was eventually combined with 'J' by an editor who made the latter the basis of his work and used only selections from 'E' to supplement it. For this reason the quantity of 'E' material in the Pentateuch is somewhat less than 'J', which means that it is more difficult to assess the theological purpose and achievement of the author of the original 'E' document.

There are a number of indications that 'E' originated in northern Israel. Thus, for example, 'E' material is prominent in the cycle of stories about the predominantly northern figure Joseph (Gen.37 ff.), and in the story of Joseph's maltreatment by his brother it is Reuben, the patriarch of one of the future northern tribes, who takes the lead in protecting him, while, as we have seen, according to the 'J' document it is Judah (Gen.37). Similarly, interest is shown in Ephraim, one of the most influential of the northern tribes (cf. Gen.48.20). In addition, northern sanctuaries such as Bethel and Shechem figure prominently in 'E'. Furthermore, the patriarch Jacob, closely associated with the sanctuary at Bethel (cf. Gen.28 'JE'), comes more to the forefront in the 'E' narrative, while Abraham, so prominent in 'J', recedes somewhat. The 'E' document knows nothing of the story of Abraham and Lot (Gen.13) or the stories about Sodom and Gomorrah (Gen.18–19), while the story about Judah, Shua and Tamar in Gen.38 contains no 'E' material.

One of the most striking differences between 'E' and 'J' is that 'E' contains no primaeval history (Gen.1–11 comprises only 'J' and 'P' material). In this respect 'E' lacks the universal dimension of 'J' and does not share the same belief in the divine commission of Israel as the agent through which Yahweh's blessing would come to the nations. Instead, 'E' begins with the call of Abraham and from here onwards follows the course of events described by 'J'. In this respect 'E' is therefore closer to the basic Pentateuch tradition ('G'), the themes of which it, like 'J', elaborates.

A further characteristic feature of 'E' is its tendency to widen the distance between God and man. There is a more sophisticated concept of God in 'E' than we find in 'J' in which Yahweh comes down and 'walks in the garden in the cool of the day' (Gen.3.8). In 'E' God is thought of as dwelling in heaven and mediating his will to man through angels (cf. Gen.28.12) or in dreams and visions (cf. Gen.20.3). And with this stress on the otherness of God comes a corresponding heightening of the wonders and miracles which he performs; the 'E' material in Ex.7–10 ('J', 'E' and 'P') augments the miraculous element in the plagues inflicted upon Egypt.

Yet another feature of the 'E' document which marks it off from 'J' is the emphasis which it places upon the figure of Moses. It was to Moses, according to 'E' (cf. Ex.3), that the divine name Yahweh was first revealed, while 'E' also has supplied many of the details about Moses's early life and call in Ex.2 ff. The uniqueness of Moses is stressed in other ways also. Thus the distance drawn in 'E' between God and man and the necessity for intermediaries throws the mediating role of Moses into prominence. Moses in 'E' is in fact the great mediator with whom God spoke 'mouth to mouth'; he is the prophet *par excellence* (cf. Num.12.7 f.). We may also observe in this connection that the author of 'E' was keenly interested in prophets and prophecy (cf. Num.11.25 ff.).

Also characteristic of 'E' is the emphasis it places upon the exclusiveness of Israel as the people of Yahweh; Israel is to be to God 'a kingdom of priests and a holy nation' (Ex.19.6). The limitation of the use of the name Yahweh to the post-Mosaic period evidences this. But it is particularly in evidence in the polemic in 'E' against pagan cults (cf. Gen.35.2,4; Ex.19.5 ff.; 32.21). It is probable that we have here further indications of the northern background of 'E', for while Judah was by no means free from the danger of the influence of Canaanite religious and cultic practices, it seems that the real threat to Israel's worship of Yahweh was centred in northern Israel. Here the main concentration of the old Canaanite population was to be found and here the predominantly agricultural environment lent itself to Baal worship with its emphasis on fertility cults. We may note also that the northern prophet Hosea was deeply concerned with the influence of Canaanite cults at Israel's northern sanctuaries (cf. Hos.2;4;10), while the Deuteronomic authors who also probably came from the northern kingdom show themselves to have been acutely concerned with pagan cults.

The period in which 'E' was written is difficult to determine. It is widely accepted that it was composed during the monarchical period in northern Israel, but whether at the beginning of it under Jeroboam I or towards the end of it under Jeroboam II is not agreed. The polemic against pagan cults more than echoes the struggle of Elijah against the worship of Baal in northern Israel, but such a struggle had already been going on even before this. Perhaps the fact that there is no hint of the threat of the Assyrians which began in the mid-eighth century may be taken as an indication that the 'E' document was composed in the earlier part of the history of the northern kingdom and the period of comparative calm in the early years of the eighth century has been plausibly suggested by a number of scholars.

Like the Yahwist, the Elohist author composed his epic as a history of salvation. But he cannot be said to have achieved the same breadth of vision and theological dimension as the Yahwist. This is particularly evident in the absence of 'E' of the primaeval history which, as we have seen, occupies a place of great theological significance in 'J'. The 'E' document is more nationalistic in character and the emphasis throughout is on the exclusiveness of Israel as Yahweh's people among the nations. The limitation of the use of the divine name Yahweh to the post-Mosaic period itself stresses this and the conservative element which pervades the work as well as the acute fear of the influence of or challenge of pagan cults further throw it into prominence. The universalism which we found in 'J' is absent and the saving activity of God is orientated towards Israel alone.

In defence of the Elohist, however, it must be borne in mind that he lived in an age and environment in which Yahwism was struggling for nothing less than its survival against the increasing popularity of Canaanite religion in the northern kingdom of Israel. In such a situation the emphasis which he placed upon the exclusiveness of Israel as the covenant people of Yahweh to whom alone their allegiance was due was of extreme necessity and was patently justified. Furthermore, in stressing Yahweh's otherness he shows himself to have been one not just concerned with coining a more exalted concept of God but with asserting his holiness and divine sovereignty over against the squalid fertility rites of the Canaanite worship of Baal. He sought to break through the superstitious practices of pagan cults and

point to a God who could not be manipulated by such practices but whose grace had throughout the past been extended in love to his people and was still directed towards them. It was against this background and with these intentions that the Elohist presented his interpretation of Israel's salvation-history.

3. The 'D' document

The book of Deuteronomy ('D') is the third of the four main documents which the Pentateuch comprises. This book purports to be Moses' farewell address to Israel just before his death and on the eve of the entry of the tribes into the promised land. This traditional view of its origin and composition can no longer be accepted, however, and it has become clear that the book of Deuteronomy as it now stands is the final product of a long history, both with regard to much of the material which it embodies and individual traditions to which it gives expression as well as the literary stages through which it has developed.

Since the work of the German scholar W. M. L. De Wette in the early nineteenth century it has been widely agreed that the 'book of the law' which, according to II Kings 22, was discovered in the temple in Jerusalem in the eighteenth year of the reign of Josiah (621 BC) was the book of Deuteronomy in its original form. The question of the contents of this original book has been much discussed, but more recently the view has been widely favoured that it comprised substantially chs. 5–26 and 28 of the present book of Deuteronomy. The latest date for the composition of this original book is clearly 621 BC while the earliest is very probably c.700 BC, since one of the dominant characteristics of Deuteronomy is the demand for the centralization of the cult to one sanctuary, a demand which, as far as we know, was first introduced by Hezekiah as part of a reformation which he carried through in the late eighth century BC (cf. II Kings 18.4,22).

The process whereby the original book was expanded into the book of Deuteronomy in its present form is no longer possible to ascertain in all its details. It is possible that the book was periodically read within a liturgical context, perhaps as part of a covenant renewal festival (cf. Deut.31.9 ff.), and this may have provided the occasion for the addition of further material. But there is every reason to believe that much of the later material in the book (chs.1–4; 27 and much of 29–34) was added by the author of a history influenced by Deuteronomistic ideas. This presents a history of Israel from Moses and the giving of the law (Deuteronomy) through the period of the conquest of Canaan (Joshua), the period of the judges (Judg.1–I Sam.7) and the monarchical period down to the fall of the northern kingdom in 721 BC and the state of Judah in 586 BC with the ensuing exile (I Sam.8–II Kings 25). Since, however, the book as a whole displays a remarkable uniformity of outlook, the authors of the original book and the later Deuteronomistic historians very probably belonged to one and the same 'circle of tradition'; for our purposes the book may be considered as a whole.

Unlike the documents 'J' and 'E' which we have examined briefly above, Deuteronomy does not present an extended narrative of the history of salvation from the creation or the call of the patriarchs onwards. Instead it centres on the Sinai covenant of which it purports to be a restatement made by Moses after the forty years of wandering in the wilderness, which followed the original covenant ceremony on Mt Sinai. This does not mean, however, that the salvation-history is of no importance in Deuteronomy; on the contrary, throughout the book it is presupposed and briefly summarized as that which called Israel into being as God's people and was as such the very basis of the covenant. It was also the record of Yahweh's grace towards Israel to which she is here called upon to respond in faithful adherence to the solemn responsibilities which the covenant placed upon her.

In its main theme as well as in its manner of presentation and the actual form which it takes, Deuteronomy is the covenant document *par excellence* in the Old Testament. As such its overall purpose is to call Israel to a full realization of her election as the people of Yahweh and the solemn obligations which this placed upon her. Accordingly, the main part of the book is a presentation of the laws governing the covenant (Deut.12–26), and the very distinctive homiletic style in which they are couched, as well as the hortatory introduction to them (Deut.5–11) and the formulation of blessings and curses which follow them (Deut.28), are all aimed at pressing home upon the minds and consciences of those to whom they were addressed the urgent necessity of obedience and faithfulness to them.

The nature of Deuteronomy and the purpose for which it was composed can be fully appreciated only when the particular period in which it made its appearance is borne in mind. At the time when the Deuteronomic authors worked the northern kingdom had already been destroyed and the best of its population exiled, while the Judaean state which had providentially escaped this disaster was in grave danger of becoming totally apostate largely due to the extreme paganizing practices which had evidently seized hold of national life during the reign of Manasseh in the first half of the seventh century BC. For those who composed Deuteronomy the problem was nothing less than the very survival of Israel as the people of Yahweh and it was in an attempt to meet the dangers which this posed that they drew up their programme of reform and renewal.

In attempting to meet the grave challenge which the age in which they lived presented, the Deuteronomic authors sought above all to assert the separateness of Israel as the people of Yahweh to whom alone their allegiance was due. To this end the book is on the one hand permeated through and through with the solemn warning against the danger of Israel becoming 'like the nations round about' by adopting their cultic and religious practices and other institutions, while on the other hand Israel's own worship of Yahweh is now brought under the strictest possible control.

The separateness of Israel among the nations is expressed in a number of ways in Deuteronomy. It is crystallized in Deut.7.6 which formulates the biblical doctrine of the election:

> For you are a holy people to the Lord your God; the Lord your God has chosen you to be a people for his own possession out of all the peoples that are on the face of the earth.

And this belief in divine election permeates the whole book forming the basis for faithfulness to Yahweh and obedience to the covenant law (cf. Deut.4.32 ff.; 6.20 ff.; 8.1 ff. etc.). It finds further expression in the warnings against entering into relationships with the nations among whom Israel is to settle in the land of Canaan (cf. Deut.7.1 ff.; 12.24 ff.; 20.16 ff.). In this respect attention must also be drawn to the marked martial spirit which pervades the book both in the form of individual laws concerning the conduct of war (cf. Deut.20; 21.10 ff.; 23.9 ff.) as well as in a number of passages exhorting Israel not to fear the peoples who shall oppose their entry into the promised land, and promising that Yahweh will himself go before Israel to fight for them (cf. Deut.7.17 ff.; 9.1 ff.; 11.22 ff.). During the period when Deuteronomy was composed the possibility of armed conflict with the inhabitants of Canaan did not exist and the idea of exterminating them was completely unreal. What these martial passages seek to do is to reinforce the demand for Israel's separateness from the nations among whom she dwelt and to protect her life as Yahweh's people against the influences of foreign culture and religion. This is further emphasized by the amount of polemic in the book against the cultic institutions and practices of the Canaanites. Israel is commanded not only to have nothing to do with them but to root them out and destroy them (cf. Deut.7.25 ff.; 12.2 ff.); any attempts to go after other gods will bring judgment upon Israel. At the same time Israel's own worship of Yahweh is brought under strict control and to this end the Deuteronomic authors formulated one of the most far reaching laws in the whole book, the law demanding the centralization of the cult at one sanctuary only which stands at the very beginning of the presentation of the covenant laws and which occurs frequently throughout the law code (Deut.12.2 ff.; 15–16).

Not only, however, does Deuteronomy attempt to control Israel's relationships with other peoples and to guard against pagan influences and to protect Israel's worship of Yahweh, it also seeks to control other aspects of her life as Yahweh's people. Thus the book contains laws to regulate the functions of important officers (judges, kings, priests, prophets in Deut.16–18), procedure in the law courts for criminal cases (Deut.19–21), and family relationships (Deut.21–22). Altogether the book attempts to regulate all aspects of Israel's life, and the motivation for this and the goal to which it was directed was to call Israel to a full realization of her role as Yahweh's holy people and to render her acceptable in his sight.

If we were to sum up the total requirement which Deuteronomy demanded of Israel we could not do better than the book itself which right at the outset and in addition to the ten commandments sets forther the *Shema* which calls for love of Yahweh in a radical manner:

> Hear, O Israel: The Lord our God is one Lord; and you shall love the Lord your God with all your heart, and with all your soul, and with all your might (Deut.6.4).

4. The 'P' document

The fourth and final document which makes up the Pentateuch is the Priestly document ('P'), the distinctive features, style and theological outlook of which render it relatively easy to isolate from the surrounding material. In addition, its relation to the other sources makes it clear that 'P' provides the framework of the Pentateuch as we now have it.

Like 'J' and 'E', the Priestly document narrates the history of salvation and in doing so presents its own interpretation of that history. The author began, like the Yahwist, with creation and the primaeval history and it is to him that we owe the first creation story (Gen.1–2.4a), which sets forth the different stages of creation, all of which are attributed to the creative word and command of God. Creation reaches its climax in the creation of the first man and woman (not, as in 'J', the first man and then the first woman). The framework of the primaeval history is provided by a series of genealogies ('generations') which culminate in the genealogy of the immediate circle to which Israel belonged (Terah the father of Abraham in Gen.11.10 ff.). The primaeval history in 'P' is tersely presented with the exception of the flood story which is narrated in some detail and ends with the giving of the 'Noachian commandments' in Gen.9.1–7. The Priestly document then proceeds, like 'J' and 'E', to narrate the history of the patriarchs where again the framework is provided by a series of genealogies, in this instance the genealogies of Ishmael (Gen.25.12–17), Isaac (Gen.25.19), Esau (Gen.36.1–30), and Jacob (Gen.37.1). This is followed by the history of Jacob's descendants in Egypt, their bondage there and God's awareness of their plight at the hands of the Egyptians. At this point Moses is called (Ex.6) and, as in 'E', the divine name Yahweh is first revealed to him. There follows a description of the exodus from Egypt and the march through the wilderness to the sacred mountain of Sinai where the legislation which is to govern the life of Israel is given to Moses by Yahweh. The 'P' document then briefly describes the forty years wandering in the wilderness and the preparation for the conquest of the promised land.

The date of the composition of the Priestly document has generally been arrived at on the basis of a comparison between some of its dominant aspects and the demands and characteristics of both Deuteronomy and Ezek.40-48. Thus in 'P' the centralization of worship is taken for granted and this probably indicates that 'P' post-dates Deuteronomy in which such centralization still requires the strongest possible emphasis. Ezekiel 40–48, which belongs to the exilic period and contains plans for the future rebuilding of the temple and the ordering of its worship, knows of no high priest and designates the Levitical house of Zadok as the priests who will serve at the altar. In the post-exilic period, however, there was a high priest and the priests who served at the altar in the second temple were the sons of Aaron, all of which accords with the legislation concerning these matters in 'P'. On these grounds, therefore, it is widely agreed that the Priestly document was composed in the early post-exilic period though it seems clear that this was only the final product of a process which began and developed already in the exilic period itself.

The purpose and significance of 'P' are revealed clearly in the stages through which it traces the salvation-history and the great amount of priestly and cultic legislation which it contains. Its main object was to present a systematic view of the origin and working of the great theocratic institutions of Israel which recognized God as the divine and only ruler, and the nation as the 'congregation' of God. Like 'E', the Priestly document postpones the revelation of the divine name of Yahweh until Moses. It admits no cult in the early period: Noah does not offer any sacrifice after the flood (as in 'J'; cf. Gen.8.20 f.), nor do the patriarchs build altars and offer sacrifices. No offering is recorded until Aaron and his sons are prepared to make sacrifice in Lev.8. Nevertheless, the Priestly author skilfully makes preparation all the way through for the establishment of the sacral institutions of the congregation: the order of creation has its ritual significance, for here the heavenly bodies serve to mark the festal times and seasons (Gen.1.14); after the creation of the world and

nature in six days God keeps the sabbath (Gen.2.2); primitive humanity is vegetarian (Gen.1.29) but after the flood the new race is to be carniverous, subject, however, to the prohibition of eating the blood in which lay the life (Gen.9.3 f.). A further advance is made with Abraham when the covenant promising him the land of Canaan is sealed with the sign of circumcision (Gen.17), while the future possession of the promised land is symbolized by the cave at Machpelah in which lie three generations of patriarchs (Gen.25.8 ff.; 49.29 ff.). Yet another step is taken when the Passover ritual is instituted on the eve of the exodus from Egypt (Ex.12.1–20) and rules were added defining the conditions under which slaves and strangers were to be entitled to partake in it (the limits of the congregation being thus incidentally defined). Everything moves forward to the detailed and expansive legislation concerning Israel's worship of God given at Sinai by Moses and recorded in Ex.25–30; 35–46; in Leviticus and much of Numbers.

The account of the revelation of the institutions of the theocratic community Israel and the sacral legislation which is to govern its life as the 'congregation of Yahweh' takes up over half the Priestly document. On Mt Sinai Moses receives instructions for the building of the tabernacle and the sacred vestments of the priesthood (Ex.25–31; 35–40). Subsequently, detailed regulations concerning sacrifices and offerings are presented (Lev.1–16). At this point the Priestly author has incorporated an originally separate document (the so-called Holiness Code, 'H', in Lev.17–26 which was probably composed in the exilic period) in order to supplement the legislation already given. There follows a series of detailed laws which are to govern the life and worship of the congregation around the tabernacle 'in the camp' (Num.1–9). In this way the salvation-history reaches its climax; from creation onwards it moves, in the Priestly document, towards the establishment of the congregation of Yahweh and the legislation and institutions which are to govern its life and the communion which it is to enjoy with God, all of which is already summed up in Ex.29.44 ff.:

> I will consecrate the tent of meeting and the altar; Aaron also and his sons I will consecrate, to serve me as priests. And I will dwell among the people of Israel, and will be their God. And they shall know that I am the Lord their God, who brought them forth out of the land of Egypt that I might dwell among them; I am the Lord their God.

The theological conceptions of 'P' are in many respects quite different from those characteristic of 'J' and 'E'. The transcendence of God is emphasized and the actions of God are not described as if they were those of men (anthropomorphism). Apart from a few passages in which God addresses or 'appears' to individuals (Noah, Abraham, Jacob) he is approached solely through the priests and the cultic rituals. For the wilderness period the manifestation of God is effected by his 'glory' which 'dwells' on Mt Sinai (Ex.24.16) and fills the tabernacle when it has been erected (Ex.40.34). The cloud which conceals God is permanent; when the camp breaks up it ascends. Characteristic of 'P' also is the place which it affords to the conceptions of sin offering and atonement (Lev.16).

This peculiar emphasis of 'P' on the sacral institutions and legislation of the congregation can be fully appreciated only when the particular period in which it originated is borne in mind. As in other documents of the Pen-

tateuch, here also there is much material and several traditions which derive from much earlier periods than that in which the author of 'P' lived and worked. Thus, for example, the tabernacle as described in 'P' is based to some extent on the traditions of the old 'tent of meeting' of the wilderness period and to some extent on the pre-exilic temple in Jerusalem. Furthermore, much of the legislation, for example, Lev.18, belongs to a very early period in the history of Israel. But, again as in the other documents, the author is here not concerned merely with describing what is past, for in recording the salvation-history in the manner in which he does he is in fact thinking of the present and the future requirements of Israel as the people of God. Working in the exilic and post-exilic period the authors of 'P' have sought to present for their generation their own interpretation of Israel's election and the system which God gave Israel for the ordering of their life as his chosen people. Israel's election had been called seriously into question in the tragedy of the destruction of Judah and the temple and the ensuing exile; here the Priestly authors have proclaimed the renewal of Israel's life as the congregation and the solemn obligations which this imposed upon her; she is to be the holy people of Yahweh who alone is her God.

The historicity of the Pentateuch tradition

From our brief discussion in the foregoing pages it has emerged that the individual documents of the Pentateuch assert that God called Israel's ancestors and promised them the land of Canaan, delivered their descendants from bondage in Egypt, made a covenant with them on Mt Sinai, led them through the wilderness for forty years, and finally brought them into the promised land. We saw also that in two of the documents, 'J' and 'P', this salvation-history is prefaced by a description of the primaeval history beginning with creation and narrating man's rebellion against his Creator, the destruction of the world by the flood, the renewed sinfulness of man after the flood, and the circumstances which led to the call of the first patriarch of Israel, Abraham. The question to which we must now turn is the historicity of the basic story of the Pentateuch as here outlined.

It is clear to begin with that Gen.1–9 cannot any longer be accepted as providing an accurate description of the origin and early history of the world and man yet the basic assertions of Gen.1–2 remain true; namely that man is a finite being and the creature of God against whom he rebels, thus alienating himself from his true life in communion with his Creator, and that man accordingly stands under judgment and is in need of grace and salvation. It is for this reason that they are of abiding value and not because of the information which they are so often thought to shed on the origins of the cosmos.

What then of the salvation-history proper, that is, those events beginning with the call of Abraham and culminating in the entry into the land of Canaan which Israel looked back upon as having called her into being as the people of Yahweh ? Modern scholarship leaves us in no doubt that here we are dealing with historical personalities and events, for few today deny that the patriarchs Abraham, Isaac and Jacob did exist and that events such as the exodus, the covenant ceremony on Mt Sinai and the entry into Canaan by Israel's ancestors did happen.

It is now widely agreed that Israel as a group of twelve tribes came into existence only on the soil of Canaan and comprised clans and groups of clans or individual tribes which had little or no relationship with each other prior to their entry into the land. Furthermore, almost certainly the entry into Canaan of the disparate elements which were eventually united to form Israel took place over a considerable period of time. It is probable that traditions and historical events which had originally been separate, that is, the property of the originally separate clans and tribes, were united to become traditions and historical events belonging to all Israel. In other words, Israel as one people living in one land and worshipping one God traced her history back through a common historical experience to a common ancestry.

Thus it is probable that the patriarchs Abraham, Isaac and Jacob were, from a historical point of view, originally unrelated to each other but were the revered founders and ancestors of originally separate clans. When, however, these clans were absorbed into the totality Israel their separate patriarchal traditions became traditions of Israel as a whole, and since the tribes of Israel eventually came to believe that they had a common origin and history, so also Abraham, Isaac and Jacob became related as father, son and grandson.

If all this is accepted, then clearly the origins of the tribes of Israel and the process whereby they became a nation living in the land of Canaan were much more complex than is suggested by the relatively straightforward account of them which forms the basis of the salvation-history narrated in the Pentateuch and elsewhere in the Old Testament. But this does not make nonsense of the salvation-history. The salvation-history witnesses primarily not to the 'bare facts' of history but to the faith of men who believed that God was concerned with the life of man and has acted and continues to act to bring salvation to man. It was in this sense, as we have seen, that the authors of the Pentateuchal documents understood the salvation-history and it is in this sense that it continues to be meaningful for us today.

ERNEST NICHOLSON

5 In the Beginning

Old Testament history begins with Abraham whose westward pilgrimage from Mesopotamia to Canaan is recorded in Gen.12. What then of Gen.1–11 ? These chapters are the prologue to that history, with much the same function as the prologue to Shakespeare's Henry V.

1. The prologue is written *after* the main lines of the action are already known. Behind Gen.1–11 lie the story of Abraham, the exodus, the settlement in Canaan and all the knowledge Israel gained, through these events, of God in living encounter with man.

2. The prologue is an appeal to the imagination, to the imagination of faith, to grasp that what was being played out on the narrow stage of Israel was of significance for all time.

The background

Increasing knowledge of the religions and literature of the ancient Near East makes it clear that the authors of Gen.1–11 are handling themes of common currency, particularly in Mesopotamia. To take three examples:

1. The Creation Hymn (Gen.1–2.4b) has marked affinities with the Mesopotamian Creation Epic *Enuma Elish*. The sequence of creative acts is the same in both documents. From cosmic matter and primaeval chaos come light, the firmament, dry land, the heavenly luminaries and man, in that order. Thereafter in *Enuma Elish* the gods rest and celebrate (cf. Gen.2.2).

2. The mysterious tree of life in Gen.2.9; 3.24 recalls the Epic of Gilgamesh with its plant of life whose name is 'man becomes young in old age'. Moreover, this plant is stolen from Gilgamesh by a serpent.

3. The flood story in Gen.6–8 has many echoes of the flood story in Tablet XI of the Epic of Gilgamesh – the construction of a boat coated with pitch, the sending forth of birds to see whether the flood waters have subsided, the sacrifice to the gods after the waters have abated.

The similarities are unmistakable, but the differences are equally striking. Behind most of Shakespeare's historical plays lie Holinshead's Chronicles. All that we mean by the genius of Shakespeare, however, consists in what he pours into the bare historical outline he inherits. Genesis 1–11 handles well-known themes; but they come to us reminted in the crucible of Israel's distinctive faith and from the hands of creative writers nurtured in that faith.

The nature of the material

These chapters are not historical, if by historical we mean the record of certain events that once happened at a particular time and place. The background Mesopotamian material is religious mythology. What is meant by myth ? 'Myth' as a word has become debased in common currency where it usually means something devoid of truth or reality: mere fantasy. It should be self-evident that this is not what is meant by describing Gen.1–11 as myth. More seriously, the word is used with a wide range of meanings in modern theology. In some cases it seems to be little more than a convenient term for religious language. Two more precise meanings of 'myth' are relevant to Gen.1–11.

1. 'Myth is to be defined as a complex of stories – some no doubt fact, and some fantasy – which, for various reasons, human beings have regarded as demonstrations of the inner meaning of the universe and of human life.' Such 'story-myths' occur in two forms. They may be traditional, popular, handed down from generation to generation, their ultimate origin lost in the mists of antiquity. On the other hand they may be the conscious creation of a great teacher. He may draw on traditional material, but he uses it for his own purposes. The myth of the prisoners in the cave in Book VII of Plato's Republic is a good example. And the purpose of such myths ? 'You are describing a strange scene and stranger prisoners,' says Glaucon to Socrates; to which Socrates replies, 'They resemble us.' Thus it would be wrong to ask where or when Adam and Eve lived. Adam is not the first man. He is 'Everyman', the 'Everyman' in us. Arguments about the dimensions or seaworthiness of Noah's ark are irrelevant. The story points to the ever present realities of the judgment and mercy of God. The background to such 'story-myths' may be fantasy, e.g., the garden of Eden; or it may be fact, e.g., the memory of catastrophic flooding, a not uncommon happening in southern Mesopotamia.

2. The ancient Near East was familiar with myth in another sense. Myth is what is said as certain religious rites are performed by and on behalf of the community. It declares in words what the ritual is designed to ensure through action. It is the word element in the sacrament. The purpose of such myths and accompanying ritual is severely practical. The 'Creation Myth' is not speculation about the origin of things, its concern is with the everyday needs of man and society, with the forces which support and threaten existence, order and chaos, life and death, fertility and drought. At the New Year festival, the triumph of order over primaeval chaos is re-enacted, re-lived, because only thus could there be any assurance of the well-being of the community throughout the coming year. Was there such a New Year festival in ancient Israel ? Many scholars believe that the feast of Tabernacles (Deut.16.13; Lev.23.34) was such a festival. It has been argued that Gen.1 originates in such a festival, the seven days of creation corresponding to the seven days of the festival.

Content and meaning

Genesis 1–11 fall into certain clearly defined sections, each of which contributes to the meaning of the whole.

1. *The hymn of creation* (1–2.4a)

This is Priestly teaching in Israel at its finest. It is hymn-like, carefully schematized, making effective use of recurring words and phrases, e.g., 'God said . . . and it was so', 'So evening and morning came . . .'. Its purpose is neither historical nor scientific. It is written by faith for faith.

A good deal of myth and ritual is concerned with the natural forces that shape man's life. In myth, however, such forces are never regarded as objects; they are always personalized as gods and goddesses. In Canaanite mythology the interplay of fertility and drought is the conflict between *Baal*, the god of the fertilizing rain, and his enemy *Mot* (Death). In the Babylonian

Enuma Elish the struggle is between *Tiamat*, primeval chaos, and *Marduk*, the champion of the gods. Just as there are many different and conflicting phenomena surrounding man, so there is an inevitable polytheism in such myths.

In contrast, Gen.1 is uncompromisingly monotheistic. The Hebrew word for 'the deep' (*tehōm*) in 1.2 is sometimes claimed to be a reflection of Babylonian Tiamat. At best it is a literary echo. The entire theme of creation coming by way of conflict between rival gods has been excised. Here there is but one God who speaks, and his word is effective to create. The same point is made in 1.14–19. Instead of speaking about sun and moon, the hymn refers to 'the greater light' and 'the lesser light'. Sun and moon were common objects of worship in the ancient Near East. It is as if the hymn is deliberately demythologizing them. It refuses to name them directly and insists that they share in the finitude of all created things. More importantly, the God of Gen.1 is not one of the phenomena of nature, not even 'Nature' with a capital N. He is wholly other, 'transcendent', standing over and against the world; the source of all its life, yet never to be equated with anything in it. The word 'create' (*bārā*) used throughout this chapter is only used in the Old Testament of God and his activity. Nothing in the world may be equated with the divine. But neither is the world in any sense the enemy of God. All is part of his good creation (cf. the summarizing verdict in 1.31). This includes man, the apex of the creation pyramid.

When the hymn comes to man (1.26), the form of expression changes. It becomes more personal: 'Let us' instead of 'Let there be'. The plural 'us' (cf. 3.22; 11.7) probably derives from the mythology of the divine council which the supreme god consults when important deci-sions are to be taken. But in the hymn, that is no more than a literary allusion; the plural 'Let us' switches immediately to the singular in 1.27: 'So God created . . . he created . . .'. Man is made *'in our image, after our likeness'* (1.26, cf. 1.27). The key word is 'image', 'likeness' being a more general term which merely emphasizes the image concept. But what does the image of God mean? Every age has tended to read into this phrase its own highest ideal of man, whether that is thought of in terms of the immortality of the soul or the possession of reason. In context in Gen.1, the phrase 'the image of God' seems to be defined by the words which follow. Just as God is Lord over all creation, so man exercises under God a secondary lordship over the rest of creation (cf. Ps.8). Inherent in such delegated lordship, however, is the thought that man is responsible to God for the way in which he exercises this lordship.

The concluding stanza of the hymn (2.2 f.) provides ultimate theological justification for the weekly keeping of sabbath. It traces it back to something in the very nature of God.

2. The enigma of man (2.4b–3)

Here the 'J' source takes us into the world of 'story-myth'. When such stories provide explanations of curious phenomena in the world, they are called *aetiological myths* (Greek *aition*, explanation, cause). Many explanations of different depth and interest may be offered within the one story. One native South African story, for instance, which is centrally concerned with why men die, also explains why the hare has a cleft lip and always seems to be on the run, why hare's flesh is taboo, and why the moon has marks on its face.

This section of Genesis has some curiously rough edges, which may reflect once independent stories – two accounts of man placed in the garden (2.8, 15), two accounts of the clothing of man (3.7, 21), two trees, the tree of life and the tree of knowledge of good and evil. It must, however, be read as a whole. It suggests answers to many questions – why the serpent is such an odd creature (3.14); why the instinctive antipathy between man and serpent (3.15); why the pain in child birth (3.16); why the farmer's lot is so hard (3.17–19); why marriage and the different sexes (2.20–25). All these 'whys', however, are peripheral to the central thrust of the story. It is not another creation story. The barren desert (2.4b–7), fertilized by super-natural water (the mist, 2.6), is a very different picture from the primaeval water chaos of Gen.1. It is merely the setting for man (Hebrew *ādām*), the 'earthling' formed from 'the earth' (Hebrew *adāmāh*). Shaped by a divine potter, this man becomes a living being or creature (*not* soul), when God breathes into him the breath of life (2.7). This man is placed in a position of responsibility in the garden of Eden, almost certainly a mythical garden paradise. All attempts to unravel the geographical references in 2.10–14 come at some point to a dead end.

The 'tree of the knowledge of good and evil' in this garden has provoked endless discussion. 'Good and evil' are perhaps best interpreted to mean 'everything' (cf. our use of the opposites 'hot or cold' to mean any temperature). The temptation which dangles before man is that of grasping at a totality of knowledge which is the prerogative of God. Once possessing all knowledge he would know the whereabouts of the tree of life, and thus be in danger of trespassing upon another divine prerogative, immortality. When temptation conquers, all goes wrong. The garden of delight becomes the garden of disenchantment. Childlike trust is replaced by the guilty conscience. Harmony turns to friction. The life of rewarding toil becomes the irksome struggle for existence. Death enters the scene.

The psychological insight in the story is profound. Note the subtlety of temptation (3.1-6), the 'passing of the buck' mentality (3.12-14). But the heart of the story is theological, that basic sin in man's nature which mars his world. He is a creature in rebellion against his Creator. He refuses to accept that he himself is not omniscient or the centre of the universe. Like Gen.1, this section knows of the greatness of man. His lordship is indicated by the way in which man gives names to the other creatures (2.19 f.). But this lordship, as Israel had every reason to know, is a marred lordship.

3. Cain and Abel (4.1–16)

Certain curious features of this story – the different types of sacrifice (vv.3 f.), sin crouching, demon-like, at the door (v.7), the blood crying from the ground (v.11), the mark placed on Cain (v.14) – have been traced back in origin to tribal customs and Babylonian ritual practice. In context, however, the meaning is plain. From rebellion against God, man progresses to fratricide. Here is the fatal legacy of man's self-assertiveness – murder, and murder capped by a classic denial of responsibility. 'Am I my brother's keeper?' (v.9). But if man disclaims responsibility, God does not. The mark on Cain is a protective mark. Cain is punished; he is banished to wander (Nod, v.16, means wandering) on the face of the earth, but he can never wander beyond the protection of God. God does not wash his hands even of rebellious man.

4. *The descendants of Cain* (4.17–24)

In terms of the family of Cain, various facets of cultural life are introduced – city civilization (v.17), the tent-dwelling herdsmen (v.12), music (v.21), and the metal working smiths (v.22). The Kenites, the descendants according to tradition of Cain, remained itinerant smiths.

Verses 23 f. preserve an ancient song which breathes the proud code of honour of the desert, the spirit of blood revenge. Perhaps in the mind of 'J', it is further illustration of human aggressiveness.

5. *The beginning of the worship of Yahweh* (4.25 f.)

This passage fits ill with Ex.3.13-15 ('E') and 6.3 ('P'), the latter passage specifically stating that worship of God under the name of *Yahweh* (the Lord) began at the exodus. The universalizing intention in Gen.1–11 is here at work. The worship of Yahweh was always the faith of the true line of mankind.

6. *The first Priestly genealogy – from Adam to Noah* (ch.5)

The Priestly writer stresses the continuity of history by way of genealogies. Abnormally long life spans, much longer than in this list, are assigned to ancient worthies in Mesopotamian tradition. No real theological significance can be read into the numbers which, in any case, vary considerably in the different versions of the Old Testament. Hebrew, Samaritan and Greek. Enoch, the seventh in the list with 365 years, is of interest, since the seventh in the list of Babylonian pre-flood worthies was a devotee of the sun god, and skilled in the art of divination. If 'P' knew this tradition, it is significant that for one skilled in divination he

has substituted a man who 'walked with God', an exemplar of true faith.

7. *The prologue to the flood story – the sons of God and the daughters of men* (6.1–4)

Stories of intercourse between gods and mortal women are common enough in religious mythology. Nor is it surprising that the offspring of such unions should be regarded as giants, the Nephilim (v.4). But this piece of pagan mythology is given new meaning by placing it as a prologue to the flood story. It now becomes an illustration of the evil which infects not only men, but even celestial beings. It points to a cosmic, demonic dimension to evil which more than justifies the judgment to come.

8. *The flood* (6.5–8.22)

The flood story (a fusion of 'J' and 'P' traditions) has many points of contact with Mesopotamian flood traditions, which survive most complete in Tablet XI of the Epic of Gilgamesh. There Noah's counterpart is Utnapishtim. The biblical narrative, however, is distinctive. Its motivation is strictly ethical (6.5–7); no such reason is given in Mesopotamian tradition. Its ethos is monotheistic whereas the Mesopotamian story is polytheistic. The Gilgamesh parallel to 8.21 reads:

The gods smelled the savour,
　　the gods smelled the sweet savour,
　the goods crowded like flies round the
　　sacrifice.

The ethical spirit and monotheistic conception of God, however, just scratch the surface of the basic difference. The entire orientation of the narrative is different. The flood story in the Gilgamesh Epic comes within the setting of a man's search for elusive immortality. The flood story in Genesis underscores some of the basic themes of Israel's faith.

(a) *The reality of judgment*. The seriousness with which God views the chaos sin brings into the world is expressed in the decision to wipe out the evil-infected age. Man bent on a 'Rake's Progress' can only progress to destruction.

(b) *Salvation*. Judgment is not God's last or only word. One man, Noah, finds favour in the eyes of God (6.8), is regarded as being 'in the right' with God (6.9; 7.1), 'blameless' he walked with God (6.9). As one age dies, engulfed in the surging waters, a new age is born, a new age grounded in a divine promise of the lasting stability of the natural order (8.21 f.).

9. *The covenant with Noah* (9.1–17) 'P'

In the new age, the age of Israel's historical existence, God's original command to man 'Be fruitful and multiply' (Gen.1.28) is repeated. Part of the harmony in nature, however, has disappeared. Man is no longer vegetarian (contrast 1.29). Two specific checks are placed upon what man may with impunity do.

(a) He is not to eat flesh with the blood in it. This ancient ritual taboo is based on the equation of the blood with life (cf. Lev.17.11–14; Deut.12.23). Orthodox Jews still eat only 'Kosher' meat in the light of this ordinance.

(b) The sanctity of human life is stressed in an ancient sacral, legal formula, 'The shedder of blood in man, by man shall his blood be shed.' This sanctity is rooted in man's kinship with God (the image of God) according to the Priestly author; and man is held responsible for the punishment of murder.

(c) The new age is above all the *covenant* age. A covenant (*berith*) is a treaty or agreement between two parties (cf. Gen.31.44; I Sam.18.3). Within the context of Israel's faith, however, covenant has a distinctive meaning. The initiative always comes from God; it is he who establishes his covenant (cf. 6.18; 9.9–11; 15). It is his gift to man. As such, the covenant contains an element of promise, the promise in 6.18 that Noah will survive when all else perishes; the promise in 9.9 f. that never again will the earth be destroyed; the promise that God will always remember (9.15 f.).

The same emphasis appears in the way the writer deals with the bow in the cloud (9.12-17). In certain mythologies, the rainbow is the bow of the warrior storm god hung up in the sky after the defeat of his enemies. Israel may have known this myth. Here, however, the bow is merely a 'sign', a 'sign' not to man but to God, a sign which guarantees that God will always remember his covenant and covenant promises. Upon the utter dependability of God, Israel staked her faith.

10. *The family of Noah – curse and blessing* (9.18–29) 'P'

The Noah of this episode is curiously different from the Noah of the flood. He is the first to plant a vineyard, and the first to succumb to over-indulgence in its produce. This episode is used by the writer to say something about the history and destiny of the peoples who struggled for possession of the land of Canaan. The three sons of Noah, Ham (Canaan), Shem and Japheth, represent three peoples whose destiny is fixed by the curse and blessing of father Noah. 'Curse' and 'blessing' are for the Old Testament not merely words. They are solemn, sacred, power-charged words, which work themselves out inexorably in events. Canaan, the indigenous inhabitants of the land prior to the Hebrew settlement, are to be abject slaves (v.25). Instead of Shem, the ancestor of the

Hebrews, being blessed, it is Yahweh, the God of Shem, who is blessed (v.26). Although this expression is not paralleled elsewhere in the Old Testament, it probably reflects the writer's conviction that the true blessing of the Hebrews lay in their worship of Yahweh. In v.27 the word 'enlarge' (Hebrew *japht*) is a play on the name Japheth. The reference here is not wholly clear, but probably it is to the Philistines who, although never in alliance with the Hebrews, struggled with them for possession of Canaan in the twelfth century BC.

11. *The table of the nations* (ch.10) 'P'

This chapter has been well described as 'a pioneering effort among the ethnographic attempts of the ancient world'. The threefold division of peoples is neither strictly linguistic nor ethnic. It is mainly geographical. Some of the names still defy reasonable explanation. What is remarkable is that all the nations of the then known world, from the Black Sea and the Aegean region in the north to Somaliland in the south, from the Iranian plateau in the east to the western Mediterranean, are gathered together as if they were the fulfilment of the command to Noah: 'Be fruitful and multiply' (9.1). All are one and under the providence of one God.

12. *The tower of Babel* (11.1–9) 'J'

Like Gen.2–3, this story has aetiological (explanatory) elements. It attempts to explain why, in this one world, there is such a diversity of languages. It gives a popular and quite unscientific explanation of the name Babel, linking it with Hebrew *bālal*, confuse. In fact, 'Babel' means 'the gate of God'. But the aetiological element does not take us to the core of the story. The setting is unmistakably Mesopotamia. Behind it is the memory of contact with the great temple towers or zig-gurats. These Mesopotamian cathedrals, with names that sometimes stressed the link between earth and heaven, were the ultimate expressions of man's piety. But not to the Bible writer. Here he sees man's pride, his self-assertiveness, his fatal attempt to seek for self-made security apart from God. The result is disaster, confusion, the fragmentation of the world.

13. *The genealogy of the sons of Shem* (11.10–32)

Against this background, one family group, Shem and his descendants, are singled out because they are to be the bearers of new hope for all humanity. This line of Shem (the Semitic peoples) leads directly to Abraham, with whom Hebrew history begins. In a few bold strokes, the prologue has introduced the main themes of the Old Testament faith. God is the transcendent Lord of all creation and all history. Man, part of the finitude of creation, is made in God's image to share in this lordship. But man is a rebel who progresses inevitably to destruction and confusion under the judgment of God. Even in the midst of judgment, however, God never renounces rebellious man; he protects, he renews, he binds himself to man in promise.

ROBERT DAVIDSON

6 The Patriarchs

The patriarchal narratives in Gen.12–50 divide into blocks of material which centre on the four main patriarchal figures:

1 Abraham (12–25.18)
2 Isaac (26)
3 Jacob (25.19–33; 27–35)
4 Joseph (37; 39–50).

Of these four, Isaac is a shadowy figure, briefly mentioned, little more than a link between Abraham and Jacob. The Joseph stories, very different in character from the other narratives, are likewise a link, a link between the patriarchal period and the exodus traditions.

The 'documentary hypothesis' finds in these chapters a fusion of the three main narrative sources in the Pentateuch, 'J', 'E', and 'P'. It is not always easy to be certain of the breakdown of the narratives into these sources. It is probably more important to begin by asking what lies behind all the sources. Each of them draws on the old traditions which must have circulated from generation to generation by word of mouth for centures before they ever achieved written form. Many of these traditions must have been wholly independent of one another. They achieved their unity only as 'Israel' found her national unity, and traditions, once the possession of separate tribal groups, became the heritage of all Israel. We cannot regard these chapters as a straightforward chronological record of the history and the religion of the patriarchal age. What then is their value historically and theologically ?

The historical question

So long as the world of the ancient Near East between 2000–1500 BC was a virtual blank as far as extra-biblical material was concerned, it was possible to treat the patriarchal narratives with marked scepticism. At best, they were a reading back, into idealized ancestors, of the beliefs and customs of later Israel. Some scholars went much further and dissolved all the patriarchs into gods or tribal symbols. Increasingly, new historical data for this period has become available, and with new knowledge, the need to revise this attitude of scepticism. Illustrations of the kind of evidence accumulating from two archaeological sites, Mari and Nuzu, will suffice.

1. *Mari* in the north-west Mesopotamia was, in the eighteenth century BC, a powerful Amorite (or proto-Aramaean) kingdom. Names similar in type to those found in the patriarchal narratives appear in many documents from Mari. These documents are engraved on tablets, made of hard-baked mud. We hear, for example, of the 'banuiamina', sons of the right hand (south); the Hebrew form is Benjamin (Gen.38.15, etc.). Social and political customs, for instance census taking, are also very similar at Mari and in the Old Testament. Since the Genesis tradition traces the coming of Abraham from Haran, in precisely the same area of north-west Mesopotamia (Gen.12.4), it is reasonable to think of Abraham and his family as belonging to one or other of the Amorite groups, whose presence at this period in

different parts of the ancient Near East is amply documented.

2. Further down the Mesopotamian valley at *Nuzu* there was, in the middle of the second millennium BC, an important Hurrian community. These 'Hurri' (Old Testament: Horites, Gen.14.6; 36.20 ff.) seem to have come from the mountains of Armenia. Documents from Nuzu contain some remarkable parallels in social customs to features in the patriarchal narratives which are not easily explicable in the light of later Old Testament law and custom.

(a) Three times in Genesis, the story is told of a patriarch passing off a wife as his sister (12.10–20; 20; 26.1–11). One form of marriage contract at Nuzu provides for a man to adopt his wife as his sister. Although the Genesis narratives no longer understand the incidents in this light, the Nuzu type wife-sister relationship may underlie the stories.

(b) In certain cases at Nuzu property could pass, not to the eldest son, but to a daughter's husband. Legal proof of this was the handing over of the 'household god' images. Rachel's conduct in Gen.31.19 ff. when she stole 'her father's household gods' becomes clear. She was furthering Jacob's claim to part of Laban's property.

(c) Two types of heir are recognized in Nuzu law, the direct heir (*aplu*) and the indirect heir (*ewirru*), who may be an adopted slave. If, after an *ewirru* is designated heir, a direct heir is born, the *ewirru* loses his legal rights. This seems to be the situation in Gen.15.3 where Abraham's heir is Eleazar, a slave born in his household. This Eleazar disappears when Isaac, the direct heir, is born.

(d) At Nuzu a childless wife was under obligation to provide her husband with a concubine. This explains Sarah's action in Gen.16.1 ff.

Mari and Nuzu, as well as Babylonian, Hittite, Canaanite and Egyptian sources from various periods in the second millennium BC refer to a certain category of people as *Habiru*. The meaning of this term is still widely disputed. It is a descriptive word – 'mercenaries', 'refugees', 'donkey caravaners' have been suggested. It seems likely that there is some link between this term and the description of Abraham as *the Hebrew* (Gen.14.13). With one exception, all references to 'Hebrews' in the Old Testament occur in passages which refer to events prior to 1000 BC.

All this evidence points to the conclusion that historically, culturally and socially, the patriarchal narratives fit meaningfully into the world of the ancient Near East at about 2000–1500 BC and into no other milieu, earlier or later. Whatever these narratives may be, they are not merely the romanticizing products of a later age.

The character of the traditions

Can we then call these narratives 'history'? It depends what we mean by history. Genesis 12–50 do not contain a record of significant public, political and social events. Very little of the political history of this period can be gleaned from them; and what there is is often incidental. An exception is Gen.14 which does preserve the memory of an expedition by four northern and eastern potentates against communities in the region of the Dead Sea. It faces the historian, however, with difficult questions. The identity of the kings involved is by no means certain. It is best to treat these narratives in the main as *sagas*. Sagas, transmitted from generation to generation by word of mouth, are stories which preserve the memory of the movements and adventures of tribal groups, and of the noteworthy deeds of tribal heroes. Sagas often concern themselves with quite trifling personal incidents, domestic intrigue, family quarrels, love and jealousy. Sagas preserve and reflect a way of life, a set of values. They mirror the way in which a community thinks about itself and its own past. As such they are of immeasurable historical value, even when they do not record historical events. In most cases there is a solid substratum of historical fact in the saga, but the task of penetrating to it is not always easy. Even when focusing upon individuals, such sagas may be retelling the fortunes and exploits of tribal groups. The Jacob-Esau stories (25.21–34; 27.32 f.) are a good example of this. The 'Jacob' of these incidents represents 'the sons of Jacob' (Israelites), Esau represents the Edomites. In the birth story, God says to Rebekah, 'Two nations are in your womb, and two peoples, born of you, shall be divided' (25.23). On the other hand, sagas may genuinely retain the memory of the exploits of individuals. This seems to be true in the main of the Abraham sagas. There is no good reason to regard Abraham as a tribal symbol.

Not all the material in Gen.12–50, however, is saga. There are passages which contain *aetiological* (explanatory) *legends*. Of these, many are *cult legends* explaining the origin of the worship of Yahweh, the god of Israel, at particular shrines in the land of Canaan. Prominent among such cult legends are those associated with Hebron (13.18), Shechem (12.6 f.; 33.18–20) and Bethel (28.19–21). Such holy places were centres of worship long before the Hebrews entered the land of Canaan. The narratives reflect a successful Hebrew religious take-over bid, the original Canaanite deity being grafted into Hebrew religion or simply being replaced by the Hebrew god, Yahweh. Thus Gen.33.20 speaks of a sacred stone at Shechem called El Elohe-Israel, i.e. El (the supreme Canaanite deity), the god of Israel; while Gen.14.22 identifies Yahweh with El Elyon (El Most High), the god worshipped in the pre-Israelite cult at Jerusalem. The fact that such stories are called legends does not mean that they lack all historical reference. There is no reason to suppose that the story in Gen.31.45–50 was invented to explain the boundary stone; the boundary stone may be the witness to a historical event. Nor is there any reason to doubt that a Hebrew patriarch may have had an authentic encounter with this god at or near a Canaanite sanctuary (32.24–31).

The Joseph story (37; 39–50) stands on its own. It is neither saga nor legend. Instead of a series of loosely connected episodes, we have a carefully constructed short story which builds up to a dramatic climax. Instead of narratives which speak at point after point of God making himself known to the patriarch, the interest is focused on the character, motives and actions of the human agents. The religious emphasis, although present, is unobtrusive. The local Egyptian colouring of the story is authentic. The story of Joseph's entanglement with Potiphar's wife is basically similar in plot to the Egyptian 'Tale of Two Brothers'. Throughout, it breathes the atmosphere of the 'wisdom' tradition in Israel. What the origin of these chapters is and whether they originally had any organic relationship to the rest of the patriarchal traditions are questions difficult to answer.

A rich variety of material, very different in character and purpose, is thus discernible in

Gen.12–50 – fragments of historical records, sagas both tribal and personal, explanatory legends, the Joseph story. That the end product is not an impossible hotch-potch is the result of a unity which has been given to this material by Hebrew writers who have used it for their own purposes to witness to the God of Israel's faith and the mystery of his choice of Israel to be his people. Genesis 12–50 is like a collection of pearls, gathered from different oyster beds. Each pearl has its own value, its own character; but all have been matched and strung together by master craftsmen to find new lustre in a new setting.

The theology of the narratives

The prologue stories in Gen.1–11 close with a family tree which narrows world history down to one tribal group, the sons of Shem, and within that group, to the person of Abraham, son of Terah (Gen.11.31). At this point, Old Testament history begins; but it is history of a peculiar kind, narrated in terms of God's activity and God's purposes. This is made immediately clear in 'J''s introduction to the Abraham sagas in 12.1–3. Certain basic themes are sounded.

1. Call or election

Whatever political or economic factors controlled the movements of the Amorites in the ancient Near East c.2000–1500 BC, this man Abraham moves in response to a call from Yahweh (the Lord):

Now the Lord said to Abram, 'Go from your country and your kindred and your father's house to the land that I will show you' (12.1).

No explanation is given as to why the call came to this man. It is left as mystery, rooted solely in the initiative of God. It is a call which looks for a response of obedience; but it is not a call which comes because of the prior goodness or merit of Abraham. The patriarchs are not idealized figures. Abraham twice resorts to deceit to save his own skin (12.10–20; 20); Isaac follows suit (ch.26). With good reason popular saga connected Jacob's name (original meaning 'may God protect') with the Hebrew words for 'heel' (25.26) and 'supplant' (27.36, cf. Hos. 12.4). Jacob had nothing to learn in the art of 'one-up-manship', as the Jacob-Esau and the Jacob-Laban stories make plain. Joseph in his childhood and youth must have been an insufferable prig (ch.37). Yet it is precisely to such men that God's call comes; it is through them that God's purposes are forwarded. Israel had few illusions about her own goodness, but even fewer about the reality of God's call.

2. Promise

Associated with this call there is a twofold promise.

(a) The promise of 'land' (i.e. Canaan) and a future 'great nation' (12.2, cf. 12.7). This promise echoes throughout the patriarchal narratives. It is repeated at significant crisis points in Abraham's life (13.14–17; 15.4–7; 18.18; 22.17); it is confirmed to Isaac (26.2–4, 24), to Jacob (28.3 f., 13–15; 35.11 f.) and to Joseph (48.15 f.). The change of the name from Abram to Abraham (17.5) – the forms are probably merely dialectal variants – is popularly explained by reference to this promise. This is a promise repeatedly called into question by events. The land of Canaan remains occupied by other peoples. Famine forces Abraham to leave this land and go down to Egypt (12.10). Jacob is sent back to north-west Mesopotamia (cf.28). The narrative closes with Jacob's burial, according to his wish, in a plot of land in Canaan purchased by Abraham. The Canaanites, however, are firmly in possession of the land, while Abraham's descendants find themselves in Egypt (ch.50). The promise of a great nation is hazarded by Sarah's barrenness beyond the normal age of child-bearing (18.11 ff.). Isaac, upon whom all Abraham's hopes focus, becomes the source of Abraham's greatest testing. Genesis 22, the sacrifice of Isaac, is a good example of the theological purpose of the narratives. Taken by itself, it could be a legend explaining the name of a place (22.14) or why human sacrifice, practised at certain Canaanite sanctuaries, had been replaced by animal sacrifice in Hebrew religion. But the opening words of the chapter make it perfectly clear that the incident is to be read as the supreme test of Abraham's faith. It is so because what God asks jeopardizes the promise which God has made. If Isaac dies, there will be no great nation. The opposite side of this 'promise'-coin is the demand made upon man to live trusting in the promise even when circumstances seem to threaten it (cf.15.6; 17.1). This is faith. Again and again in the narratives it is solely God's initiative and God's intervention which keep the promise in being, sometimes in unexpected ways. Compare Joseph's words to his brothers, 'God sent me before you to preserve life' (45.5). The strongly God-centred emphasis surrounding the promise of land and a great nation prevented, or ought to have prevented, Israel from thinking of her destiny in purely imperialistic or political terms.

(b) On the other hand, there is the promise of blessing to come through Abraham's descendants to other nations. The destiny of other nations is linked for good and for ill, in blessing and in curse, to that of Israel. 'By you all the families of the earth shall bless themselves' (12.3). What Abraham becomes under God is to be the desire of all nations. They will use his name in invoking blessing upon themselves. This note of universal promise is repeated at 22.18 and 26.4.

These two aspects of the promise, the one inward looking, the other outward looking, were often to be in tension in the history of Israel. It was only too easy for Israel to forget that what she was, she was for the sake of others.

3. Covenant

Many of the strands we have touched upon in call and promise come together under the concept of the covenant. The tradition of a covenant between God and Abraham appears in two forms in Genesis, the one in 15.7–21 ('J'), the other in 17.1–14 ('P'). Both traditions lay stress upon the fact that the covenant is rooted in God's self-revelation and initiative. The 'J' tradition begins with a formula in which God identifies himself and declares his past mighty acts.

I am Yahweh your God who brought you from Ur of the Chaldees to give you the land to possess (15.7, cf. Ex.20.1; Deut.5.6).

The narrative goes on to describe an ancient ritual for covenant making which lies behind one of the common Hebrew expressions for making a covenant, namely 'to cut a covenant'. The contracting parties pass between the severed halves of sacrificial animals or birds. They thus bind themselves to one another, and invoke upon themselves a fate similar to that of the victims if they violate the solemn terms of the covenant (cf. Jer.34.18 f.). In the mysterious and awesome imagery of this narrative, however, only one of the contracting parties participates in the ritual. While Abraham lies in the grip of a deep sleep, Yahweh, in the symbols of smoke (a smoking oven) and fire (a torch), passes between the severed victims. It is thus Yahweh who initiates the covenant, who binds himself to Abraham to fulfil his promise of the possession of the land. The 'P' tradition in 17.1–14 makes the same point by its repeated emphasis upon 'my covenant':

I will make my covenant between me and you (17.2,7).

My covenant is with you (17.4,9,13).

The speaker in each case is God. What is offered to Abraham is an 'everlasting covenant' (17.7) which binds God to be for ever the God of Abraham and of his descendants. In this tradition, circumcision is introduced as the 'sign' of the covenant. It is not the condition for belonging to the covenant people; it is simply the outward sign that a man does belong to that people. Circumcision was commonly practised among many of the peoples of the ancient Near East and beyond. Usually it is a rite associated with puberty or marriage. It is characteristic of the Old Testament that it takes such a practice and baptizes it into the faith of Israel, where it becomes the sign of a lasting theological truth (cf. the 'bow' in Gen.9.8 ff.).

Both 'J' and 'P' covenant traditions point towards the future (15.13 ff.): 'J' to the fact that the promised possession of the land will only come after a long period (400 years) of apparent frustration; 'P' (17.6) to the coming of nations and kings out of the line of Abraham. These elements in the tradition may represent a reading back into the past of hopes fulfilled in the establishment of the Davidic kingdom. Whatever their origin, they point to the unity of all Israel's history under the sovereignty of the one God.

4. The presence of God

Throughout the Abraham, Isaac and Jacob sagas there is a repeated emphasis upon *theophany*, the appearing of God to the patriarchs in one form or another. Many such theophanies occur in close proximity to holy places and sanctuaries (e.g., Gen.12.6 f.; 18.1 ff.; 28.10 ff.). Sometimes the narrative simply says Yahweh or God 'appeared' (cf. 17.1); sometimes it is the word of Yahweh that comes (15.1); sometimes God's presence is revealed in a dream, an emphasis which is usually thought to be characteristic of the 'E' source (e.g., 20.3; 28.13); sometimes it is the angel (or messenger) of Yahweh who appears (e.g. 16.7 ff.; 19.1 ff.; 21.17 ff.; 22.15 ff.); sometimes God appears, at first unrecognized, in human form (e.g., 18.1 ff.; 32.4 ff.). Behind certain of these theophanies lie ancient cult legends which at one time had no reference to the patriarchs of Israel or to their God. Genesis 32.24 ff., the mysterious story of Jacob's nocturnal wrestling, is a good case in point. Its origin is probably a legend about a demonic night assailant who disputed the passage of the ford Jabbok. Whatever their origin, such stories communicate a lively sense of the continuing encounter between God and man in the patriarchal era.

The names of God in the narratives point in the same direction. Many of them are divine titles, familiar in Canaanite religion before the Hebrews entered the land. This is true of numerous divine titles in which the first element is 'El, the supreme God'; e.g., El Shaddai (17.1): God of the Mountain, El Olam (21.33):

Everlasting God, El Elyon (14.22): God Most High, El Bethel (31.13; 35.7): the God Bethel. There is, however, another category of divine names which links God to a patriarch. Thus God is 'the God of Abraham and the God of Nahor' (31.53); he is the Fear (or Kinsman) of Isaac (31.42,53), the Mighty One of Jacob (49.24). All such titles indicate a relationship between God and a particular person, usually the head of a clan-group. This emphasis upon personal revelation and personal relationship with God seems an authentic element in the religious experience of Israel's patriarchal forefathers.

The patriarchal narratives will always be a happy hunting ground for the social anthropologist and the religious historian. Behind the present form of narratives lie many old, and in certain respects primitive, traditions, some of which have been uneasily assimilated into Israel's faith. In their present form, however, the narratives breathe a rich spirituality. There will always be differences of opinion as to how much of this spirituality is a reading back into patriarchal times of a knowledge of God which only came to Israel later in her pilgrimage. At every point in that pilgrimage we come up against the mystery of God's initiative and self-revelation. Why should this not have as its starting-point, as Old Testament tradition affirms, the moment when a man called Abraham left north-west Mesopotamia in response to a call from God ?

ROBERT DAVIDSON

7 Moses

Moses is a key figure in the history and religion of Israel. He is regarded as the ideal prophet, the true servant of God, the trustworthy mediator of God's word to the people (Num.12.1–8; Deut.18.15–22). In later Jewish tradition, the supremely authoritative section of the Old Testament – *TORAH*, the Law (Genesis, Exodus, Leviticus, Numbers and Deuteronomy) – is known as the five books of Moses. To him the Old Testament traces back much that came into Israel only later and from a variety of sources. To him is ascribed the calendar of the religious year with its fixed festivals (Ex.23.14 ff.; 34.22–24; Lev.23; Deut.14); the entire cultic system with its sacrifices, offerings and priestly ministrants; the various codes of law, the earliest of which, the 'Book of the Covenant' (Ex.20.22–23.33), already presupposes the settled agricultural life in Canaan (cf. the Holiness Code, Lev.17–26, and the Deuteronomic Code, Deut.12–26). So important for Israel were the events associated with Moses, that all Israel was regarded as participating in these events (cf. the figures given in Ex.12.13 and the census lists in Num.1 and 26). Historically this is incredible, but theologically it is true in the same sense as one may speak of all Chrstians being 'there' at Calvary and the Empty Tomb. Moses was not given this dominant position without good reason. Much that was distinctive in Israel's faith, much that was to be decisive for Israel's later history was there, in at least seminal form, in the revelation that came to Moses and in the events of Moses' time.

The historical problem

The very centrality of Moses in tradition, however, poses serious historical problems.

1. The events recorded, the institutions described in the sources which lie behind Exodus, Leviticus, Numbers and Deuteronomy, were never in Israel cold historical facts. They are handed down to us across centuries of retelling and reliving in family worship and in the liturgies of the community. They speak of the mystery and wonder of God's mighty acts on behalf of his people, of a past which had no significance in Israel apart from faith. This does not mean that we are faced with 'take it or leave it' choice with respect to narratives steeped in the supernatural and the miraculous. The Old Testament is never naïve enough to believe that God's presence in the world is to be equated with the supernatural. The kind of questions raised are well illustrated in the story of the plagues which afflicted Egypt as narrated in Ex.7–12. With the notable exception of the final climactic blow, the death of the first-born in every Egyptian household, all the plagues are well authenticated as natural phenomena which occur in the Nile valley. The quails and manna in the wilderness (Ex.16), the water spurting forth from the rock (Ex.17) similarly admit of a natural explanation. What seems naturally explicable and what remains inexplicable are both equally God-centred in the narratives. It is impossible to eliminate the sense of wonder from the tradition.

2. The narratives tell a connected story in each part of which Moses has a crucial role to play. Beginning with the harsh enslavement of the Hebrews in Egypt, they lead us through the wonder of deliverance from bondgate to the encounter with God and the making of the covenant at the sacred mountain. The subsequent years of frustration and wandering in the wilderness come to a climax with the children of Israel poised on the verge of entry into the land of promise. There at Mt Nebo, looking out across the Jordan valley to Canaanite Jericho, Moses dies (Deut.34). Many scholars believe that, as in the case of the patriarchal narratives, this connected story is the result of the bringing together, into the religious and literary treasury of later Israel, of once separate traditions belonging to different tribal groups. In particular, on the basis of the omission of all references to the covenant at Mt Sinai in many credal passages which refer to the deliverance from Egypt (e.g., Deut. 26.5–11; Josh.24.2–12), it has been argued that originally there was no historical link between the stories of the exodus from Egypt and the covenant at Mt Sinai. The arguments for this division of the traditions are hardly conclusive. Even if they were, it remains true that from a very early date, the tenth century BC with the 'J' source, the link between the exodus and Mt Sinai had been made and was to be significant for the subsequent faith of Israel.

Whatever the problems posed for the historian by the narratives, the centrality of the personality of Moses can hardly be denied unless the traditions are drastically rewritten.

Extra-biblical evidence

At points where we can bring extra-biblical evidence to bear, it tends to corroborate the basic authenticity of the narratives.

1. Legend may have contributed its share to the stories about the infant Moses. The very name Moses, however, fits in well with the Egyptian background. Although Old Testament tradition links the name Moses with the Hebrew verb *mashah*, to draw up (Ex.2.10), the name in fact comes from an Egyptian root meaning 'beget'. It is found frequently, added to the name of a god, in Egyptian personal names, e.g., Thut-mosis, Ra-messes. Other names belonging to the family of Levi also have Egyptian associations.

2. Exodus 1.11 speaks of the Hebrew slaves building for Pharaoh the store cities of Pithom and Raamses. Both these towns are in the Nile Delta region. Raamses is almost certainly Avaris, rebuilt as the royal capital of the vigorous nineteenth Egyptian dynasty. It was called 'the house of Ramesses' by Ramesses II (thirteenth century BC), the second ruler of that dynasty. Egyptian tests of the period provide ample documentation of *Apiru (Habiru)* working as slaves on royal building projects. The name 'house of Ramesses' soon disappears from Egyptian texts and after the eleventh century it is always referred to as Tanis. It seems that the narratives at this point have drawn on authentic pre-eleventh-century BC tradition.

3. Two dates have been frequently canvassed for the exodus.

(a) Fifteenth century BC. This fits in well with the evidence of the fifteenth-century Amarna letters. In these letters, Egyptian satellite rulers of Canaanite city states send repeated appeals for help to the ruling Pharaoh. They allege intrigue and counter-intrigue against one another and make reference to attacks by Habiru. This date can also claim support in biblical tradition. I Kings 6.1 states that the fourth year of Solomon's reign, i.e., 958 BC, was the 480th year after the people of Israel came out of the land of Egypt.

(b) The main thrust of present evidence, however, points to the thirteenth century BC. This fits in well with the reference in Ex.1.11 (see above). Further, the story in Num.20–21 of the Israelites seeking permission from the Edomites to travel north along the King's Highway assumes a fair degree of Edomite settlement in the area. Archaeological evidence, however, reveals no trace of settlement in the region for centuries prior to the thirteenth century BC. Any date for the exodus is inevitably related to the date of the subsequent settlement in Canaan. There is evidence of severe destruction of several Canaanite cities in the late thirteenth century including Debir and Lachish in the south (Josh.10.31 ff.), Bethel in the centre (if Bethel is to be equated, as seems likely, with the Ai of Josh.8) and Hazor in the north (Josh.11). There is, of course, no conclusive proof that it was invading Hebrews who inflicted such destruction, but where archaeological evidence and biblical traditions seem to illumine each other, it is hypercritical to deny a link between them.

The significance of Moses

By the very nature of the case, we must deal with probabilities rather than certainties when we discuss the historical background to the age of Moses. The Old Testament has no hesitations, however, about the significance it assigns to Moses.

1. *The revelation of the character and name of God*

Moses, although brought up in the Egyptian

court, retained his sense of identity with his enslaved fellow-countrymen. He slew an Egyptian taskmaster whom he had seen maltreating a Hebrew slave (Ex.2.11–21). In consequence he fled to Midianite territory where, near the 'mountain of God', he had an encounter with God which was to be decisive, not only for his own life, but for the future of his people. At a mysteriously burning bush, he was confronted by a god who revealed himself as the 'God of your father, the God of Abraham, the God of Isaac and the God of Jacob' (Ex.3.6). In many respects, this encounter resembles the divine appearances in the patriarchal narratives. There is the same sense of direct personal relationship, a relationship enshrouded in mystery. Moses stands on 'holy ground'. The word 'holy' denotes separateness, that which belongs peculiarly to God. When applied to God it indicated the essential difference between God and even the best and greatest of men, the divine 'otherness' which evokes from man a response of reverent awe. Yet this 'otherness' is not remoteness. This God is concerned about the oppression of the people (Ex.3.7,16,17). These two aspects of God's character are held together in later Old Testament thinking by the description of God as 'the Holy One of Israel' (cf. Isa.1.4; 5.9,24; Ps.71.22). Moses' experience also points forward to later prophetic experience. His encounter with God is not an end in itself, not an invitation to share in mystical union with God. It issues in a word of command which commits Moses to action and obedience, a word of command from which Moses at first shrinks (Ex.4; cf. Isa.6; Jer.1).

Linked with this encounter there is the revelation of the name YHWH. The Priestly narrative in Ex.6.2 f. specifically claims that this is the revelation of a new name, not known to the patriarchs. The original meaning and even the pronunciation of these four consonants YHWH are matters of considerable dispute. Some have traced the name back beyond Moses to the worship of the Kenites or Midianites. The evidence for this lies mainly in the relationship between Moses and his father-in-law Jethro, the priest of Midian (see Ex.3; 18.10–12, 13–27). This is possible, but it is a case of explaining the unknown by an even greater unknown, since nothing is really known of the religion of the Kenites in pre-Mosaic times. Old Testament scholarship today usually renders the name *Yahweh*, which is probably as near as we can get to the original pronunciation. Most modern English translations use 'the *Lord*' (AV had Jehovah, which is an impossible form which was first coined in the Middle Ages). Whatever its origin, the narrative in Ex.3.13 ff. links it with the Hebrew verb HYH, 'to be' or 'to become'. 'God said to Moses "I am who I am" [or "I will be who I will be"]. And he said "Say this to the people of Israel, '*I am*' [or 'I will be'] has sent me to you" ' (Ex.3.14). YHWH therefore means 'He is' or 'He will be'. It is also possible that it may be a causative form 'He causes to be'. The emphasis is upon a God whose character is essentially dynamic and active. But the form of the statement '*I am who I am*' also indicates a certain reserve or mystery. The request to know God's name is a request to know his nature. The reply declares that God cannot be known in the sense of being neatly defined or labelled. He is a God who is and will be known through his active presence in the history of his people. The definition of his name is a challenge to go on into the unknown future with only one assurance: 'I will be with you' (Ex.3.12). The fact of the presence of Yahweh is stressed in various ways in the narratives of the period of the wandering in the wilderness. He is present in the pillar of cloud by day and fire by night that accompanies the Israelites (Ex.13.21; 14.19 f.), and in the 'tent of meeting' which, according to the earliest tradition in Ex.33, was a sanctuary outside the encampment where Yahweh could be consulted by his people. A sacred box, the ark, embodied Yahweh's presence. Numbers 10.35 preserves a very old tradition which addresses this ark as Yahweh: 'When it moved, Moses said, "Arise Yahweh, and let thy enemies be scattered" . . . and when it rested, he said, "Return, Yahweh, to the ten thousand thousands of Israel." ' Yahweh is therefore a pilgrim God present with his people. He is henceforth for Israel a God known by what he does.

It is important to notice that Moses' encounter with God and the revelation of the name YHWH come before the deliverance of the people from enslavement in Egypt. This gives Moses the standpoint of faith from which to declare what is going to happen, and from which to interpret the meaning of what does happen. Whatever took place at the exodus, it was not something self-explanatory as an 'act of God' to anyone who lived through it. Moses taught the people to accept it as God's action on their behalf, because of a faith in God which he already had.

2. *The exodus*

The exodus from Egypt is central to the faith of the Old Testament. If there is one description of God which, above all others, is characteristic of the God of the Old Testament, it is this: 'I am Yahweh your God who brought you out of the land of Egypt.' The prophets are the heralds of this God:

I brought you up out of the land of Egypt

(Amos 2.10; cf. Jer.2.6).

When Israel was a child, I loved him,
    and out of Egypt I called my son (Hos.11.1).

Psalmists praise this God:

Thy way was through the sea,
    thy paths through the great waters,
    yet thy footprints were unseen.

Thou didst lead thy people like a flock
    by the hand of Moses and Aaron
    (Ps.77.19 f.; cf. Pss.66.6; 78.11 ff.;
    136.10 f.).

When a son asked his father the meaning of the commandments binding on Israel, the father is instructed to reply:

We were Pharaoh's slaves in Egypt, and Yahweh brought us out of Egypt with a mighty hand, and Yahweh showed signs and wonders, great and grievous, against Egypt and against Pharaoh and all his household before our eyes . . .' (Deut.6.21 f.; cf. Ex.20.2; Deut.5.6).

The significance of the exodus for faith is unquestionable; what actually happened was probably sober enough. A group of Hebrew slaves under the leadership of Moses left Egypt. They safely negotiated a stretch of water called the Sea of Reeds (not the Red Sea). The location of the Sea of Reeds is uncertain; the likelihood is that it lay in the general region of what is now the Suez canal or further east along the Mediterranean coast at Lake Sirbonis. The earliest narrative strand 'J' speaks of a strong east wind blowing all night to push the water back (Ex.14.21–28). The pursuing Egyptian chariots stuck in the soft sand and were drowned by the returning water. Naturally, Egyptian records have nothing to say about what was at most, from their point of view, a minor frontier incident. In the Old Testament, however, this is never an escape bid engineered by Moses, but always a mighty act of God in which he delivered his people out of enslavement. What is probably the earliest Old Testament witness to the event, the triumph-song of Miriam, grasps the essence of what happened:

Sing to Yahweh, for he has triumphed
    gloriously,
the horse and the rider he has thrown into
    the sea (Ex.15.21; cf. 15.1).

This was Yahweh's victory over his enemies, a victory on behalf of his oppressed people. That it was so interpreted from the beginning must be attributed to the prior revelation of God's purposes given to Moses. The exodus is the heart of the Old Testament gospel, the good news of what God has done.

Just as the memory of central events in the New Testament gospel was preserved in the worship of the early Christian community, so the exodus was handed down in Israel in one great family religious festival 'Passover'. Alone among the festivals of the Hebrew religious year, Passover goes back beyond the time of settlement in Canaan, back in all probability beyond the exodus. In origin, Passover is the festival of a pastoral community. Celebrated in the spring, at full moon in the first month of the year, it contains a rite, the smearing of the blood of a lamb on the tent posts, which was probably designed to ward off demons of destruction or infertility. The lamb is roasted in nomadic fashion and eaten with desert food, unleavened bread seasoned with bitter herbs. The participants in the meal are ready to move at a moment's notice to defend the flock, belt fastened, sandals on feet, staff in hand. All of this is explicable without any reference to the exodus. But, just as Christmas has gathered to itself many pagan customs to give them new meaning in Christ, so Passover finds a new meaning in the Old Testament through being linked to the exodus. The name of the festival 'Pesah', a word of very uncertain meaning, is linked in the earliest source, 'J', with Yahweh's 'passing over' (Hebrew: *pasah*) the blood-smeared lintels of Hebrew homes when the destroying angel smote Egypt (Ex.12.21–27). In the 'P' tradition in Ex.12.11, the fastened belt, sandalled feet and staff in hand are memorials of the haste with which the Hebrews left Egypt at God's command. In Deut.16.3, the unleavened bread is called the 'bread of affliction', again a memorial of the people's flight in haste from Egyptian bondage. The date of the celebration is the month of Abib (April: 'the month of the green ears of corn'), 'for in the month of Abib Yahweh your God brought you out of Egypt by night' (Deut.16.1; cf. Ex.23.14 ff.; 34.18).

Passover is an illustration of something that happened to most of the festivals of the Hebrew year. Festivals such as *Massoth* (Unleavened Bread), *Qasir* (Harvest) and *Asiph* (Ingathering) are native to the agricultural life of Canaan. But whatever their origin, the Old Testament gives them a historical reference, and in most cases that historical reference is to the exodus or the events associated with it. *Asiph*, for example, is the great harvest thanksgiving festival. The farmer's work for the year is successfully completed; the mood is one of unrestrained rejoicing. In Deut.16.13, however, this festival is called *Sukkoth* (Huts). The origin of these 'huts' is disputed. Some find here a reference to the sacred booth in which the marriage between the god and goddess of fertility was consummated, others think the 'huts' are the temporary shelters which Palestinian agricultural workers from time immemorial have erected in the fields at harvest time to give shelter from the sun in the heat of the day. According to

Lev.23.42 f. these 'huts' or 'booths' have a different significance: 'You shall dwell in booths for seven days; all that are native in Israel shall dwell in booths that your generations may know that I made the people dwell in booths when I brought them out of the land of Egypt. I am Yahweh your God.'

3. *The covenant*

Closely associated with the exodus in Old Testament tradition is the story of how the Israelites journeyed to a mountain where there was ratified a covenant between Yahweh and the people. Much is uncertain about this mountain of Israel's destiny. Its very name is variously given in tradition. Two of the sources ('E' and 'D') consistently refer to it as Horeb, two ('J' and 'P') call it Sinai. Its location is likewise in dispute. Tradition places it near to the southern tip of the Sinai peninsula at the Jebel Musa (mountain of Moses). Many scholars hold to a much more northerly location near Kadesh (Ex.15.12), while others place it further east beyond the Gulf of Aqaba. This latter location is based mainly on the supposition that the language describing God's coming to his people on the mountain implies volcanic activity. Exodus 19.16–18 speaks of thunder, lightning, thick cloud, trumpet blast, smoke like the smoke of a kiln. The language might equally refer to a violent mountain storm. It is doubtful, however, whether we ought to press literally words and images which are traditionally associated with the divine appearances (cf. the covenant with Abraham, Gen.15). The tradition as to what happened at the mountain is exceedingly complex. There are three different appearances (Ex.19–20; 24.10–18; 34) and with each there are associated laws and regulations, governing worship and social relationships within the community. Many of these regulations are obviously of later date. What is the authentic historical kernel in all this ?

First we can assert with confidence that at this mountain a group of Hebrew refugee slaves from Egypt became conscious of their destiny as 'the people of God' through a covenant ceremony. The covenant ritual is described in Ex.24.4–8. It involves sacrifice and the sprinkling of half the blood upon the altar, symbol of God's presence, and half upon the people. God and people are now bound together in one common life. In one respect this covenant ceremony echoes the covenant traditions in the patriarchal narratives. The emphasis is heavily upon God's initiative. It is God who comes to the people in the awesome imagery of the mountain scene. When Moses sprinkles the blood upon the people he declares, 'Behold the blood of the covenant which Yahweh has made with you' (Ex.24.8). Exodus 34 contains what has been called a 'Ritual Decalogue' prescribing the religious acts to be observed by the community throughout the year. Its emphasis in terms of initiative is one-sided. No ceremony of covenant ratification is described, but this is a covenant which Yahweh makes (cf. Ex.34.10, 27). In another respect, however, this covenant is different from those in the patriarchal narratives. It is made by God no longer with one man such as Abraham, but with a community. The covenant is not between God and Moses. Moses simply acts as the priestly mediator in a covenant that binds God and people. Henceforth Yahweh is the God of Israel, and Israel the people of Yahweh. This means that Israel is no longer merely a tribal or racial group, but a religious community, committed to a certain kind of loyalty to a God who

had chosen them to be his people.

Two points are worth stressing about the covenant bond.

(a) It is in no sense a natural or inevitable relationship based on any ties of kinship between God and people. Rather is it a relationship of grace. It was inaugurated at a particular time and place in history as the outworking of God's revealed compassion for an oppressed people. Its continuance, therefore, depends solely upon the consistency of character of this God who had chosen Israel, upon what the Old Testament repeatedly refers to as the *hesed*, steadfast love, and the faithfulness of God (cf. Ex.34.6 f.).

(b) Although there is a historical 'once and for all' aspect about this covenant, its significance is not tied to any one point of time in Israel's history. Since it called the people to commitment, it is a covenant which, from the side of the people, must be accepted anew by each succeeding generation. Every generation was present or ought to be present at Mt Sinai.

4. *The Decalogue*

The various laws and regulations associated with the divine appearances in the exodus tradition are attempts to spell out for Israel the implications of this covenant relationship. The only element in them with any claim to be Mosaic is the Decalogue, the Ten Words. They come down to us in two versions, Ex.20.2–17 ('E') and Deut.5.6–10, both of them probably later theological variants of an original shorter form. The theological expansion is evident in the different reasons alleged for the observance of the sabbath: the Exodus version rooting it in the creation tradition of Gen.1, Deuteronomy making it a sacrament of the deliverance from Egyptian bondage. Many scholars regard the

Decalogue as a distillation of the teaching of the great prophets of Israel and no earlier in date than the exile of the sixth century BC. There are, however, no compelling reasons against it being in essence of Mosaic origin. In context, the Decalogue is distinctive because it consists of words addressed by God to the people, in contrast to the surrounding ordinances, regulations and statutes. Such ordinances are, in the main, in the form of 'case law' of a type common to the great law codes of the ancient Near East – the ordinance concerning Hebrew slaves in Ex.21.1–11 is a good example. The Decalogue throughout is in the form of direct address from God to the people. This has been compared with Hittite treaty documents of the fourteenth and thirteenth century BC. Such treaty documents begin with a prologue in which the Great King identifies himself and lists his beneficent acts towards his vassal people. The obligations upon loyal vassals are then listed. They include no dealings with the king's enemies and the fulfilment of all duties incumbent upon the king's subjects. The form of the Decalogue is remarkably similar. The prologue identifies God, 'I am Yahweh your God'; it declares his gracious deeds on behalf of the people: 'who brought you out of the land of Egypt out of the house of bondage'. Obligations are then laid upon the people, including the demand for exclusive loyalty to Yahweh, and the following of a code of conduct befitting Yahweh's people. Later Assyrian treaty documents have provided further close parallels notable to elements in the book of Deuteronomy. We may therefore think of the covenant at Mt Sinai as a treaty covenant, establishing the kingship of Yahweh over his subject people. The Decalogue is the charter document of this treaty.

The character of Yahweh revealed in the Decalogue is remarkable. There is the demand for *an exclusive loyalty*: 'no other gods "before" or "besides" or "in preference to" me'. In a world of many pantheons where gods and goddesses had their places in appropriate family groups, Yahweh was to stand alone in his people's loyalty. There is the demand for *imageless worship*. In a world where gods and goddesses were represented in myriad forms – human, animal, bird, fish – there was to be no representation of Yahweh. Deuteronomy 4.15ff. see this as a safeguard to the element of mystery in the nature of Yahweh. The people saw no form on the day that Yahweh spoke to them at Horeb out of the midst of the fire.

There is the demand to take the claims of Yahweh with *utter seriousness*. 'Not to take the name of Yahweh your God in vain' is far more than the prohibition of equivocal oaths. The best commentary on it is Josh.24.19–22 where Joshua warns the people against any glib or light-hearted pledge of loyalty to Yahweh. There is the demand to keep *sabbath*. The origin of and background to sabbath are obscure. The essential character of sabbath in the Old Testament, however, is that of a day which belongs to Yahweh, a tithe on time, proclaiming Yahweh's lordship over all time.

The last six demands are concerned with regulating human relationships within the covenant community. These six words focus attention on the character of the worshipper and the community in which he lives. They deal with what the prophets were later to summarize as 'justice' and 'righteousness'. If we take an organic link between religion and morality, both social and personal, for granted, it is only because we stand within a Judaic-Christian heritage which stems from the Decalogue. It was not always so in the world of the ancient Near East, where religion often centred on the forces of nature rather than on the demand for righteousness.

The legacy of Moses

Considerable discussion has centred upon whether, and in what sense, Moses can be described as a monotheist. Partly this is a question of terminology. Monotheism, in the sense of a theological or philosophical doctrine that there is in fact only one divine reality in the universe, had no relevance to Moses' situation. With belief, however, in a God who shapes the forces of nature and history, who brooks no rival, who has no female consort, who demands the exclusive loyalty of a people, monotheism of a practical kind is there in seminal form. It has been well said that the poet-prophet author of Isa.40–55, many centuries later, was but pushing Mosaic religion to its logical conclusion when he unequivocally declared:

> Turn to me and be saved, all the ends of the earth, for I am God and there is no other (Isa.45.22; cf. 44.6–8).

The history of Israel's religion from the time of the settlement in Canaan is a history of conflict: conflict between the many who demanded a 'Comprehensive Religious Insurance' policy covering the gods of Canaan as well as Yahweh and the few who stood for the exclusive claims of Yahweh; conflict between those who thought of religion basically in cultic terms and those who never lost sight of the essentially ethical element in Hebrew faith; conflict between the many who viewed Yahweh as the private patron saint of Israel and the few who saw judgment upon Israel springing inevitably out of the demanding nature of Israel's God.

That it was a history of conflict, not merely compromise; that a distinctive Yahwistic faith survived instead of being assimilated into the religious culture of Canaan, that it outlived the political disintegration of the Hebrew states; this is the legacy of the revelation that came to Moses, and the decisive shape that revelation gave to Israel's faith.

ROBERT DAVIDSON

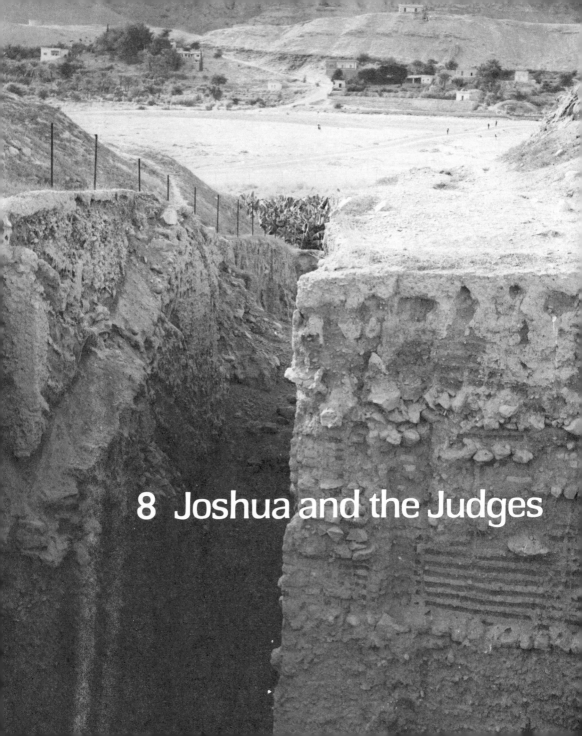

8 Joshua and the Judges

The evidence

1. Biblical material

This is to be found almost exclusively in the Old Testament books called 'Joshua' and 'Judges'. The former is concerned with the career of Joshua after the death of Moses; the latter covers the period from the death of Joshua to the emergence of Saul as the first king of Israel somewhere about 1000 BC. At first sight, the picture of the events given in these books appears comparatively straightforward. Under the leadership of Joshua, the twelve tribes of Israel that have come out of Egypt invade Palestine and conquer the whole country in a short space of time, as the result of three rapid campaigns – against the central part of the land (Josh.1–9), against the south (Josh.10) and against the north (Josh.11). As a result, Joshua is able immediately to divide Palestine among the twelve tribes, each of which settles in its allotted area (Josh.13–21). The book of Joshua fittingly concludes at ch. 24 with the account of a great ceremony in which, at Joshua's direction, all the tribes pledge themselves to the sole worship of the God Yahweh. After the death of Joshua, the nation broke this solemn obligation and began to worship other gods: as a result, they incurred divine judgment, which took the form of their falling under the rule of foreign enemies (Judg.2.6–3.6). When this happened, the nation repented, in consequence of which Yahweh chose a 'judge' ('ruler' conveys better the sense of the original) who first led the people to victory over their oppressors and then governed Israel during his lifetime. After his death, Israel again fell away from Yahweh: the same sequence of events occurred and the same pattern was repeated many times (Judg.3–16). Samuel was the last of these 'judges' and it was through his agency that a new system of government, the monarchy, was introduced.

2. Archaeological evidence

The evidence provided by the excavation of Palestinian sites is often adduced to support the biblical picture of a speedy and violent conquest of the whole country by the Israelites under Joshua. This evidence shows that there was a tremendous destruction of four towns mentioned in the conquest narrative as being destroyed by the Israelites, and that in each case the town was destroyed between 1300 and 1200 BC, and most probably in the latter half of the century. The towns in question are: in the south of Palestine, Lachish (Josh.10.31 f.) and Debir (Josh.10.38 f.); in the centre, Bethel (Judg. 1.22–26); in the north, Hazor (Josh.11.10–13). Thus, the biblical tradition and the archaeological evidence appear to agree that these places were all violently destroyed and within a comparatively brief span of time.

A reconstruction of events

When both the biblical records and the archaeological evidence are examined more closely the picture appears a good deal more complicated.

The first chapter of the book of Judges gives a markedly different account of the Israelite occupation of Palestine from that to be found in the book of Joshua. First, this account makes it clear that in a number of areas the Israelites were able merely to settle down alongside the already existing inhabitants, the peoples called Canaanites and Amorites (see, e.g., Judg.1.29, 31 f.), and that, even where they became the dominant power, they did not attempt to expel or exterminate the native population (Judg.1.21, 27 f., 30, 33–35). Most of the places referred to in this connection are towns and this would appear accurately to reflect the contemporary situation. Palestine at this period consisted mainly of a number of independent city-states, usually ruled over by a king and generally situated in the plains. It would seem that for a long time the area of Israelite occupation was restricted to the hilly districts and did not extend to the plains (so Judg.1.9). The Canaanite cities retained their independence and only became incorporated in the organization of Israel with the establishment of an Israelite state when kingship was introduced. Relations between the incoming Israelites and these cities no doubt varied from place to place. Often they would be hostile, which accounts for the traditions of attacks on cities that are to be found in the book of Joshua. On the other hand, Judg.1 indicates that the two groups frequently lived side by side in a state of relatively peaceful co-habitation and there are instances of actual confederations between them. Such is the reality behind the story in Josh.9 of how four Canaanite cities made a treaty of alliance (which is what the word 'covenant' means in this chapter) with the Israelites. In Judg.8.29 f.; 9, we seem to have the picture of a similar alliance, cemented by inter-marriage, between the tribe of Manasseh and the still Canaanite city of Shechem which continued the worship of its own special god (see Judg.9.4, 27, 46). A similar marriage relationship between the tribe of Benjamin and the city of Shiloh is probably the real explanation of the story in Judg.21.19–23. The continued existence of Canaanite populations, and the friendly relations of the Israelites with them in many cases, meant that the newcomers were often tempted to worship Canaanite deities or to fuse them with their own god, Yahweh, and to introduce Canaanite religious practices into his worship.

Canaanite religion

The Canaanites worshipped a group of gods, of whom the chief were El, the creator deity and the head of the group, Baal, the young storm-god and most active member of the group, and three goddesses, Anath, Ashtaroth and Asherah, all of whom were consorts of Baal. Canaanite religion was basically concerned with fertility, with securing a plentiful supply of crops, animals and children. The 'myths' or stories about the gods' doings all have this as their underlying theme and it seems likely that these stories were enacted year by year, in a kind of sacred drama, to bring about the fruitfulness and prosperity of the country and thus to ensure the people's continuing existence. It is not hard to see why this sort of religion appealed so strongly to the Israelites. It was concerned with survival and rooted in the soil and agriculture of Palestine: the problem for the Israelites was to survive in a strange country and to adapt themselves to the new agricultural way of life, in contrast to their previous semi-nomadic existence. Agriculture was the affair of the Canaanite gods: it was natural, therefore, for the Israelite farmer to turn to them for help or to invest Yahweh with their functions. Whatever may be thought of the worship of deities other than Yahweh – and the Old Testament universally condemns it – the development by which such a god as El was assimilated to Yahweh was not wholly bad. For it brought about a widening and deepening of the whole idea of Yahweh. He came to be seen as the Creator, the Lord of all nature as well as the Lord of the history of a particular people. Thus the seed which was to grow into the idea of one universal God was already planted in this early period of Israel's history.

A gradual conquest

The first chapter of Judges (in contrast to the book of Joshua) suggests that the occupation of Palestine was not carried out by a single operation of all the tribes acting together under a united leadership. Rather, in this chapter, we have a picture of individual tribes, or even smaller groups, acting independently of one another, each one moving separately into a particular area on its own initiative. In a number of cases, exploits which elsewhere are attributed to all Israel are here presented as the work of a single tribe: thus, in Josh.10.36–39 Hebron and Debir are captured by a united nation under the leadership of Joshua; in Judg.1.8–15 Hebron is taken by the tribe of Judah and Debir by a small clan represented as an individual, Othniel, without any mention of Joshua at all. Further, on closer examination, even the book of Joshua tends to confirm that this picture of a piecemeal settlement in Palestine probably corresponds to what actually happened. The account of the wholesale con-

quest of the country is in fact confined to Josh.10–11 and is in very general terms. By contrast, in chs. 1–9, which are in much greater detail, the territory said to be conquered or occupied is limited to the area belonging to the tribe of Benjamin alone. It may well be that the kernel of the book of Joshua was originally the tribe of Benjamin's own account of how it came to possess its own particular territory. It would thus be parallel to the individual tribal traditions of settlement to be found in Judg.1 and elsewhere. Joshua himself was perhaps to begin with just the local Israelite leader in this region: he seems to have originated not from Egypt but from the neighbouring hill country, where his family held property and where he was buried (Josh.24.30).

At this point, the archaeological evidence must also be looked at again. We saw that, from the fact of the destruction of certain towns, it has been held that there was actually a sudden and fairly rapid Israelite conquest of Palestine within the period 1300–1200 BC. There are three points to be noted in connection with this. First, there is no *direct* evidence from archaeology that these particular towns, or indeed any others, were destroyed by the Israelites. Most excavated Palestinian cities suffered frequent destructions between 2000–1000 BC and not all these can be attributed to the Israelite tribes: we simply do not know who was responsible. Secondly, the archaeological evidence from some cities which are said in the Bible to have been taken by the Israelites does not allow their destruction to be placed in the century 1300–1200 BC. To refer to the most striking examples, Joshua and the Israelites are said to have captured and burned the cities of Jericho and Ai (Josh.6–8). But the latest excavations show that the site of Jericho was probably unoccupied, and certainly did not possess a city wall, during the century in question, while Ai had been left abandoned some hundreds of years before. Thirdly, there is the evidence of the Amarna letters, so called because they were discovered at Amarna in Egypt. These are letters written somewhere between 1450 and 1350 BC to the king of Egypt from the rulers of various Canaanite cities. Some of them mention attacks on cities in Palestine by a people called the *Habiru*, and this word is probably closely connected with the name *Hebrew*. It is not possible simply to equate what is said of the *Habiru* disturbances with the biblical record of the Israelite conquest, as has sometimes been done, but it seems likely that there is some link between the two and that the *Habiru* movement probably was a part, though not the whole, of what we call the Israelite conquest and settlement of Palestine.

Taken in conjunction with the biblical witness to the piecemeal character of the Israelite occupation of Canaan, the archaeological evidence too, suggests that the 'conquest' was probably a very slow and gradual process, extending over some hundreds of years and by no means completed even during the period covered by the books of Joshua and Judges. The difficulties and discrepancies of the Old Testament narrative, some of which have been mentioned, can probably best be accounted for by some such reconstruction as the following. To begin with, we have to think of a number of separate groups, though no doubt of much the same racial stock, which formed the basis of the later Israelite tribes. Each of these, at different times and in different circumstances, pushed into Canaan from the desert region on its eastern border and settled down there, and each group preserved its own tradition of how

this happened. What we have in the Bible is, in the first place, the collecting together of these often very divergent tribal recollections, and this came about when the various tribes joined together on the soil of Palestine to form the entity which the Bible calls 'Israel'.

In the second place, the different traditions of conquest and settlement are in the Old Testament unified and harmonized, and again it is perhaps possible to suggest how this happened. One or more of the groups, though not all, that came to constitute 'Israel' migrated to Egypt and eventually experienced the events of the exodus and the desert wanderings. It was this group's tradition of those events which became the dominant one in Israel and was adopted by all the other groups as part of their own tribal history. That this was possible, it may be surmised, was because of the tremendous effect of Yahweh's greatness made on those who heard of his mighty works at the exodus. The different tribal groups came to see that the God who had been active in the deliverance from Egypt was in fact the one who had also led them in their own migrations to Palestine: that is, acceptance of the exodus tradition also meant recognition of Yahweh. Perhaps we can see signs of the process we have just outlined at work behind the narrative in Josh.24, although this chapter has no doubt been worked over by editors of varying dates. Here a great assembly of the tribes of Israel gathers together at the holy place of Shechem, but it is clearly stated that their ancestors were not Yahweh-worshippers (v.2) nor are many of them now (vv.14 f.). The purpose of Joshua's speech is to win over the whole body to the worship of Yahweh, who is the God of his own group (v.15). This he does by reciting a statement of Yahweh's saving acts in history up to the occupation of the Promised Land (vv.3–13). The statement includes mention of Yahweh's care of Abraham, Jacob and Esau (vv. 3–4), and these patriarchal names almost certainly represent originally independent groups. Thus once separate histories of particular groups are here linked with the exodus tradition and with the God of the exodus. The climax is reached when all the people recognize Yahweh and make their own his deliverance of them from Egypt and his settling of them in Canaan (vv.16–18). Finally, Joshua makes a covenant (v.25), a solemn agreement which joins all the tribes together in a common service to the one God, Yahweh. Joshua 24, therefore, does seem closely to reflect the manner in which we have suggested the different tribal traditions came together.

Judges and the Deuteronomic history

We saw that, in its present form, the book of Judges presents the nation as a whole, and the judges appear as rulers over the entire people, succeeding one another in chronological succession. But closer study shows that this presentation is the result of the final editing of the book, the purpose of which was to give a particular interpretation to the much older material which the editor used and to set out a particular understanding of Israel's history. It is now widely accepted that this editing was done by the school of writers who produced the book of Deuteronomy and were guided by its outlook, and that the books of Joshua and Judges now form part of a much larger book, a 'Deuteronomic history', recounting the story of the nation from the settlement in Palestine to the fall of Jerusalem at the end of II Kings, for which Deuteronomy is the introduction and the

programme. The Deuteronomic school always views Israel as a single whole, so that all the laws of Deuteronomy are given to the nation as one unit. Again, the Deuteronomic literature has a very definite purpose and a very distinctive theological position. Its writers were also preachers who wanted to convince the people of the need to remain faithful to Yahweh and they tried to achieve this by constantly driving home the point that disobedience to Yahweh automatically involved national disaster and vice versa. Both these characteristics are very marked in the book of Judges, but, as we have already partly seen, they represent an *interpretation* of historical events rather than an accurate picture of conditions in the age before the rise of the monarchy. When we look at the actual stories of the judges which the editor used, such narratives as those of Ehud (Judg.3), Gideon (Judg.6–8), Jephthah (Judg.11–12) or Samson (Judg.13–16), we can see that these are about the popular heroes of particular tribes and particular localities, who emerged to save their own group when it was threatened with attack by some other neighbouring people. The exploits of the judges were on a comparatively small scale and probably they were often contemporary with one another, active in different parts of the country at the same time. The judge was not even the regular or permanent leader of his group, in which authority normally resided in the 'elders' (see, e.g., Judg.11.5 f.), the senior men whose wisdom and experience fitted them for controlling the affairs of the tribe and for settling legal disputes between its individual members. Rather, the judge appeared in response to a grave crisis, almost always a dangerous external attack, which the elders could not cope with, and when his task was successfully completed he retired again to his ordinary life. He was marked out for his calling when he was possessed by the 'spirit of Yahweh' (see, e.g., Judg.6.34), a violent seizure which enabled him to perform superhuman feats of strength and military prowess. The Israelite judge is thus an example of a kind of leadership characteristic of simple societies and which is often described by the term *charismatic*, from the Greek word *charisma*, a gift: the judge was one who had the 'gift' of Yahweh's spirit, and he was therefore very close to the prophet. Hence it is not surprising that the institution of the judges disappeared with the formation of the Israelite state, when the overriding authority which he had temporarily possessed was permanently transferred to the figure of the king. So the book of Judges, too, gives a picture of the Israelites at this period divided into comparatively small and separate groups, occupying only restricted areas of the country and maintaining a precarious existence in the face of the threat from other groups pushing into Palestine as they themselves had previously done.

The people of Israel

Yet the fortunes of individual groups is not the whole story. As well as each particular tribe, and however different the past history of any one tribe may have been from that of any other, it seems clear it was at this time possible to recognize something called 'Israel', as a living reality over and above the individual tribes. We now have to go on to say something of the actual life of the tribe on the one hand and of Israel on the other, and to consider the relationship between them.

The individual tribes seem to have gained their form and identity as the result of the actual process of occupying specific territories in Palestine and growing into settled communities there. In not a few cases, we can see fairly clearly how the nature of the country and its inhabitants were the decisive factor in the formation of particular tribes. So, some tribal names seem to derive from the geographical area where the tribe settled, such as Ephraim from 'Mount Ephraim': again, the tribe of Judah seems to be much more a confederation than a single unit, built up by the joining together of Israelites with a number of other small groups living in the southern part of Palestine. The organization of a tribe was that of a simple agricultural community, but even the simplest society must have some rules for common living and it is the emergence of these, at the very beginning of national life in Palestine, which is one of the most interesting features of this time. There are a number of such laws, in various parts of the Old Testament, which seem to take their rise in this early period, and perhaps the most important collection of them is to be found in Ex.21–23, which are often referred to as the 'Book of the Covenant'. Three points, among many, may be singled out for attention.

1. The regulations of the Book of the Covenant are clearly concerned with an agricultural, farming community, not a semi-nomadic one. They deal with cattle, with corn, with fields and vineyards, and the people are living in well-built houses.

2. When the Book of the Covenant is examined, it can be seen to consist of two distinct types of laws. For the moment, only one of these types will be discussed because it is this type which seems to be most directly concerned with the daily life of the local community. The type in question is commonly termed *casuistic*

law, from the Latin *casus*, a case, and it is so called because it first states a typical case and then draws a principle of general application from it. Casuistic laws can be easily recognized from their opening formula: 'When a man does so and so.' A considerable number of law codes from the ancient Near Eastern world are known, from which it can be seen that this type of law was commonly used throughout the area which formed the background to Israelite life. Hence it is reasonable to think that the Israelites in Palestine may have borrowed these laws from their Canaanite neighbours: it was part of their adaptation to their new way of life. By their nature, these laws were based on custom, and sprang from the needs and problems of everyday social life.

3. The public religious life of each tribe centred on one or more holy places in its neighbourhood, and it is with these local shrines that many of the regulations about worship were originally concerned. These holy places were of greater or lesser elaboration and reputation and drew their worshippers from wider or narrower areas, but each had its own priesthood of some kind, although there was as yet no idea of a single hereditary priestly family such as came to be the case later on in Israel. It is also clear that the great majority of these sanctuaries long pre-dated the Hebrew settlement and that the Israelites took them over from, or often even shared them with, the Canaanites. The heart of the tribe's worship were the three annual feasts of 'Unleavened Bread', of 'Harvest' and of 'Ingathering' mentioned in Ex.23.14–17. 'Feast' here properly means 'pilgrimage' and these were occasions when all males had to be present at the shrine: this is the reason why the Israelite festival most familiar to us, the Passover, is not included

among them, for this was not kept publicly at the sanctuary but at home. All these feasts are linked with key moments in the farmer's year. Their original purpose was to secure the divine blessing on the basic needs of human life. The same is true of the original meaning of the presentation of the first-fruits (Ex.23.19) and of the first-born (Ex.22.29–30) and accounts for the central place given to these observances in the regulations. Here again we can see how close at this time were the basic concerns of popular Israelite religion to those of Canaanite worship.

The tribal league

Over and above the local pattern of family and tribe, there was a wider grouping to which all the tribes belonged and to which the Old Testament gives the name 'Israel'. This was a league of tribes, built on bodies of people and not on a territorial area as were many of the states of the ancient world: so, whatever the word 'Israel' may originally have implied, it early became the alternative name of a person, Jacob, from whom all the tribes were supposed to have been descended. It would be wrong to think of the tribal league as being anything like so well-defined or so closely-knit as a state, whether ancient or modern, but it did have its central organization and functionaries. Modern scholars often use the word *amphictyony* to describe what Israel was like in the centuries before the establishment of the monarchy. This is a Greek term meaning 'those who dwell round about', a league of near neighbours. In the classical world, it denoted a distinctive organization, a group of twelve or six tribes who were united together because they worshipped at a common sanctuary, with each tribe being responsible for the upkeep of this central sanctuary for one or two months in the year. It would be dangerous to think of pre-monarchic Israel as conforming very closely to the classical *amphictyony*. Whether the twelve-tribe system was a reality, at any rate at this time, is doubtful – in the very early poem, known as the 'Song of Deborah', for example, in Judg.5, there are at best only ten tribes mentioned – and there is no clear evidence in Israel for each tribe in turn being responsible for the monthly upkeep of a central sanctuary. Nevertheless, there are enough similarities to make it illuminating to apply the term *amphictyony* to early Israel, as long as it is not pressed too far.

As we have seen, the tribes were held together by a covenant which bound them to worship Yahweh alone: the basis of the Israelite league was the religious obligation of this covenant. But it was necessary from time to time to remind the Israelites of their covenantal obligations and also to make these known to succeeding generations. Thus there would seem to have come into being an annual ceremony, attended by all the tribes, when the covenant was solemnly renewed. On this occasion, the terms of the covenant – the demands of Yahweh – were read out to the people, who then undertook to observe them. These demands are what is meant by 'law' in the Old Testament and there all the different law-codes are represented as expressions of the will of the covenant God. In the period with which we are concerned, we can probably see the character of the covenant law in a second type of legal material found in the Book of the Covenant, which is often called *apodictic*, a word meaning 'absolute', something which admits of no exception. *Apodictic law* is recognizable by the formula 'thou shalt' or 'thou shalt not': because it

expressed the will of Yahweh, it could not be modified by changing circumstances as could casuistic law. A description of the ceremony at which the terms of the covenant were read out is in Deut.31.9–13, though here the reading of the law takes place at seven-year intervals. Here the law is entrusted for keeping and reading to the priests and the elders, but there may also have been a single individual who, as the covenant mediator, was responsible for transmitting the law, and this person may be the source of some features in the biblical picture of such figures as Moses and Joshua. He may also have had the functions of a judge in the proper sense, settling disputes which were too difficult for the local elders (see Deut.17.8–13). Judg.10.1–5 and 12.8–15 is perhaps a list of such central judges.

The central sanctuary and the ark of the covenant

The renewal of the covenant implies a sanctuary where the ceremony took place and where a copy of the law was kept. This sanctuary did not replace the local shrine, but its distinguishing feature was that it was a central place where the tribes all assembled on solemn occasions. In the books of Joshua and Judges, we read of various shrines at which the tribal league came together and it is possible that different places were the site of the central sanctuary at different times during this long period. But, towards its end, the central sanctuary seems to have been firmly established at Shiloh, about which we learn a great deal from the first three chapters of I Samuel. There, we find that the main celebration was a great harvest festival in the autumn to which people came from considerable distances on pilgrimage (I Sam.1): this is the festival which is known elsewhere in the Old Testament as the 'feast of Tabernacles' and it should be noted that this was also the occasion of the reading out of the law (see Deut.31.10).

At Shiloh, we find a priesthood which had the special responsibility of looking after the ark, which, at this time, was the chief religious symbol for the Israelite nation. The exact nature of the ark is much disputed, and no doubt it meant different things at different times, but it is always closely associated with the covenant and the tribal league; indeed, in the Old Testament it is very frequently described as the 'ark of the covenant'. Sometimes the reason for this title is given as being that the ark was a kind of container in which the copy of the covenant law was kept (so Deut.31.26): but perhaps the ark was rather the symbol of the covenant God and the community in fellowship with him. So we find the title 'the ark of the covenant of Yahweh of hosts' (I Sam.4.4), where the word 'hosts' probably refers to the massed gathering of the tribes of Israel. Above all, the ark, as many Old Testament passages show, represented the living, active presence of Yahweh among his chosen people, so that it could sometimes be virtually identified with him (see I Sam.4.6–8). Yahweh was felt to be specially active on behalf of his people when, the ark going at their head, he led them out to victory against their enemies (see Num.10.35); and here we come to what, apart from the renewal of the covenant, was at this period the chief function of the tribal league.

The holy war

Not all wars – for example, battles between individual Israelite tribes – were 'holy': the holy war was fought by Yahweh's people and in his name against foreign enemies and their gods. Its distinctive feature was that Yahweh was considered to be the actual leader of the Israelite forces and he alone won the victory by sending a panic on the enemy which decisively routed them (see Judg.7.22). Therefore all the spoils of battle belonged not to Israel but to Yahweh: Israel could not enjoy them in any way; they all, human captives as well as animals and material objects, had to be offered to him in sacrifice (see Josh.6.17–21).

Such was the inspiration by which Israel fought its wars of conquest in Palestine. We may feel that it is almost blasphemous to call such warfare 'holy', but we need to understand the outlook of a people who believed that Yahweh had promised them possession of the land of Canaan and that he would fulfil his promise in the real situation of war and conquest. The institution of the 'holy war' is another example of the fact that it was a common loyalty to Yahweh which was the real bond holding together the tribal league, and a genuine expression of Israel's faith in this early period that its entire existence and success belonged solely to him.

J.R. PORTER

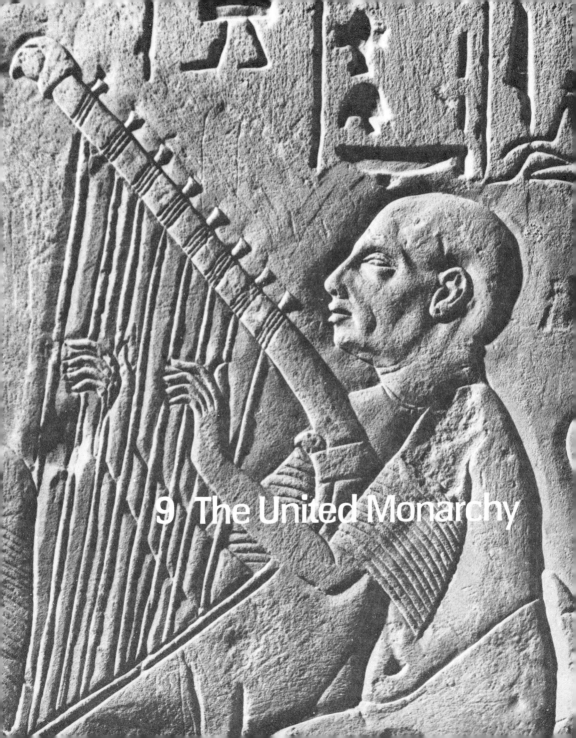

9 The United Monarchy

The evidence

1. Biblical sources

(a) The main narrative source for this period is I and II Samuel; I Kings 1–11. This contains an unusually large amount of thoroughly reliable information, especially for the reigns of David and Solomon, although a skilled critical examination is necessary to distinguish history from legend, saga and later religious or nationalist comment.

(b) The other narrative source, I Chron. 10–29; II Chron.1–9, is much less reliable. In its general outline it follows the account in Samuel-Kings for the reigns of David and Solomon, but it deliberately omits large sections of material in order to create an idealistic picture of these two kings, and adds much new material, especially concerning David's supposed preparations for the building of the temple and for the organizing of its worship, which is generally held to be wholly or almost wholly unhistorical. Chronicles was written many centuries after the events which it describes.

2. Archaeological evidence

The chief contribution of archaeology to the study of this period is a negative, though useful one: discoveries which specifically confirm details of the biblical narrative are few, but the discoveries which have been made are completely compatible with the biblical statements. Discoveries which can be directly related to the biblical narrative include the discovery of a small citadel of the period at Gibeah, Saul's capital; Solomonic fortifications at Megiddo and elsewhere; and buildings at Ezion-geber on the Red Sea where Solomon established his shipyards and seaport. A copper refinery, also at Ezion-geber, provides us with one piece of information about Solomon's activities not found in the biblical narrative. Finally the plan and the furnishings of a number of temples of the period excavated in Syria and Palestine confirm the description of Solomon's temple in I Kings.

Becoming a nation

The 'Israel' of the tribal league was not yet a nation. Although there had been moments of crisis in the past when something like a feeling of nationhood had momentarily united the tribes, there had been no external pressure sufficiently prolonged to allow this tendency to develop.

About the middle of the twelfth century this impetus towards nationhood was provided by the Philistines, a non-Semitic people which had originally formed part of a great wave of migrating peoples which swept down the eastern coast of the Mediterranean from the north in the late thirteenth century, destroying whatever lay in its path. This mass movement had been checked, though with great difficulty, by the Egyptians; and when it broke up, some of its constituent groups settled in a small district bordering on the southern coast of Palestine, probably under Egyptian auspices. This occurred shortly after the arrival of the central Israelite tribes under Joshua. Egyptian dominance of Syria and Palestine was rapidly collapsing; and the Philistines began to advance from their original base. They soon obtained control of a large part of Palestine, not only in the plains where the Canaanite cities mainly lay, but also in the Israelite hill country.

Our information about the early stages of this process is very incomplete. According to the biblical narrative Israel suffered an initial defeat (I Sam.4.1–10), but then found a leader in Samuel, who inflicted total and lasting defeat on the Philistines simply by asking as Moses did before him for divine assistance (I Sam.7.7–14). This story cannot be historical, for two reasons: first it assumes a degree of national cohesion which did not then exist, and secondly it fails to explain why only a few years later Israel was still completely under Philistine control (I Sam. 13.2–7, 19–23).

The role of Samuel has evidently been greatly exaggerated. The actual facts are difficult to assess; but it is probable that there was some movement towards national unity during this period, and that Samuel was closely associated with this. Probably he was recognized as head of the religious assembly of the tribes, and from this position played a decisive part in creating an awareness that the time had come for a greater degree of political unity. The multiple traditions which associate him with the institution of the monarchy (I Sam.8; 9.1–10. 25; 11.12–15) can hardly be without a historical basis.

The statement in I Sam.8.5,20 that the elders of Israel came to Samuel and asked him to 'appoint for us a king to govern us like all the nations' and to 'go out before us and fight our battles' has the ring of authenticity about it.

This amounted to a recognition by the tribal leaders that only the establishment of a permanent military commander who would be authorized to enforce obedience from all the tribes could save them from the Philistines. That they should turn to the surrounding nations for the model of the new institution was natural. But it was equally natural that they should want to combine the new office with their own traditional kind of leadership. Consequently, from the very moment of the institution of a monarchy in Israel there was a tension between conflicting ideas of what the monarchy should be. The words of Samuel in I Sam.8.11–18 show a realistic grasp of political realities: a military leader to whom such extensive powers were to be given would never be content to be a military leader only: he would have to be a king 'like all the nations', having power over his subjects in other aspects of their lives besides war; and this would always create the danger of tyranny. It seems that this danger was recognized from the beginning, and that some Israelites thought it to be an even greater danger than that of Philistine domination (I Sam.10.27): hence the hesitations and opposition of which we read in these chapters.

Saul: the first king

The decision was taken; and, perhaps about the year 1020 BC, Saul was chosen as the first king. There are several conflicting accounts of the manner of his selection (I Sam.9.1–10.16; 10.17–24; 11.1–15), but all agree that he was designated by God; it is also taken for granted that his tenure of office depended on continued divine approval. Nothing is said at this stage about any dynastic principle: it was Saul, not his family, who was appointed.

At first all went well. We read of successful attacks by Saul and his son Jonathan against Philistine forces (I Sam.13.2–7, 15b–23; 14.1–23, 31–35, 52). But our information is very incomplete. These battles may have been little more than local skirmishes against occupying forces. Whether Saul ever securely held any large tract of territory we do not know; certainly the statement in I Sam.14.47 that he inflicted defeats on the neighbouring states of Moab, Ammon, Edom and Zobah can hardly be correct. The impression given by the narrative as a whole is one of a reign wholly occupied with a war of independence (cf. I Sam.14.52) which ultimately ended in total defeat for Israel, with the Philistine power once more supreme (I Sam.31). Probably there were moments of success and times of defeat – the situation was evidently a fluid one. The absence of any details about the establishment of a permanent administrative system in Israel is also significant, in that it suggests that Saul's 'kingdom' was at best a precarious one, and that there was never any respite from war which would have made consolidation possible.

Saul and David

The ultimate failure of Saul's reign was due to three main causes; his quarrel with Samuel (I Sam.13.8–15; 15.10–35) and the priesthood (I Sam.22.11–19); the split in loyalties due to the emergence of David as a rival; and the deterioration of Saul's own character. These are mutually related. Behind the accounts of Saul's dispute with Samuel there almost certainly lie reasons other than those which are given to us: the real nature of Saul's 'disobedience' to God was probably that he was not content to remain under the tutelage of Samuel but was deter-mined to have freedom of action. It is clear also from I Sam.20.31 that he came to regard his office as hereditary, and intended to found a dynasty; and the statement in I Sam.14.52 that 'when Saul saw any strong man, or any valiant man, he attached him to himself' shows that he attempted to build up a *corps d'élite* loyal to himself and independent of the tribal organization.

But to have made enemies of Samuel and of the priests, representatives of the old order, who still exercised great influence, proved fatal to his position. His mental deterioration (I Sam.16.14 and subsequent stories), whether the result of his failures or independent in origin, made him increasingly incapable of competent leadership.

Both of these things played into the hands of the upstart David, who was one of the young men especially recruited by Saul. It was Saul's misfortune to have in his entourage a man of such outstanding ability, who had no difficulty in exploiting the situation. The stories of David's relations with Saul are so patently concerned to convince the reader of David's unswerving loyalty and disinterestedness that we can be sure that the opposite was the case. The realistic Jonathan understood quite clearly that David both intended to be, and would be, king (I Sam.20.13b–17).

David's outstanding qualities as a military commander soon won for him great popularity (I Sam.18.6–9), and equally made him an object of suspicion to Saul. Eventually there was an open breach between the two, and David became a fugitive, fleeing from place to place and ultimately driven to seek refuge with the Philistine Achish king of Gath. The stories concerning this period of David's life reveal him as almost uncannily astute. He built up a useful band of followers amounting to a private army (I Sam.22.2; 23–31 *passim*), acquired great possessions in Judah by an astute marriage (I Sam.25), and while in the employ of Achish succeeded in preparing the way for the future by establishing friendly relations with the Judaeans while at the same time convincing Achish that he was making enemies of them (I Sam.27.8–12). He also had the good sense to bide his time.

The opportunity for David came when the Philistines inflicted a decisive defeat on Israel at the battle of Mount Gilboa (*c*.1000 BC), in which both Saul and Jonathan were killed (I Sam.31). The Israelite kingdom, it seemed, was at an end. But the Philistines reckoned without David.

The reign of David

After the battle the Israelites were leaderless and Philistine power unchallenged. It is therefore clear – although the biblical narrative leaves the reader to infer this – that David's first steps towards national leadership were taken under Philistine auspices. They thought that they had every reason to trust him, and no doubt approved of his first action, which was to advance upon Hebron, the chief city of Judah (II Sam.2.2–4). They were unaware that to the Judaeans David was more of a national hero than a traitor, and that they needed no show of force to choose him as their king. To the Philistines, this 'kingship' of David's was a title without substance: he was their vassal, governing Judah on their behalf. But all the time David was laying plans to give it substance, and also to extend it.

The Philistines continued to look on with approval while David carried on hostilities against what remained of the forces of Saul. Abner, Saul's cousin and commander-in-chief, had withdrawn to Mahanaim to the east of the Jordan, beyond the reach of the Philistines, and had there set up an Israelite kingdom with Ishbosheth (or Ishbaal) as puppet king (II Sam.2.8–10). But after military successes and some strokes of good fortune had removed both Abner and his protégé (II Sam.2.12–4.12), David accepted the invitation of the local elders to become king of the north and east also (II Sam.5.1–3). That they should have submitted themselves to the rule of the enemy of Saul shows a realism and sense of national unity which came as a complete surprise to the Philistines. When they realized that they had been outwitted, and that David had established an independent rule over the whole of Israelite territory under their very noses, they hastily assembled a large army; but they were too late: they were resoundingly defeated (II Sam. 5.17–25). Their empire had been swept away almost overnight by a man who, though admittedly he had had his share of good luck, had won his way to power through sheer intellectual ability.

David spent the next few years in consolidating his position. His defeat of the Philistines was decisive, but he did not annex their home territory: he left them still independent but powerless to harm him (II Sam.8.1). But he went on to conquer the neighbouring states of Moab, Edom and Ammon, and the Aramaean kingdoms of Zobah and Damascus (II Sam.8; 10.15–19; 12.26–31) in such short order that more distant states such as Hamath and Tyre, recognizing the fact that a new and formidable power had appeared in Palestine, hastened to establish friendly relations with him. Others no doubt followed suit: no foreign power ever attacked Israel during David's lifetime.

Apart from the story of David's capture of Jerusalem we are not told what happened to the city states of Canaan. Some of these (e.g., Bethshan, I Sam.31.10) had been conquered by the Philistines; others had presumably remained independent until now. But from this point in the biblical narrative there is no further mention of them except, later, as cities in Israel. We may therefore assume that they capitulated to David. It is unlikely that he would have tolerated independent enclaves within his home territory when he set out on his foreign campaigns.

Thus an entirely new situation was created. Only a few years previously, 'Israel' had consisted of a few loosely organized tribes under foreign domination; there was now an Israelite empire stretching from the border of Egypt to the Euphrates. Its creator, David, was to rule it for forty years (c.1000–961; cf. II Sam.5.4 f.).

Jerusalem: capital of the kingdom

Internally also David took some shrewd steps to consolidate his position. He captured Jerusalem, using only his private army (II Sam.5.6–9; this event probably took place later than the biblical narrative suggests), and transferred his capital there. He thus not only secured an extremely strong fortified city as the centre of his government, but at the same time forestalled possible tribal jealousies: ruling from Hebron, he might have seemed to the northern tribes like a Judaean usurper; but Jerusalem had no tribal connections at all. David was determined to be regarded as impartially king of 'all Israel'. As later events were to show, he was not entirely successful in this attempt to secure the loyalty of the north;

but for the time he succeeded well enough.

Even more astute was his transfer to Jerusalem of the ark of God. This sacred object, once the rallying-point of the tribal league, had earlier been captured by the Philistines; and in spite of the story of its return to Israelite territory (I Sam.6) it is probable that it had remained ever since within Philistine control: it plays no part in the stories of the reign of Saul. But it evidently still had the power to command the old loyalties. By placing it permanently in his new capital, David made a shrewd move to strengthen Israelite loyalty to himself and to allay the suspicions which many conservative Israelites must have had that he intended to sweep away old traditions and institutions and to establish a new type of monarchy on a pagan model. By this action he showed himself to be after all a pious Israelite of the old type, concerned above all to restore and maintain the old institutions and to give to the old tribal league a permanent centre where the traditional worship of the God of Israel would be carried on as before.

He was greatly assisted in this policy by the fact of his immense and – as it must have seemed – miraculous success in everything which he did: no-one, it was believed, could be so successful without a special degree of divine favour. This is, indeed, the constant theme of almost all the stories which are told of him; and it was expressed as a 'theological dogma' in II Sam.7 where God is represented as confirming David's position as the divinely appointed leader through whom God's will for his people has been achieved.

That David firmly believed himself to be the servant of the God of Israel there is no reason to doubt. At the same time he was well aware that his kingdom was a composite one, composed of Canaanites as well as Israelites. The co-operation of the Canaanites was not only essential for the safety of the state, but also potentially of great benefit to it. Heirs of centuries of civilized urban life, they were superior to the Israelites in the arts both of war and of peace. Unassimilated, they constituted a serious danger; assimilated, they provided David with much needed administrators and military experts. In return for their loyalty, David seems to have left them to continue their own local administration, and to a very considerable extent to practise their own religious traditions.

Thus in his religious policy David steered a sagacious middle course. At Jerusalem, the worship of the God of Israel centred upon the ark was modified by elements taken from the pre-Israelite Canaanite cult. Canaanites who worshipped there would thus not feel that the worship was something entirely strange, imposed by a foreign conqueror. A similar policy, even more 'liberal' was adopted in the other former Canaanite cities, and the worship of the gods of Canaan, thus tolerated, continued to flourish throughout the period of the monarchy. David, although he believed himself to be under the especial protection of the God of Israel, was no religious fanatic; and this fact contributed not a little to his success.

The organization of the state

The monarchical system established by David was thus a very different thing from the *ad hoc* rule of Saul. As a powerful political state, Israel now rapidly developed institutions which were politically necessary but entirely new to the Israelites, and which in many ways resembled those of Israel's neighbours. Efficient government required a professional civil service. David recruited this partly from native (Israelite and Canaanite) sources; but he also found it necessary to employ skilled scribes from other countries who had greater experience of administration, especially from Egypt. This central government at Jerusalem provided the king with advice on political problems, in the wisdom tradition of the ancient Near East; it also administered justice under the king as chief judge, collected taxes and dues, organized a state labour force, kept administrative records, and dealt with foreign affairs, maintaining a diplomatic correspondence with foreign powers and negotiating international treaties.

These administrative developments had far-reaching consequences. In particular they facilitated the development of greater social distinctions than Israelite society had ever known before. The Canaanite cities were already accustomed to a highly stratified social structure; but this was the first time that the freeborn Israelites had experienced rule by a wealthy, urban ruling class whose interests were far from identical with their own. In the reigns of David and Solomon Jerusalem became a wealthy, cosmopolitan city in which this ruling class enjoyed a standard of living beyond anything which could have been dreamed of; but, apart from the fact that they were now free from foreign oppression, the ordinary Israelite population, which still consisted mainly of farmers, hardly felt the benefits of Israel's new imperial status.

Supreme above the new upper class stood the king. Whatever the divine sanctions by which he claimed to rule, and however much he might rely on the loyalty of the ordinary Israelite, one of the main sources of his power was his professional army, which owed him a purely personal loyalty. Many of its members were foreigners who had no reason for loyalty to Israel or to its God (II Sam.8.18; 11; 15.18–22; 20.7, 23). It was these 'servants of David' who, during Absalom's rebellion, defeated the rebels (significantly referred to as 'the men of Israel'), and restored David to the throne (II Sam.18.7).

His position secured by this personal army, David was able to a considerable extent to play the part of an oriental monarch, gathering round him a court which imitated the splendour and ceremonial of foreign courts, and tending to become isolated from the common people (II Sam.15.3 f.).

He was, however, too shrewd to allow this tendency to go too far. He knew that ultimately he could not retain his throne without the loyalty and affection of his people, and also that too great a departure from the old Israelite social and religious traditions would put his throne in danger. It is unlikely that the Israelite monarchy, at this or at any other time, succumbed to the temptation of claiming for itself that semi-divine character which was characteristic of some of the other monarchies of the time. It is true that both in the narrative sources and also in the Psalms and elsewhere we find phrases (such as 'the king is like the angel of God to discern good and evil', II Sam.14.17; the divine word to David, 'You are my son, today I have begotten you', Ps.2.7) which seem to suggest that this was so; but we have to distinguish between high-flown language and actual political realities. David was certainly, like Saul, 'the Lord's anointed', the man who because of his especial relationship with God had brought 'salvation' to his people; but there were too many men in his entourage who knew the facts of his rise to power, such as the old

general Joab (II Sam.19.5–7), for any more extravagant notions about his office to gain currency.

David did, however, firmly adopt one aspect of the monarchical concept which hardly accorded with Israelite ideas of charismatic leaders, that is, men chosen personally by God: the principle of a hereditary monarchy. We have already seen that Saul also had intended that his son Jonathan should succeed him. Under David the principle seems to have been taken for granted, and it was given religious sanction in the divine promise to David in II Sam.7.

However, neither David's own position nor the future of his family was really secure. The very power and prosperity of the Israelite state made it an attractive prize for the would-be usurper; and such men found no lack of disaffection which could be made to serve their purposes. There were those who had remained loyal to Saul and his family and regarded David as a usurper and murderer (e.g. Shimei, II Sam.16.5–8); there were those who disapproved of David's arrogant and sinful actions such as his adultery with Bathsheba and his murder of Uriah; in the north there were those who resented being ruled by a man of Judah; and there were those who felt that the old religious and social traditions were being overthrown. First David's own son, Absalom, and then a man called Sheba, of Saul's tribe of Benjamin, exploiting these feelings of discontent, rose in rebellion (II Sam.15–20). Although both rebellions were crushed, the feelings of discontent remained.

The accession of Solomon

The situation of the later part of the reign was

complicated by uncertainty with regard to the succession to the throne. David had a number of wives, several of whom had borne him sons. In the hereditary monarchies of the ancient Near East there was no rule that the eldest son must succeed: the king had the right to choose his own heir, and it was obviously desirable that this should be done in good time. After the death of Absalom there remained Adonijah and Solomon, half-brothers, as obvious candidates. Between them David, now old and feeble, was unable to make up his mind. Their rivalry caused a dangerous cleavage between the leading men in the state; but Adonijah made a false move, and paid for it with his life, dragging down with him some of the most important personalities of the reign which was now ending. Solomon was king; but he had to begin his reign with a bloodbath (I Kings 2).

The reign of Solomon (961–922), in spite of the splendid outward appearances, was a period of stagnation and of the beginning of decline. This was probably inevitable: even another David could probably not have succeeded in holding together the heterogeneous empire for a second generation; and Solomon was far from being a second David.

On the economic plane things might have continued to go well. Although the agricultural resources of Israel were not great, it was well placed in other respects. Possession of the Canaanite plain had given David control of the only land route linking Egypt in the south, Mesopotamia in the east, and Asia Minor in the north; and Solomon ensured his control over it by extensive fortifications of the key cities (I Kings 4.26; 9.15–19; 10.26). He was thus able, like his father, to derive considerable wealth by levying tolls and by import-export activities of his own (I Kings 10.28 f.). He also established,

with the help of his Tyrian ally, a lucrative sea trade, based on a seaport which he built at Ezion-geber on the Red Sea; and he mined and refined copper in Edom, presumably partly for export. There was also trade with Egypt (I Kings 10.29), Tyre, the Sabaeans of South Arabia (I Kings 10.2,13) and elsewhere.

These activities undoubtedly brought considerable profit to Israel (cf. I Kings 10). But Solomon succumbed to a fatal *folie de grandeur*, attempting to imitate the splendours of Egypt and Mesopotamia by erecting buildings of great magnificence. Since Israel possessed neither the necessary materials nor skill, he had to import these from Hiram of Tyre, and as a consequence found himself in financial difficulties (I Kings 9.10–14). At the same time he did much to alienate popular support by not only burdening his people with the support of an extravagant court (I Kings 4.7–19, 22 f.), but also extending the forced labour scheme which David had begun to such an extent that it seriously impaired agricultural efficiency (I Kings 5.13–18).

The empire began to break up. Judah remained loyal, and the Canaanite cities gave no trouble; but Edom and Damascus revolted, re-establishing their independence and becoming dangerous enemies (I Kings 11.14–25); and the northern tribes of Israel produced a leader, Jeroboam, who, when his first attempt at revolt proved unsuccessful, retired to Egypt where he was given protection and bided his time (I Kings 11.26–40).

Solomon's most enduring achievement was the building of the temple at Jerusalem. But he certainly can have had no inkling of the importance which this was to have in later times. The building of the temple was, from one point of view, merely the corollary of

David's bringing of the ark to Jerusalem: Solomon provided a magnificent shrine for it. From another point of view it was simply one example of Solomon's extravagance. Since it was designed and furnished by Phoenician craftsmen (I Kings 7.13 ff.), it is likely that the most immediate religious consequence of its construction was to increase the Canaanite element in Israel's worship.

Solomon is praised in several biblical passages for his wisdom (I Kings 3.9–14, 16–28; 4.29–34; 10.1–10). In only one of these passages does 'wisdom' mean statesmanship. Solomon may have been wise in other respects, but statesmanship was certainly not one of them. The early promise of political greatness for Israel was not fulfilled.

Nevertheless, Israel during the reigns of David and Solomon had undergone fundamental changes which would never be reversed. It had been brought into the world not only of international politics, but also of international culture. This expressed itself chiefly in literature, of which the most remarkable example is the so-called 'Succession Narrative' (II Sam.9–20; I Kings 1;2) in which characters and events at David's court are described with unequalled brilliance and subtlety. The striking advance in literary craftsmanship shown in this literary masterpiece over all earlier efforts in the same *genre* clearly indicates the extent of Israel's cultural transformation. Much of this was undoubtedly due to the influence of the Canaanite cities and of Egypt, but the Israelite literature of this period is by no means merely imitative: its authors applied the newly acquired techniques and insights to their own historical traditions, in which the new confident, national spirit inspired by the achievements of David had given them a new pride.

R.N. WHYBRAY

10 The Divided Kingoms

The evidence

1. Biblical sources

(a) The main biblical narrative source for this period is I Kings 12–II Kings 25. It is based mainly on reliable documents to which the compilers have added their own comments, chiefly moral and religious judgments on the various kings. Some stories, however, especially those concerning Elijah, Elisha and Isaiah, are derived from less objective sources and present a rather idealized picture.

(b) The second narrative source, II Chron.10–36, mainly follows Kings, but confines itself to the southern kingdom (Judah). Where it differs from Kings it also tends to present an idealized picture, although in a few instances it probably preserves accurate information not available to the compilers of Kings. The books of the prophets Isaiah (chs.1–39), Jeremiah, Hosea, Amos and Micah are also valuable as they depict the social and religious conditions of Israel and Judah during this period; their words need, however, to be disentangled from later and irrelevant material.

2. Archaeological evidence

A vast quantity of written sources dealing with the international setting of the history of Israel has been discovered. Egyptian, Assyrian and Babylonian records have provided a very full account of the history of those empires, including their relations with the Israelite kingdoms. In a few instances they contain independent accounts of events described in the biblical narrative. Besides these sources the Moabite Stone, erected by Mesha, king of Moab, gives that king's version of his relations with Israel, also described in II Kings 1.1; 3.4 ff. From Palestine itself come two texts, written in Hebrew; the Siloam Inscription, written by Hezekiah's engineers inside a water tunnel (cf. II Kings 20.20), and the Lachish Letters, a correspondence between Judaean army officers during the campaign which ended with the fall of Jerusalem to the Babylonians. The excavation of Samaria, the Israelite capital built by Omri, brought to light the Samaria Ivories, probably part of the decoration of Ahab's palace, the 'ivory house' of I Kings 22.39.

The revolt of the northern tribes

The political history of Israel during this period (922–587) is a story of increasingly rapid decline, punctuated by brief periods of partial recovery but ending in total annihilation. This fate befell not only Israel but all her neighbours as well. The rise of new centres of imperialism in Mesopotamia probably made this inevitable, though it was accelerated by the foolish policies frequently pursued by the victims.

Rehoboam (922–915), the son and successor of Solomon, either was unaware of, or chose to ignore, the weakness of his position in the northern part of his kingdom. On his accession he brusquely rejected the demands for reform made by the northern tribes; and at once all their resentment at being ruled by a Judaean, which had already manifested itself under

David and Solomon, came to a head. The northern tribes declared their independence, and selected Jeroboam, their former champion, who had just returned from exile in Egypt, as their first king (I Kings 12.1–20).

The new kingdom took for itself the name of Israel, which had previously been used to designate the whole undivided kingdom; the remnant in the south, which remained loyal to the dynasty of David, became known as Judah. With this division into two separate kingdoms, at first bitterly hostile to one another, the era of Israelite glory was over.

Of the two kingdoms, Israel was both the larger and the more prosperous. It included most of the larger Canaanite cities, the main trade routes, and the best land on both sides of the Jordan, including the former kingdom of Moab. Judah by comparison was a small state in the hills, remote from the main roads and from the sources of wealth. This remote position was to prove to be both favourable and unfavourable to Judah: unfavourable in that it was inevitably overshadowed by Israel, whether as an enemy, or, later, as a junior partner; favourable in that, being both strategically and economically less important to the great empires, it was able to survive for more than a century longer than its northern neighbour.

The monarchy thus established in (northern) Israel was somewhat different in character from that of Judah. The Judaeans remained loyal to the house of David to the very end; apart from the usurper Athaliah, no one other than a descendant of David ever sat on the throne of Judah. But in Israel the election of Jeroboam by the assembly (I Kings 12.20) seems to have been a conscious attempt to return to the old idea of kingship as an office conferred on an individual in view of his per-sonal merit. Whether the kings of Israel were regarded primarily as elected by the people or designated by God is not clear: in some cases the biblical narrative seems to suggest the former, in others the latter. In practice neither principle was strictly observed: many kings attempted to found dynasties, some – especially Omri and Jehu – successfully; on the other hand the fact that of all the kings of Israel only half came to the throne by dynastic succession shows that the dynastic principle was never fully accepted. The effect of this uncertainty about the succession was to make the kingdom of Israel extremely unstable: no less than eight of its nineteen kings obtained the throne through the assassination of their predecessors.

Like David, Jeroboam (922–901) made certain religious changes in an attempt to strengthen his position (I Kings 12.26–33). In order to discourage the annual pilgrimages which his subjects continued to make, in spite of the political schism, to Jerusalem, he established two royal temples of his own, choosing for this purpose the ancient sanctuaries of Bethel and Dan, where the God of Israel had been worshipped for centuries. Here, as a kind of compensation for the ark, he set up golden bull images. These were probably not intended to represent pagan deities, but to be used for the worship of the God of Israel; but they did later become centres of a debased, if not wholly pagan, worship (Hos.8.5 f.; 10.5; 13.2).

During this time the political vacuum in the Near East which had made it possible for David to establish his empire had continued to favour the independence of the Israelite kingdoms. Egypt, it is true, still hoped to re-establish its former empire in Syria and Palestine; and a few years after the division of the Israelite kingdoms its king, Shishak, invaded Palestine and devastated large parts of both Judah (I Kings 14.25 f.) and Israel (according to his own statement). But this was an isolated, though painful, incident and had no permanent results. Egypt's age of imperial power was over.

For some years there was also no threat from the other traditional centre of imperial power, Mesopotamia. Babylonia was hopelessly weak, and Assyria in a temporary state of decline from which she only began to recover at the end of the tenth century. Nearer at hand, the Aramaean kingdoms to the north of Israel were not yet ready for hostile action.

But in the ninth century the situation began to change. The first recorded interference of the Aramaean kingdom of Damascus in Israelite affairs well illustrates the fatal effects of the division of the Israelite kingdoms. Asa of Judah (913–873), hard pressed by an attack by Baasha of Israel (900–877), formed an alliance with Benhadad of Damascus and invited him to attack Israel, which he did with considerable success (I Kings 15.18–21). This was the beginning of a long history of alliances, intrigues and counter-intrigues between these three states which was to continue until Damascus was swept away by the Assyrians in 732 (I Kings 20; 22; II Kings 5–7; 8.28 f.; 10.32 f.; 12.17 f.; 13.3–7, 22–25; 14.28; 15.37; 16.5–9). Mainly it was a struggle between Israel and Damascus for the possession of territory lying between them in the north and north-east. On more than one occasion one or other of the two states came close to annihilation by the other.

The threat from Assyria

These squabbles between small states were serious enough in themselves; but they were suicidal in view of the threat soon posed for them all by the growth of the power of Assyria. Assyrian expansion began with Adad-nirari II (912–890); but it was not until the reign of Asshur-nasir-pal II (883–859) that the Assyrians turned their attention to the west. By 877 Asshur-nasir-pal's successive campaigns had taken him as far as the Mediterranean coast, and opened the way south towards southern Syria and Palestine.

Israel seems first to have become aware of the danger after the accession of his successor Shalmaneser III (859–824), who continued his predecessor's policy. For a few years Benhadad of Damascus and Ahab of Israel dropped their quarrel, and joined with other neighbouring states in a coalition against Assyria. We learn from Shalmaneser's own account of his campaigns that Ahab was one of the leaders of the coalition, and that when the Assyrians met the allied forces in Syria at Qarqar on the river Orontes (853), his was one of the largest of the allied contingents.

Shalmaneser claimed the battle as a victory; but in fact it appears to have been indecisive, and temporarily to have checked further Assyrian advances. For the time being the threat seemed to have abated. But neither Israel nor Damascus had learned its lesson. Instead of maintaining the coalition by a permanent defensive treaty, they reverted to a state of intermittent mutual warfare, and so were unready for the new threat when it came.

Israel was at this time relatively powerful. Omri (876–869) was a military commander who seized the throne after a period of dynastic conflict (I Kings 16.8–22). Although the compilers of the books of Kings found little concrete to say about him (I Kings 16.23–28), he was one of the more able Israelite kings, and his policies were continued by his son Ahab

(869–850), who, however, was constantly involved in wars with Damascus. In these wars, which continued to the end of the dynasty, the successive kings of Judah, Jehoshaphat (873–849), Jehoram (849–842) and Ahaziah (842) appear as the allies, willing or unwilling, of Israel.

The books of Kings devote a great deal of space (I Kings 16.29–22.40) to the reign of Ahab because of his religious apostasy and tyrannical behaviour, against which the prophet Elijah waged a vigorous campaign. Seen through the eyes of fervent admirers of the prophet, the character of Ahab appears far blacker than it actually was. Omri and Ahab, as kings of some consequence in the contemporary world, were necessarily subject, for political reasons, to influences of various kinds from the neighbouring states, and their wise renewal of David's policy of alliance with the powerful Phoenician state of Tyre had been sealed by Ahab's marriage to Jezebel, the daughter of the king of Tyre (I Kings 16.31). Jezebel was a woman of great determination, inspired with an ambition to introduce the religion and customs of her own people into Israel. According to the Elijah stories (I Kings 17–19; 21) she came near to exterminating the worship of the God of Israel in favour of that of Melqart, the god of Tyre (known to the Old Testament simply as 'Baal'). But this is certainly an exaggeration. It is clear that Ahab regarded himself as a worshipper of the God of Israel: not only did he on occasion recognize (if unwillingly) the authority of Elijah, but more significantly he gave to two of his sons (Ahaziah and Jehoram) names which imply devotion to the God of Israel. The truth of the matter is probably that under the influence of Jezebel he permitted or encouraged the worship of other gods as well, a policy which was by no means without precedent in Israel.

Of Ahab's tyranny the only specific example given to us is the story of Naboth's vineyard (I Kings 21), in which Ahab is represented as weak rather than tyrannical, allowing his ruthless and foreign wife to commit murder in order to obtain a piece of property which the owner had refused to sell. This story doubtless illustrates a tendency of Israelite kings towards autocratic rule; but it is important to notice that, as in the case of David and Uriah, the queen was obliged to carry out her crime by secret methods, and that when the deed became known it was regarded as an outrage. This shows that, even in the time of Ahab, tyranny in Israel was an exception and had not yet been accepted as normal.

The stories of Elijah and his successor Elisha show that the policies and actions of the kings of the dynasty of Omri were nevertheless regarded by an increasingly influential body of prophets as an apostasy from true religion which justified its overthrow. This came to pass in 842 with the murder of king Jehoram, Ahab's second son, by an army officer, Jehu, at the instigation of Elisha (II Kings 9.1–13).

Jehu (842–815) was placed on the throne because he was a fanatical champion of the God of Israel. He did not disappoint his sponsors. Besides Jehoram and Jezebel, he killed the whole of Ahab's family and all his associates, Ahaziah, the king of Judah, and his family and all the priests of Baal in Israel (II Kings 9.14–10.14; 10.18–27). No trace was left of the old regime. One learns with some relief that these 'pious deeds' were regarded with horror rather than admiration by a later prophet of greater sensibility than Elisha (Hos.1.4).

The reaction against religious apostasy had

its counterpart in Judah, though not immediately. After the murder of Ahaziah there followed a six-years' usurpation of the throne by his mother Athaliah (842–837), who may have been the daughter of Ahab and Jezebel, although this is not certain (cf. II Kings 8.26). She used Jehu's methods – the extermination of the royal family – to achieve an opposite end, the establishment in Judah of the worship of Baal (II Kings 11.1–3). On this occasion it was not a prophet but a priest, Jehoiada, who put an end to the apostasy. Athaliah and the priests of Baal were executed, the sole surviving descendant of David, Joash (837–800), placed on the throne, and the return to the faith of the God of Israel inaugurated by a solemn covenant between God, the king and the people (II Kings 11.4–20). But neither of these 'restorations' was to keep Israel or Judah permanently loyal to the God of Israel.

These events were followed by a period of weakness both in Israel and Judah. The Assyrians, in spite of their check at Qarqar, still remained a menace: Jehu was forced at one time, as we know from Assyrian sources, to acknowledge the overlordship of Shalmaneser, and Judah also suffered serious defeats and loss of territory at the hands of Hazael of Damascus (II Kings 12.17 f.).

Both countries were, however, to enjoy one final period of prosperity. Damascus, Israel's traditional enemy, was crippled by the Assyrian king Adad-nirari III (811–783) in 802, and thereafter Assyria left Syria and Palestine in peace for half a century. During the long reigns of Jeroboam II (786–746) in Israel and Uzziah (Azariah) (783–742) in Judah, both countries made a swift recovery. Jeroboam recovered the whole of his northern and trans-Jordanian territory at the expense of Damascus and

Hamath, pushing his northern frontier back to that of Solomon (II Kings 14.25, 28). He may also have recovered control of Moab, which had been lost to Israel after the death of Ahab. Judah had already reconquered Edom in the reign of Amaziah (800–783; II Kings 14.7,22) and went on under Uzziah to further conquests (II Chron.26.6–15). The two kingdoms together were now almost as extensive as Solomon's empire had been.

These successes, which restored to Israel and Judah their former sources of wealth, brought in their train a sudden new prosperity with inevitable social consequences. Once more the new wealth went into the pockets of a small privileged class, while the majority of the population found itself exploited to an unprecedented degree. These social changes are fully documented in the teaching of four contemporary prophets: Isaiah and Micah in Judah, and Amos and Hosea in Israel. The wealthy classes controlled the processes of law and so could prevent the under-privileged from obtaining redress when they were squeezed out of their holdings and forced to become the hired labourers or even slaves of the new proprietors, who in this way built up huge farms whose produce was used to support them in luxury (cf. Isa.3.16 f.; 5.8–12; 28.1–8; 32.9–14; Amos 2.6–8; 4.1–3; 5.10–13; Micah 2). Most of these arrogant magnates saw, or pretended to see, no incompatibility between their actions and their professions of religious faith: they regarded religion and ethics as two separate spheres, unrelated to one another. For them, religion was mainly a matter of the assiduous performance of cultic duties – by no means free, especially in Israel, from corrupt and pagan elements – in recognition of a God who, they believed, had guaranteed permanent safety and prosperity to his chosen people (cf. Isa.1.12–23; 29.13–16; Amos 5.21–24; Micah 3.9–12).

The prophets of this time startled and scandalized their hearers by proclaiming the unheard-of message that the God of Israel, after vain attempts to persuade his people to reform their ways, would withdraw his protection from his people and, becoming their enemy, bring about the destruction of the two kingdoms. These predictions were fulfilled; and, in the case of Israel, with very little delay.

The end of Israel

The dynasty of Jehu had lasted almost exactly a century (842–745). Six months after the death of Jeroboam in 746, it came to an abrupt end. Jeroboam's son and successor Zechariah was murdered by an usurper, Shallum, who a month later was himself murdered by Menahem (II Kings 15.10–14). Israel now lapsed into a state of disintegration, political, religious and social, which is well chronicled by the prophet Hosea. Of its last five kings, three were assassinated. Law and order broke down. And this collapse coincided with the active return of Assyria to Syria and Palestine, and in a new mood: no longer content to bully the small states into submission, but bent on permanent conquest. The inaugurator of this new policy was Tiglath-pileser III (745–727). During the reign of Menahem (745–738) he invaded Syria and the coastal cities of Phoenicia and annexed some territory which he put under direct Assyrian rule. Menahem escaped this fate by the payment of tribute (II Kings 15.19 f.). But such acknowledgment of Assyrian overlordship was now intended to be permanent. The Assyrian frontier was now very close, and Tiglath-pileser clearly would not tolerate disloyalty.

Nevertheless, hopes of resistance were not yet dead; and a few years later one of Menahem's successors, Pekah (737–732), formed an anti-Assyrian alliance with Rezin of Damascus. Jotham of Judah (742–735), the son of Uzziah, was invited to join the coalition, but refused. Pekah and Rezin then took the fatal step of trying to force Judah to join. Ahaz of Judah (735–715), who had now succeeded his father Jotham, was faced simultaneously with one attack by Israel and Damascus and another by the Edomites, who at this point rose in rebellion; and in spite of the warning of the prophet Isaiah he felt obliged to turn to Assyria for help. This involved the acknowledgment of vassal status; but it brought the desired relief. Tiglath-pileser attacked Damascus and Israel, abolishing the kingdom of Damascus altogether and in 732 annexing a large part of the territory of Israel (II Kings 15.29; 16.5–9; Isa.7.1–17). Pekah had now been murdered by the usurper Hoshea, who immediately surrendered to Assyria and was permitted to retain the remaining territory as vassal (II Kings 15.30; 17.3).

But Israel still continued its disastrous policies. Some years later, soon after the accession to the Assyrian throne of Shalmaneser V (727–722), Hoshea committed the incredible folly of withholding tribute from Assyria and making a treaty with 'So, king of Egypt' (II Kings 17.4), a petty local ruler of part of Egypt, which at that time had fallen into a state of anarchy. Such an ally was quite useless against the might of Assyria, and Shalmaneser made the final move. He attacked Israel in 724 and besieged the capital, Samaria. After a siege of more than two years, in the course of which Shalmaneser died and was succeeded by Sargon II (722–705), Samaria fell; and Sargon put an end to the kingdom of Israel. Following a policy which had been instituted by Tiglath-pileser for preventing further rebellions among conquered peoples, he deported a large number of the inhabitants to other parts of his empire, and replaced them with people of other races (II Kings 17.5 f., 24).

The kingdom of Judah

Judah was now left alone. During the century which followed, the fear of Assyria continued to dominate the actions of the little states which remained in and around Palestine. The policies of the kings of Judah fluctuated wildly according to their assessments at various times of the possibility of adopting an attitude of defiance. It is important to observe that their foreign and religious policies went hand in hand. Assyrian domination meant the acceptance of the worship of the Assyrian gods side by side with that of Yahweh, and was also marked by a decline in moral standards and social justice; rebellion against Assyria was accompanied by a revival of national pride which led to religious reform and greater justice.

The details of these fluctuations are fairly clearly set out in II Kings, although the Assyrian records are needed for a full picture, and in one case at least – Hezekiah's rebellion and Sennacherib's suppression of it – there remains considerable doubt about the exact course of events.

Ahaz, having placed himself under Assyrian protection, remained loyal to his overlord all his life, and as a consequence was forced to introduce Assyrian religious practices into the temple (II Kings 16.10–18). His son Hezekiah (715–687), however, encouraged by what he took to be signs of an Assyrian collapse, joined forces with other states and attempted to assert his independence (II Kings 18.7). At the same time he instituted a religious reform, purging the temple of alien cult-objects of all kinds (II Kings 18.4). But his rebellion was crushed by the Assyrian king Sennacherib (705–681; II Kings 18.13–16; Isa.36.1).

Hezekiah's death was followed by a period of forty-seven years during which Assyrian power, under Esarhaddon (681–669) and Asshurbanapal (669–631), was at its height, and Hezekiah's son Manasseh (687–642) and grandson Amon (642–640) accepted the Assyrian yoke. In contrast with the reign of Hezekiah, this was a time when the religion of Israel reached its lowest ebb, and the people of Judah were subjected to a cruel tyranny, hardly less severe than if they had been directly ruled by the Assyrians (II Kings 21.1–16).

The reign of Josiah (640–609), the son of Amon, was as great a contrast to those of his father and grandfather as can be imagined, and recalled that of his great-grandfather Hezekiah. Josiah is the only king of Judah who is praised without reservation by the compilers of the books of Kings (II Kings 22.2; 23.25). Like Hezekiah, he reasserted Judah's political independence; but this time the action seemed to be justified by political facts. After the death of Ashurbanapal in 631 the long dominance of Assyria had come to an end. Its last two kings were not of the calibre of their predecessors, and the collapse was very swift. Its two capitals, Ashur and Nineveh, fell to the combined attacks of Babylonians and Medes in 614 and 612 respectively, and a last attempt at resistance at Haran failed in 609. Assyria was no more.

Some years before the final collapse of Assyria, Josiah took advantage of its weakened condition and not only restored the independence of Judah but also regained some of the territory of the former kingdom of Israel. He was intensely devoted to the service of the God of Israel, and carried out a religious reform which is said to have been suggested to him by the reading of a law-book, generally believed to be related to Deuteronomy, which was discovered in the temple (II Kings 22.3–23.24). The reform was much more thorough than that of Hezekiah. Not only was the temple once more cleansed of alien rites and the worship of the God of Israel fully restored; sacrificial worship was now confined to this one place alone, and all other sanctuaries, whether Israelite or pagan, were abolished throughout both Judah and the newly acquired territories. The life of the nation was re-established as far as possible in accordance with ancient Israelite traditions.

Josiah has the unique distinction of being praised by the prophet Jeremiah as one who 'did justice and righteousness' and 'judged the cause of the poor and needy' (Jer.22.15 f.).

His religious reform, whose principles were preserved and developed during the years of exile by the Deuteronomic school of religious thinkers, eventually proved to be one of the most significant events in the religious history of Israel. But its immediate effectiveness as national policy depended on the person of Josiah himself, and in this sense it perished with him.

The threat of Babylon

No new golden age for Judah had dawned. The collapse of Assyria was not followed by a political vacuum. The bulk of the Assyrian empire fell immediately to the Medes and the Babylonians, while the south-western districts – Syria and Palestine – became the object of a conflict between Babylonia and Egypt, which after a period of Assyrian rule had now recovered sufficiently to make its last attempt at empire under Neco II (609–593). Recognizing that the real enemy was now Babylonia, Neco marched north in 609 to go to the aid of Assyria. Josiah foolishly attempted to stop him as he passed through Palestine, and at Megiddo Judah was defeated and Josiah killed (II Kings 23.29). Judaean independence was once more at an end, and Judah passed again under foreign control, this time that of Egypt. Neco deposed Jehoahaz, the son of Josiah, who had assumed the throne, and replaced him by his brother Eliakim, whom he renamed Jehoiakim (II Kings 23.30–35).

Jehoiakim (609–598) was thus from the first a vassal king. But before long his overlord Neco was decisively defeated at the battle of Carchemish (605), Egyptian hopes of empire came abruptly to an end, and Judah fell into the hands of the Babylonians under Nebuchadnezzar (605–562). Jehoiakim was confirmed in his office (II Kings 24.1).

Jehoiakim proved to combine the cruelty and religious apostasy of a Manasseh with the foolhardiness of a Hezekiah or a Josiah. Despite the defeat of Neco, Egypt was still plotting the overthrow of Babylonia, and there was a party at Jerusalem which believed that this could be achieved, and that it would be to the advantage of Judah. The intrigues with Egypt were discovered (II Kings 24.1), and in 597 Nebuchadnezzar arrived in Judah and besieged Jerusalem, which surrendered to him. Meanwhile Jehoiakim had died, and his son

Jehoiachin was deported to Babylon together with a great number of the upper classes of society, while his uncle Mattaniah, his name changed to Zedekiah, was placed on the throne as a puppet king.

Even this disaster did not bring the Judaeans to their senses. The 'new men' who were now appointed to the offices of state were worthless even by comparison with their predecessors: the prophet Jeremiah did not recognize their authority at all. The king was weak and unable to control them. Within ten years news of further intrigue with Egypt came to the ears of Nebuchadnezzar, who now determined to put an end to the kingdom of Judah once and for all. In 588 the Babylonians invaded; the whole country was devastated and its cities destroyed. In 587 Jerusalem itself was captured and destroyed, together with the temple. King Zedekiah was forced to witness the execution of his sons, and along with many of his people was taken to Babylonia (II Kings 25.1–21).

So the Jewish people was torn in two. It is difficult to say which part was in worse plight: the exiles in Babylonia, deprived, it seemed, of the hope of ever returning to their homes, or the wretched lower classes, left mainly to their own devices in a land devastated, its crops ruined and its houses destroyed, a prey to hunger and disease and to the depredations of wild beasts and of the Edomite tribes from the south who now invaded the land, eager to revenge themselves on the Judaeans who had been their oppressors in the past.

R.N. WHYBRAY

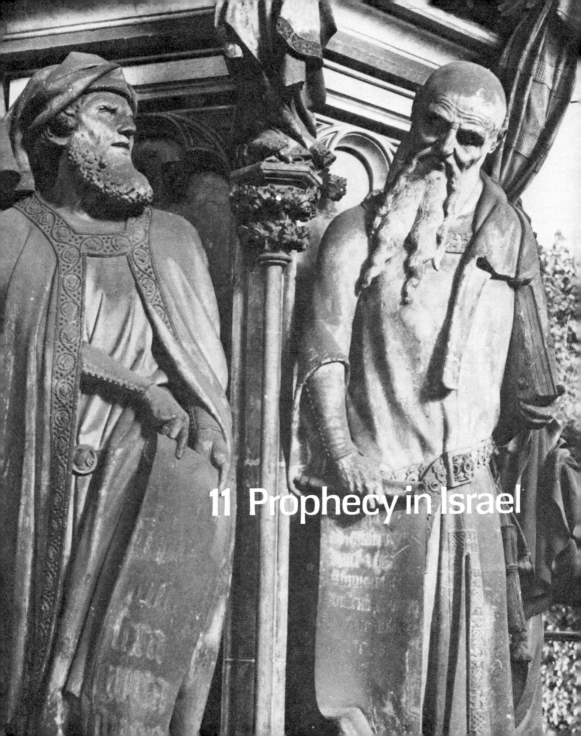

11 Prophecy in Israel

The nature of early prophecy

Already in the historical accounts of early Israel we are introduced to certain prophets and seers who were active both in Israel itself and among its neighbours. Numbers 22–24 describes how a Moabite seer, Balaam, was called to pronounce a deadly curse against Israel, but was unable to do so under God's restraint, and instead responded by uttering a prophecy declaring the future greatness and prosperity of Israel as a nation. Besides this evidence from within the Bible of a Moabite prophet there are references in non-biblical texts to prophets in Phoenicia and at Mari in Mesopotamia, which show that prophecy was not unique to Israel, and certainly did not originate within it.

Within Israel the political interest of prophecy is revealed by the part played by the prophet Samuel in foretelling the rise to kingship of both Saul and David (I Sam.9.15 ff.; 16.1–13). In these two cases, even though the accounts were certainly drawn up after the respective rulers had assumed the throne, the message given by the prophet was a way of setting the divine authority upon the separate claims of kingship of the two men. The word of the prophet not only predicted the future, but interpreted it by affirming what did, and what did not, lie within the divine purpose.

In view of this political activity of prophets, it is not surprising to find that they came to be attached very closely to David, both in his period as an outlaw and afterwards in the Jerusalem court. The seer Gad appears as a special confidant and adviser to David when he was being hunted by Saul (I Sam.22.5), urging a particular course of action on the basis of a claim to a divinely given understanding of the outcome of events. Later he became a person of influence in David's court, assuming the role of a court prophet, and appearing as a judge of David's actions (II Sam.24.10–17). He was responsible for advising David to built an altar on the threshing floor of Araunah (II Sam.24.18–25), and in this way was concerned with the choice of the site where the temple of Jerusalem came to be built (II Chron.3.1). Even better known in David's court is the prophet Nathan, who twice intervened very decisively in matters of state. On the first occasion, after David's disgraceful affair with Bathsheba, Nathan declared God's condemnation of David's action, and foretold a punishment upon him (II Sam.12.1–15). In this we can see very well the two parts which go to make up the typical saying of a prophet. There is an interpretation of a situation, in this case David's sin with Bathsheba and his virtual murder of Uriah, which is followed by a threat foretelling future trouble and setbacks as a punishment for these actions. David will be involved in fighting to the end of his days, he will suffer a rebellion in his own family, and the child born from his illicit affair with Bathsheba will die (II Sam.12.10–14). Together these threats make up a comprehensive sequence of punishments which the further history bears out in its tragic details. These two elements, a prediction of future events and an explanation, or motive, showing why such events will take place, are the basic ingredients of prophecy.

The second recorded occasion of Nathan's intervention in David's personal history is of a very different character (II Sam.7). Here he appears as a defender of the early traditions of Israel's religion, voicing God's opposition to David's proposal to build a temple, and promising instead that God will build a house (= dynasty) for David. The prophet's message here is of a very positive kind, providing a religious foundation for the political claims of the Davidic dynasty to rule as kings over Israel. Later this prophetic message was to provide the basis for the messianic hope of Judaism. Prophetic utterances therefore were not always necessarily of a threatening kind, but could take a very positive and affirmative form.

From these descriptions of the activities and preaching of prophets in Israel's early days we can form an instructive picture of their work. Their purpose was first and foremost to foretell the future, and this predictive element can never be removed from their preaching. This set them in rivalry to other means of foretelling future events which enjoyed considerable popularity in the ancient world: the consultation of omens (augury); the inquiry of departed spirits (necromancy) and the interpretation of the movements of the stars and planets (astrology), cf. Deut.18.9–22. In fact in Israel these other more impersonal means of inquiry into the future were almost entirely displaced by the prophets, who claimed to foresee events through their immediate communion with God. Such techniques of divination came to be rejected by the official representatives of Israel's religion, even though some popular attachment to them remained.

In regard to the prophet's status we find that both Gad and Nathan were closely attached to David's court, and were almost certainly paid a regular remuneration by the king. So also Balaam's close association with Balak, the king of Moab, suggests that he, too, was in the pay of the Moabite royal court, which highlights still further the extraordinary and unexpected nature of his message. The indications are, therefore, that all these prophets operated in close association with the monarchy, and that prophets were often attached to existing religious and political institutions. This is borne out still further by other Old Testament evidence. Saul's close link with bands of prophets (I Sam.10.5–13; 19.20–24) shows that the latter could be formed into organized companies who apparently lived and worked together, not unlike the monastic communities of later years. The mention of their appearing close by sanctuaries suggests that they had a permanent home, or camp, there, and thus formed a prophetic guild living as a self-supporting religious community. These prophetic companies of Saul's time reveal another distinctive feature of the prophetic activity in their irrational and frenzied behaviour. I Samuel 10.5 indicates that they could prophesy to the accompaniment of musical instruments, and I Sam.19.24 reveals that Saul, after being seized by the prophetic spirit, stripped off his clothes and lay naked for a day and a night. This strange and uncontrolled behaviour is more fully illustrated in the story of Elijah's contest with the prophets of Baal on Mount Carmel (I Kings 18.20–40), when the prophets of Baal reinforced their prayers with a wild dance in which they cut themselves with knives. Such a psychological state is usually termed 'ecstasy', meaning 'being beside oneself'. Quite a variety of forms of abnormal behaviour are covered by such a term, not all of which are appropriate to prophesying, but essentially it signifies the extraordinary appearance which such prophets gave of being 'possessed' by another spirit. Whether all prophesying was performed in this manner is hard to tell. Most probably it was not, but in any case the manner of delivery does not greatly affect the content of the message, although it undoubtedly affected the popular attitude towards the prophets. Hosea 9.7 reveals the ordinary man's distrust of this extradinary behaviour in repeating the popular saying 'The prophet is a fool, the man of the spirit is mad'.

Bearing in mind this picture of the nature of the activities of Israel's prophets, we can see the fascinating way in which the author of the great history of the Israelite kingdoms (Joshua–II Kings) has made use of such figures to interpret events (cf. I Kings 13.1–10 with II Kings 23.15–18). There is a remarkably adept interweaving of prophetic assurances of hope (e.g. Nathan's prophecy in II Sam.7) with prophetic announcements of doom (e.g., Nathan's condemnation of David in II Sam.12.1–15), which could easily at times have appeared contradictory in the hands of a less skilful writer. Instead of clumsiness, however, the author achieves a compelling picture of the hidden activity of God which operates behind human affairs and events. God's purposes, man's sinful disobedience, and the hopes and ambitions of a whole nation, are all taken up in a continuing story of that nation's history which is seen as the working out of a divine purpose. Victory and defeat are both seen to arise out of the attitudes which men adopt towards God and his known will.

The nature of developed prophecy

With the appearance of Amos a new form of prophecy arose in Israel, which is distinguished by the fact that, instead of a brief account of the prophet's work recorded in a historical narrative, we have a separate book, collecting together his sayings and containing a few brief biographical details about him. This emergence of written prophecy was a new departure with Amos, and clearly marks a significant stage in the making of the Old Testament. It can only be explained by the particular character of Amos' message and that of the great prophets who followed him. It is improbable that Amos himself wrote down his words, and more likely that hearers and disciples of his did so, because of the intrinsic importance of what he had to say, and also because the political and religious leaders to whom it was addressed rejected it (Amos 7.10–17). In view of the unbelief with which Amos' message was received, he himself may have taken the first steps to see that it was remembered and recorded so that when its threats were realized the people would know that he had spoken the truth.

1. *Amos*

Amos prophesied in the northern kingdom, Israel, towards the end of the reign of Jeroboam II (786–746 BC). Although a native of Tekoa in Judah (Amos 1.1), he made a dramatic appearance at the ancient sanctuary of Bethel, and proclaimed there the coming downfall of the nothern kingdom, with its royal house (Amos 7.7–9). This would be the end of the kingdom of Israel (Amos 8.2; cf. 5.2), and this disaster is described in terms which foretell a military defeat, with Israel's citizens being carried off into exile (Amos 4.2–4; 6.7 f.). Nowhere does Amos say precisely who the enemy will be who will carry out this threat, although he invites Egypt and Assyria to come as spectators (3.9). In a series of five visions (7.1–3, 4–6, 7–9; 8.1–3; 9.1–4) this threat of the destruction and 'end' of Israel is signified. The first two foretell natural disasters which are called off after the prophet pleads with God. The remaining visions imply an impending military defeat and occupation of the land. It is possible that the fifth vision, threatening the destruction of a sanctuary (Bethel ?), was thought to have been fulfilled by the earthquake which occurred two years after Amos had prophesied (1.1).

We have already noted from the example of Nathan that prophets could threaten disaster, so that this prediction of doom by Amos was not in itself a new departure within prophecy. What does appear to have been new was the threat of such utter doom upon both the dynasty and political existence of Israel. The extent of the threat was unprecedented, and undoubtedly contributed to its being remembered and written down. So far as its fulfilment is concerned, the decades after Amos had preached witnessed the resurgence of the imperial ambitions of Assyria in the west, which gave a political focus and reality to his warnings. When the final downfall of the northern kingdom came, with the destruction of Samaria in 721 BC, Amos' threats had been turned into a fearful reality.

Although the visions of a coming catastrophe contained the vital core of Amos' message, they say nothing to explain the reasons for it. For this we have to look elsewhere in the prophet's preaching to those oracles where he attacks the social conditions and conduct of Israel. Here we find that it is especially injustice which calls forth his bitterest attacks. The people 'sell the righteous for silver' (Amos 2.6), which must refer to the selling of people, usually women and children, into slavery in order to pay off personal debts. The immorality which the prophet condemns (2.7) probably refers primarily to the abuse of female slaves, who were not being granted the moral protection demanded by the law (cf. Ex.21.7–11). In particular Amos implies that the administration of justice had broken down so that by bribery and the popular indifference the wealthier citizens could manipulate the law to their own advantage and to the oppression of the poor (Amos 5.10 f., 15).

In the face of this undercutting of the basic supports of morality and justice Amos saw the organized worship of Israel as a useless sham (5.4 f., 21–24). Even worse, it positively hindered any redress of the wrongs being committed because it encouraged a sense of security and complacency. While the hymns sung in worship declared such assurances as 'The Lord of Hosts is with us' (Ps.46.7), the truth was that God was about to exact a terrible punishment from such people for their abuse of elementary justice. Only if the prevalent lack of justice were amended would God be with the people in reality (Amos 5.14). Thus Amos found himself thrown into opposition to the historic traditions of worship and priesthood which governed the religious life of the people. Not only was this traditional religion failing to make known the truth that no worship could please God which was divorced from the elementary demands of right and justice, but it even encouraged a misplaced sense of security and divine approval. Thus Amos championed a new and radical emphasis within the traditional pattern of Israel's religion, setting justice and right dealing above the more formal conventions of organized worship (5.21–24). To those who looked eagerly forward to the coming 'Day of the Lord', the great New Year's Day of the Autumn Festival, Amos warned that it would mean darkness and not light (5.18–20). Those who expected to celebrate in hymn and ritual service the righteous kingship of God would find that the divine righteousness fell in judgment upon them. The people could not praise God for a justice which they refused to apply to themselves and their own behaviour.

The sharpness with which Amos predicted the coming downfall of the northern kingdom, Israel, is matched by the simple clarity with which he interpreted and explained it. Far from this disaster signifying a divine indifference to his people, it would reveal the reality and intensity of God's concern that Israel should be his people (3.2). Such a message was perhaps not surprisingly rejected by Amaziah, the chief priest of the great sanctuary of Bethel where Ámos proclaimed it (7.10–13). Amaziah had Amos formally expelled from the kingdom, maligning him as a greedy scaremonger who was concerned to frighten people into paying him generously, though he was in reality motivated by nothing deeper than a narrow patriotism for his native Judah. In defence Amos could only appeal to the divine source and authority of his message. We are left to assume that Amos was deported to Judah, his life alone being spared by the fact that a traditional religious regard for prophets saved him from being executed for treason (cf. Jer.26.16).

2. Hosea

Shortly after Amos' sudden appearance at Bethel, which must have occurred sometime during the decade 760–750 BC, another prophet appeared in the northern kingdom, this time a native of that country. His name was Hosea, and, unlike Amos whose activity probably lasted no longer than a year or two, he prophesied at intervals for a period of about twenty years (*c*.750–730 BC, cf. Hos.1.1). In upbringing, temperament and religious background he was a very different person from Amos, yet the overall substance of his message had much in common with that of the prophet from Tekoa. Most striking of all, chs.1-3 of the book of Hosea concern the significance of the prophet's marriage and the children that were born to him. Two events are recorded: in ch.1 there is a biographical account, recorded in the third person style, of God's command to the prophet to marry 'a wife of harlotry' (1.2), whose name is Gomer. In ch.3 we have an autobiographical account of a further command to the prophet to marry an unnamed woman, who is an adulteress (3.1). A majority of scholars accept that this woman must also be Gomer, and that this event must have concerned the same marriage as mentioned in ch.1, but at a later stage. This carries the implication that Hosea had either divorced Gomer for her unfaithfulness, or more probably that Gomer had left Hosea without actually being divorced by him. She had then fallen into slavery from which Hosea bought her back. This certainly appears to be the intended interpretation of the present structure of the book, since Hos.2, which interprets Hosea's marriage as sybolic of God's relationship to Israel, hints at divorce (2.2), or separation, and points to a desire on the part of the unfaithful wife to return to her husband (2.7). Those scholars who regard the woman of ch.3 as someone other than Gomer, a view which is certainly not impossible, do tend to weaken the force of the marriage symbolism which expresses the permanence of the divine love for Israel, and to overrule the lines of interpretation which are indicated by ch.2.

There are several aspects of Hosea's marriage to Gomer which remain unclear. The main features and religious importance of the marriage for the prophet are not in doubt. At the time when Hosea married her, Gomer could already be called 'a wife of harlotry', which must be taken literally, and not be regarded simply as the prophet's later reflection on the character of the woman whom he had taken to be a pure and innocent girl at the time of his marriage to her. It probably indicates that she was a woman who had taken part in the immoral rites of Baal in which the worshippers imitated the divine marriage of Baal with his consort the goddess Anat. By doing so the worshipper sought to activate the creative and fertilizing powers of nature in order to ensure rain and fertility in the fields and among the flocks and herds. Such immorality, practised in the very name of religion, epitomized the extent of Israel's turning away from God, and is roundly condemned by Hosea (4.13–15, 18; 5.3 f.; 6.10; 7.4; 9.1,10). By himself marrying a woman who had shared in such a perverted religion, Hosea was made to realize the full shame of Israel's behaviour. God's command to Hosea, however, was not only to marry Gomer, but to have 'children of harlotry', who would be a testimony to Israel's gross behaviour. In consequence the main part of the story of Hosea's marriage is concerned with recording the births of his three children, and the symbolic names which the prophet gave to them (Hos.1.3–11). The message of the prophet, therefore, was not so much conveyed by his marriage, as has often been suggested, but by his children whose names warned of the coming divine judgment. The first child was called *Jezreel*, recalling to Israel the violent revolution by which Jehu had assumed the crown of Israel (II Kings 9–10), and threatening punishment upon Jeroboam II, who was of the dynasty of Jehu (cf. Amos 7.11). The second child, a daughter, bore the name *Not Pitied*, indicating that God could no longer take pity on his people Israel, but had reached the time when he must punish them (cf. Amos 7.8). The third child was called *Not My People*, declaring that God now disowned Israel from being his people, and that he revoked the very promise of the covenant. 'You shall be my people, and I will be your God' (cf.Amos 8.1). The message of Hosea, therefore, in its essential character was not unlike that of Amos in that it was a warning of the coming disaster to the northern kingdom, Israel, including a threat against the throne of Jeroboam II. At times the military character of this disaster is clearly hinted at, with pictures of the desolation of the land (Hos.5.9), the death of its inhabitants (7.16) and the deportation of others into exile (9.6; 11.5). Most directly, however, Hosea threatens disaster as the just and inevitable punishment for Israel's sins, insisting earnestly that sin carries with it its own retributive punishment. 'They sow the wind and they shall reap the whirlwind' (Hos.8.7).

In explaining why Israel was faced with this coming catastrophe we find in Hosea, as in Amos, a bitter attack upon the people for their neglect of elementary justice (4.2; 5.1; 6.8 f.; 8.12). More deeply, however, this lack of justice is itself traced back by Hosea to a 'spirit of harlotry' (4.12; 5.4) within the people. Israel is the bride of God, but has dealt faithlessly with her husband and has forsaken him for her lovers, the Baals (2.8,13,17; 7.16; 11.2; 13.1).

121

These were the various local forms of the great god Baal-Hadad, who was worshipped by the Canaanites as the controller of storms and rain, the giver of life and fertility, and the great warrior among the gods. He was acclaimed as king of the gods, superior in strength and vitality to all the other gods, and the conqueror of the dread powers of death. In particular, as we have already seen, the ritual devotion to Baal included among its rites the practice of sacred prostitution, in which young women sacrificed their virginity to Baal. Hosea could thus include a literal, as well as metaphorical, significance in his condemnation of Israel's harlotry and unfaithfulness to God. As in Amos, Hosea, too, condemns the formal worship of Israel's sanctuaries as a useless pretence at love and loyalty to God which had no real substance (6.6; 7.14; 8.13). Israel's worship is idolatry (4.17), and in particular the bull-calf images of Bethel and Samaria are singled out for attack (8.5; 10.5; 13.2). What the people regarded as symbols of divine strength and vigour were in reality nothing but occasions of disloyalty to the true God.

Where Amos had given little word of hope for Israel's future, Hosea is more positive and reassuring. While disaster threatened the nation in the immediate future, this would provide the opportunity for God to begin again with his people. Here the metaphor of Israel as the bride of God becomes very significant, especially when it is related to the symbolic action of the prophet in restoring his wife from slavery as recorded in ch.3. As Hosea could still love his own faithless wife, so God could not give up his love for wayward Israel. The most moving expression of this enduring divine love, however, is given, not in relation to the metaphor of marriage, but to that of Israel as God's son (Hos.11.1–9). The coming punishment of the nation is thus seen by the prophet not as an end, but as the opportunity for a new beginning. As the historical origin of the nation had taken the form of a deliverance from Egypt and a journey through the wilderness (Hos.11.1, 5; 2.15), so Israel would have to go back to the wilderness, and to enter the land afresh (2.14 f.). This time the settlement in the land would be the entering of Israel into a new hope and a new and faithful relationship to God (2.16–23). Significantly the very names of Hosea's children, which had warned of the coming judgment, would then take on a new meaning as indicative of God's mercy and patient love (2.22 f.).

We see both in Amos and Hosea a very sombre message of doom, alleviated in Hosea particularly by a strong insistence that the love of God for his people is such that he will now allow his last word to Israel to be one of judgment. In neither prophet, however, is a specific political danger referred to as the source of the coming judgment. While Amos can speak of exile to 'Harmon' (Amos 4.3), which is not otherwise identifiable, and Hosea threatens deportation to both Egypt and Assyria (Hos.9.6), there is no direct reference to the coming downfall of the norther kingdom as an event to be brought about by Assyria. In reality, however, there can be no doubt that the Assyrian menace to Israel in the mid-eighth century, culminating in the siege and fall of Samaria in 721 BC, represented the fulfilment of the warnings of the two prophets. It is in the preaching of Isaiah, who began to prophesy *c.* 746 BC, and who continued at least until the end of the century, that we have a very clear and direct reference to the Assyrians as the agents of God's punishment upon Israel.

3. Isaiah

What is immediately striking with Isaiah is the distinctive religious and cultural background which distinguishes him from Amos and Hosea. The latter two prophets had both proclaimed their warnings in the northern kingdom, even though Amos was from Tekoa in the far south of Judah. They both reflect the rural background of life in Israel, with its traditional adherence to the old ideals of tribal society and family life. In Hosea the particular political and religious emphases of the northern kingdom are apparent, with a scathing hostility towards the monarchy as a divinely ordained institution (Hos. 5.1; 8.4; 10.3,7,15; 13.10 f.), which reflects the unhappy experience of the kingship among the northern tribes. In Isaiah, however, the upbringing of the prophet in the city environment of Jerusalem is very apparent. Here two great events stood out in the city's history, and served to mould its religious understanding. David had brought the ancient ark of God into Jerusalem, and set it permanently there, making Mount Zion the site for a temple of the God of Israel. From the religious viewpoint this was interpreted as God's election of Mount Zion to be his dwelling-place. The second major event was Nathan's prophecy that David's sons would retain a divinely appointed kingship over Israel (II Sam.7). This meant the divine election of the Davidic dynasty to provide the kings of Israel. These two great events, with their abiding religious significance, were celebrated in the hymns sung in the Jerusalem temple (cf. esp. Pss.78,67–72, 132). Jerusalem was 'the city of the great king' (Ps.48.2), referring to God's temple there, and from it his presence shone forth in splendour (Ps.50.2). It was also the city of David, through whom the divine justice was administered to Israel (Pss.89.19–37; 132.11 f.). These focal points of the religious background of Jerusalem find a prominent place in the preaching of Isaiah, the prophet of Jerusalem in a very special way. He views Israel as a divinely governed state with its centre at Jerusalem, where the presence of God is made known.

Isaiah's call to be a prophet (Isa.6) came to him while he was worshipping in the Jerusalem temple, and the emphasis which it placed upon God's status as the diving 'King' of Israel suggests that this may have been during the Autumn Festival, which particularly stressed this aspect of God's power and authority. What is most startling in the commission which accompanied Isaiah's call is the warning of the great disaster which was about to befall the land (6.11–13). This can only have meant a military defeat of Judah with the accompanying devastation of cities and the countryside. The terms in which this commission is given, and the cry of alarm and despondency which it called forth from the prophet (6.11), indicate the severity and extent of this coming catastrophe (cf. esp. 6.13). There can therefore be no doubt that Isaiah began to preach a similar message to the earlier prophets, warning of the danger in which Judah stood and foretelling an impending defeat and conquest of the land. In explanation of these events Isaiah followed Amos in pointing to the injustice, violence and dishonesty which marred the life of the people (1.4,21–23). Even Jerusalem, which prided itself on its good administration of law and regarded itself as a city of righteousness and faithfulness, had become filled with every kind of wrong.

Not many years after Isaiah had received his call to be a prophet, a major political crisis occurred in Judah (735–732 BC). Uzziah, the king whose death had occurred in the year of Isaiah's call, had been staunchly anti-Assyrian in his policy, participating in an alliance of minor kingdoms for mutual defence against Assyria. His son Jotham, who reigned for a brief period, continued this policy, but it was reversed when his early death put Ahaz on the throne. Ahaz preferred to seek a compromise agreement with Assyria rather than accept the risks of the existing treaties with neighbouring kingdoms. As a result, two of these kingdoms, the Aramaean kingdom of Damascus and the northern kingdom, Israel, took military action against Judah, intending to depose Ahaz and to place a puppet ruler, who is referred to as the son of Tabeel (Isa.7.6), on the throne of Judah. Things soon went badly for Ahaz, and Jerusalem was reduced to a state of siege. Ahaz was in panic and planned a strong appeal to Assyria (Isa.7.1 f.). Isaiah, with his son Shear-Jashub, met Ahaz to assure him that the attack by the Israelite-Aramaean alliance would come to nothing, and to give him some sign in confirmation of this (7.3–11). Ahaz refused to seek any such sign, perhaps because he had already decided his policy, and may already have sent his appeal to Assyria. Isaiah then promised his own distinctive sign that a child would shortly be born whose name, Immanuel, would affirm the presence of God with Israel, with its implication of divine defence and protection. This child, whose birth was expected in the near future, appears most probably to have been a child of the king's, whose birth at this time of crisis would serve to re-affirm God's promise that only David's descendants should sit upon the throne of David in Jerusalem (7.12–17).

The key idea which underlies the prophet's thinking is expressed in 7.9:

If you will not believe, surely you shall not be established.

Since Jerusalem was a city built upon the two great promises of divine support for David and the dwelling of the divine presence in the temple there, Ahaz was displaying a complete lack of faith in God by his appeal to Assyria. Thus the very assurances upon which his kingdom rested would be to him warnings of judgment because of his unbelief. With striking paradox, therefore, Isaiah warned Ahaz that the Assyrians would come, but would not in the outcome prove to be his deliverers, as he hoped, but his tormentors (7.7; 8.5–8). In fact the result of Ahaz's appeal was an Assyrian expedition to Israel which compelled the Aramaeans and Israelites to lift the siege of Jerusalem, and enforced a settlement of the dispute which left the borders of Israel seriously curtailed. Thus the already divided kingdoms of Israel and Judah fell further apart, and the first major step in the political ruination of the northern kingdom took place.

In Isaiah the threats of coming disaster for Israel and Judah are specifically linked with the rise of the Assyrian empire. Assyria is the rod of God's anger, which he is using to punish his erring people Israel (Isa.10.5 f.). This in itself is a remarkable interpretation of faith, since the Assyrians regarded themselves as the servants of their god Ashur, and they ascribed all their victories to him. In their view the conquest of other nations was to bring greater honour to their god by bringing more people under his power. For Isaiah this was nothing but an arrogant illusion, since in reality the God of Israel was using them for purposes which they did not discern, and which therefore included the possibility that not only Israel and Judah, but in turn Assyria also would be punished for their violence and pride (10.7–19). At what point Isaiah began to proclaim this turn in the fortunes of Assyria, and to predict the sudden and dramatic intervention of God to humiliate and punish them, is not clear. Most probably it was not until Assyria had destroyed the northern kingdom of Israel and carried off many of her people as exiles in 721 BC (II Kings 17). With this defeat the Assyrian hold upon Judah also became tighter.

Although we cannot be sure at what point in his prophetic career Isaiah became convinced that God planned to inflict a humiliating defeat upon the Assyrians in Judah, the intensity of this conviction and its central place in his message cannot be doubted. For the prophet it supplemented his earlier warnings of the punishment which the Assyrians would bring upon Judah and Jerusalem, rather than cancelled them out. The nature and motive of this changed pattern of coming events is well described by the prophet: 'When the Lord has finished all his work on Mount Zion and on Jerusalem he will punish the arrogant boasting of the king of Assyria and his haughty pride' (Isa.10.12).

The form that this defeat of the Assyrians would take is described in different ways by the prophet. God would trample upon the Assyrians to remove their yoke from Judah (Isa.14.24–26). He would rebuke them, and they would flee away (17.12–14). He would terrify them with thunder, earthquake and great noise (29.5–8). The point that is firmly insisted upon is that it would be God, and not men, who would bring this defeat upon the Assyrians (31.4 f.; 10.33 f.), and there is a hint that this defeat would be caused by a sickness among the Assyrian soldiers (10.16–19). In this way God would be fulfilling his plan of punishing in turn the arrogant Assyrians who boasted that their victories were the consequence of their own greatness. In foretelling this crushing divine blow upon the Assyrian armies on the soil of Judah, Isaiah was able to use and re-apply ancient hymns which celebrated God's power and victory on behalf of his people (Pss.46; 48; 76). In this way Isaiah referred the imagery of the hymns to a specific historical situation, and interpreted it of a particular military threat to Judah.

In order to appreciate the relevance of this prophetic interpretation of the situation it is necessary to consider the main outlines of what took place. After the Assyrian action to prevent the suppression of Judah by the Aramaeans and Israelites in 732 the borders of Israel were greatly reduced, and conditions of subservience to Assyria imposed. In 724 the Israelites joined a rebellion against Assyria and invited more drastic punishment upon themselves. After a long siege Samaria fell to the Assyrians in 721, and large sections of the population of the northern kingdom were deported. At this time Ahaz was no longer on the throne of Judah, having been succeeded by his son Hezekiah. For a time Hezekiah continued his father's policy of submission to Assyria in return for protection, but then he, too, was tempted into joining an anti-Assyrian coalition, and into taking active steps of hostility towards his Assyrian overlord. Sennacherib, the Assyrian king, sought to inflict swift punishment upon Judah. He marched through the land, besieging and capturing Lachish, and then enforcing a siege against Jerusalem (701 BC). What happened next is not exactly clear, although it is described in detail in II Kings 18–19; Isa.36–37. From Assyrian records it is certain that Sennacherib compelled Hezekiah to capitulate and imposed heavy and humiliating demands upon him, although Jerusalem was not destroyed and Hezekiah retained his throne. It is possible that this unexpected leniency was itself regarded by the general populace as a remarkable vindication of Isaiah's preaching. Since, however, there are accounts of two deputations to Hezekiah, many scholars accept that Sennacherib relented of his leniency and later returned in an unsuccessful attempt to enforce harsh terms upon Jerusalem. Whatever the precise course of events, which now present an almost insoluble historical problem, the citizens of Judah celebrated a remarkable deliverance, and came to regard Isaiah's prophecies as having been fulfilled. Thus Isaiah, as the prophet of Zion, came to be remembered especially as a preacher of divine deliverance for Jerusalem. This must, however, be related to the very severe warnings of coming judgment with which he began his ministry.

In a famous oracle the hope of God's righteous rule from Jerusalem is presented by Isaiah (Isa.2.2–4). Since this prophecy also re-appears in the prophet Micah (Micah 4.1–4), its authenticity has often been questioned. Yet it may well have originated with Isaiah. The picture which it draws of the future age of peace, in which many nations will be united in the worship of the Lord God of Israel, is an adaptation of a traditional image of Jerusalem as a kingdom of peace, perhaps stemming from the time of David's empire. This ancient hope was undoubtedly at one time that of Jerusalem as the capital of a great empire, but with Isaiah it has been transformed into a more spiritual conception. Similarly the tradition of the Davidic kingship has been taken up and

re-applied by the prophet in Isa.9.2–7; 11.1–9 to present a picture of the coming ruler of God's people. How this was related to the existing monarchy of Judah, and whether it was in any way intended to foretell the refounding of the Davidic dynasty is not wholly clear.

4. *Micah*

We have the work of another Judaean prophet, who was contemporary with Isaiah, in the book of Micah. The nucleus of his message is to be found in chs. 1–3 of his book, where it is predominantly a warning of coming disaster for both Israel and Judah. That the northern kingdom had not yet fallen to the Assyrians is evident from 1.6, where the destruction of Samaria is foretold. In 2.1–5 there is a sharp rebuke against the wealthy landowners of Jerusalem, where we have a prophetic threat that their estates will be ravaged, and the owners evicted from them. The prediction in 2.5 that the land will afterwards be re-allocated by the old tribal system of division by line for a limited period points us to a situation in which the city landowners of Jerusalem had been unscrupulous in taking advantage of the different legal systems of land tenure that operated in the cities of Israel and Judah from that which applied to the rural areas (cf. Isa.5.8–10; Lev.25.29–34). In Micah 3.5–8 there is a vigorous condemnation of certain prophets who deceive the people by their assurances of 'peace', when they are well paid for their preaching, but who threaten war against anyone who fails to reward them sufficiently. This is one of the earliest references that we have to the existence of false prophets in Israel (cf. I Kings 22.5–28), and it is significant that their falsity is especially linked with their prophecies of 'peace', and their dishonourable professionalism. In punishment for these offences Micah threatened that even Jerusalem itself would be destroyed, and the temple left in ruins (Micah 3.9–12). That this oracle caused much consternation is clear from the way in which it was still recalled a century later (Jer.26.18), when a similar threat of the destruction of the temple was made by Jeremiah. Since we do not know exactly when Micah delivered his threat it is impossible to know precisely how it relates to the preaching of Isaiah. We must not suppose, however, that all the prophets proclaimed a uniform message, or that we can fit their preaching together into a consistent pattern.

5. Jeremiah

The next of the really outstanding prophets of the Old Testament was Jeremiah, who received his call to prophesy in 626 BC, three-quarters of a century after the great Assyrian crisis towards the close of Isaiah's ministry. Born in Anathoth, a small village five miles north of Jerusalem, of priestly parents, Jeremiah appears as a sensitive and discerning personality, whose work brought him persecution and forced him into isolation, reducing him nearly to despair. The book of Jeremiah is formed from large collections of material which reflect the history of their preservation. Of first importance is the collection of prophecies in chs. 1–25, which contains the most characteristic of the prophet's oracles, although it is difficult, and sometimes impossible, to date many of them. Chapters 26–30 and 34–45 form a 'biography' of Jeremiah, and since this concludes with a personal message for Baruch, the friend and scribe of the prophet, it is reasonable to assume that Baruch played a part in preserving this information about the prophet's life, although he may not have been the final author of it. Into this 'biography' there has been inserted a collection of assurances for Israel's future in chs. 31–33, which is often called 'the Book of Consolation'. Most of the remaining chapters of Jeremiah contain prophecies against foreign nations.

Jeremiah's priestly links with Anathoth are of interest since this was the town to which the priest Abiathar, who had been a close friend and adviser to David, had been banished by Solomon (I Kings 2.26 f.). The likelihood is that Jeremiah was a direct descendant of this historic priestly family.

When Jeremiah received his call to be a prophet (Jer.1.4–10), Josiah was on the throne of Judah, and almost a complete century had passed since the northern kingdom had been swallowed up in the Assyrian empire. During this long period of political survival Judah had remained a vassal state of Assyria. Nevertheless the mere fact of survival, in contrast to the sad fate of the northern kingdom, had greatly strengthened the popular belief that a special divine favour was being shown to Jerusalem for the sake of David, who had first made it an Israelite city, and because God had chosen Mount Zion for his divine dwelling-place. A mixture of patriotic pride and religious fervour lent to the city a unique importance in the minds of its citizens. In consequence the belief was encouraged among the people that God could certainly be relied upon to maintain his protection of the temple and of the city in which it stood.

Jeremiah's first prophecies were warnings that military and political disaster would soon overtake the land (1.11–16; 4.5–8; 6.22 f.); Jerusalem would be besieged and destruction would come at the hands of a mysterious foe from the north. The obscure way in which this enemy is described has caused much discussion, and several scholars have linked it with an invasion by marauding bands of Scythians from the north which the Greek historian Herodotus mentions from this period (Herodotus, *Histories*, 1.105 f.). Since, however, there is no reference to such an invasion in the historical books of the Old Testament, the reality of it is thrown in doubt. Most probably Jeremiah himself was at first not clear about the precise political nature of the threat to Judah, and alluded vaguely to 'the foe from the north' on the basis of older prophetic imagery. Since these warnings came at a time when Judah felt secure under the umbrella of Assyria, Jeremiah's threat gained added sharpness.

When we look to see how Jeremiah justified this impending catastrophe upon Judah we find a very close similarity with Hosea. Both prophets repeatedly accuse Israel of being the unfaithful bride of God, and point specifically to the worship of Baal with its immoral practices in support of this (cf. Jer.2.1–8; 2.20–25, 33–37; 3.1–5, 19 f., etc.). The contacts between Jeremiah and Hosea are sufficient to suggest that the later prophet was familiar with an account of the earlier prophet's message, and reflected upon it in his own prophecies. If anything the accusation against Israel that it has been unfaithful becomes even more poignant and challenging in Jeremiah's oracles.

One of the most memorable of them was a threat of the coming destruction of the temple, which would not, contrary to the popular belief, be safeguarded by the divine protection (Jer.7.1–15). Because of the sins of the people (Jer.7.9), even the ancient promise that God would always dwell within his temple (I Kings 8.13; Ps.132.13 f.) had come to mean nothing. Jeremiah himself was forbidden to pray for such a people (Jer.7.16–20; 14.11 f.), since to intercede for such hardened sinners could only be to no purpose. The personal consequences of this temple sermon for Jeremiah are described in ch. 26, where we learn that certain priests and prophets sought to have Jeremiah put to death for treason (26.10 f.). However, the earlier (unfulfilled) threat of Micah was recalled by a number of the princes, who pointed out that Jeremiah had not spoken of his own will, but in the name of God (26.16–23). In the outcome the intervention of Ahikam ben Shaphan, an influential and pious government official, secured Jeremiah's release (26.24). Already in 11.21–23 we are told how some of Jeremiah's own townspeople, the men of Anathoth, sought unsuccessfully to kill him. Neither the occasion nor the reasons for this plot are given, but it has been suggested that it may have been a consequence of Jeremiah's initial support for the religious reforms instituted by King Hezekiah which would have been resented by the priests of Anathoth because it deprived them of their livelihood.

The strong hostility and threats against his life which Jeremiah encountered brought tension and a prolonged spiritual crisis in his own life. Jeremiah rebelled against his own sufferings and came to feel that they were all in vain, since the threats of judgment upon Jerusalem failed to materialize. In a number of passages, often called Jeremiah's 'confessions', the prophet gives vent to his own feelings and complaints (Jer.11.18–23; 12.1–6; 15.10–12, 15–21; 17.12–18; 18.18–23; 20.7–18). In the most outspoken and despairing of these utterances Jeremiah openly accused God of having deceived him and of having made him into a laughing-stock. Yet when the prophet made up his mind that he would not prophesy any more, he could not restrain himself from doing so, since the message of God was like a fire shut up inside him (20.7–12). All that he could do was to plead for vengeance upon his enemies.

The reign of Josiah came to a tragic end in 609 BC when the king was killed at Megiddo by the Egyptian Pharaoh Necho, and for a brief period Shallum ruled until he was deported to Egypt (Jer.22.10–12). By this time the Assyrian empire was in ruins and the capital Nineveh had fallen to the Babylonians and Medes in 612 BC. The passing of Assyrian power, with its reputation for brutality and violence, did not go uncelebrated in Judah and the prophet Nahum offers a vivid picture of the sense of divine justice which accompanied the expectation of Nineveh's fall. Thus Nahum gave voice to the more nationalistic feelings of Israel. Yet the end of Assyrian power did not result in any lessening of foreign domination of Judah. Jehoiakim was placed on the throne of Judah instead of Shallum by the Egyptians, and his reign was marked by oppression and bloodshed. Jeremiah condemns him as an evil tyrant over his people (Jer.22.13–19). In 605 BC control of Judah passed into the power of Babylonia, and Jehoiakim secured himself before his new masters by a transfer of loyalty. It is in this year that a major event occurred in Jeremiah's ministry, recounted in Jer.36. The prophet was personally debarred from entering the temple, and so he employed Baruch to write out a scroll, at his dictation, containing his prophecies of coming disaster upon Jerusalem. Baruch then read out this scroll in the temple on a fast day, when a large crowd would be present. The year in which this occurred strongly points to the view that Jeremiah was now openly interpreting his earlier warnings of 'the foe from the north', as referring to

Babylon. Baruch was greeted with the same kind of hostility that had earlier been shown personally to Jeremiah. The scroll was confiscated and taken to the royal palace, where its contents were read out to Jehoiakim the king, who promptly cut up and burnt the leather roll as a sign of his disdain. When he learnt of this Jeremiah simply had a second, even longer, scroll written by Baruch.

In 601 BC Jehoiakim rebelled against the king of Babylon, inviting severe retaliation. This came in 598 when Jerusalem was besieged and forced to capitulate. Before the final blow fell, however, Jehoiakim died, leaving his son Jehoiachin to face the wrath of the Babylonians. The surrender terms were severe: the king was taken as a hostage to Babylon, along with several thousand of the leading citizens of the land, and his uncle Zedekiah was placed upon the throne as a Babylonian puppet ruler.

Jeremiah now actively campaigned for complete and utter submission to the Babylonians. He regarded it as the will of God that 'all the nations' should serve the king of Babylon (Jer.27.1–11). At this time the voices of certain nationalistic prophets were raised to encourage further rebellion against Babylon, and Jeremiah vigorously opposed them and their policies (Jer.27.14 f.). A remarkable and distinctive example of this confrontation of views is recorded in Jer.28. A nationalistic prophet, by name Hananiah, foretold that within two years the Babylonian yoke would be removed. At first Jeremiah appears to have accepted the possibility that Hananiah's words would prove true, until a prophetic message from God reassured him of the folly of such nationalistic hopes (28.12–17). Not only did Jeremiah reaffirm that God willed complete submission to the Babylonians, but he now also foretold the imminent death of Hananiah, apparently in punishment for his having deceived the people in God's name.

Zedekiah appears not to have been altogether inattentive to Jeremiah's preaching (Jer.37), but he finally allowed himself to be persuaded into joining an anti-Babylonian revolt (589 BC). Inevitably stern and overwhelming retribution came. Jerusalem was besieged and destroyed in 587 BC, and Zedekiah was forced to witness the death of his own sons before himself being blinded and exiled. Throughout the siege Jeremiah consistently urged the people to surrender, even encouraging individuals to desert to the Babylonian camp (Jer.38).

After the fall of the city Jeremiah was given the choice of either going to Babylon with the exiles or staying, and he chose the latter course. He seems well content to have accepted the governorship of Gedaliah whom the Babylonians now installed as controller of the Province in place of a king (Jer.40.1–12). It may be that at this time he felt most certain of the coming renewal of Israel, and of the divine grace which would bring into being a new covenant with Israel and Judah (Jer.30–31). We cannot, however, be at all sure of the date of these assurances in 'the Book of Consolation'.

The period of Gedaliah's governorship was brief, and he was tragically murdered by a member of the royal house named Ishmael, who afterwards escaped to the Ammonites. The remainder of the people were afraid of further Babylonian reprisals, and fled to Egypt, forcing Jeremiah to accompany them, in spite of his advice not to go and his warnings that to do so would only result in their own ultimate death and destruction (Jer.42.1–17). The last oracles that we hear from him came from his place of

enforced exile in Egypt, where he was still rebuking his fellow Jews for their disobedience and idolatry (Jer.43.8–13; 44).

With the fall of Jerusalem in 587 the last surviving political entity of the old nation of Israel broke up into separate, and politically subservient, communities. Many of the old nation were in exile in Babylon, where we hear more of their activities from the prophets Ezekiel and Deutero-Isaiah. Some had fled to Egypt and probably other countries where their ultimate fate is unknown. A large number remained in the land of Judah to face the pitiful sufferings of a devastated land, and to seek to build up afresh the conditions and means of a stable social and economic life. The appalling conditions are well described in the book of Lamentations, which is not from Jeremiah, but an anonymous poet, or group of poets, who lived in Judah during the period following Jerusalem's destruction. Aside from the horror of famine and disease, brought about by the ravages of war, there was the theological problem of finding some divine meaning or explanation for catastophe. Why had God disowned his people (Lam.2.5), his sanctuary (Lam.2.7) and his chosen king of the line of David (Lam.4.20)? Only by accepting the interpretation given by the great prophets that it was a divine punishment for Israel's sins could sense be made out of such an appalling situation.

The prophetic interpretation of history

Although, as we saw at the beginning, prophets were not unique to Israel, no other nation seems ever to have been so deeply indebted to them as was Israel. Furthermore, in Israel the greatest period of such prophetic influence extended over no more than two centuries, stretching from the middle of the eighth to shortly after the middle of the sixth centuries BC. Again, although very many prophets were active during this period, it is only the work of a few individuals from among them which has had a lasting influence upon human history. By these few, whom we name the 'classical' or 'writing' prophets, a significant transformation of the religion of Israel was brought about.

The prophets laid great stress upon their divine 'call', which placed the authority for what they said upon God, and so looked beyond their own feelings or desires. They worked in quite a different way from the modern politician, philosopher or sociologist in their reflections upon the character and destiny of the society in which they lived. They were not looking for intrinsic laws of cause and effect which could be seen to operate in the affairs of men, but were threatening the direct personal intervention of God in judgment upon his elect people. They ascribed their message to divine inspiration, and not to their own thoughts about the future state of the world in which they lived. It was this awareness of divine authority and commission which enabled the prophets to face rejection, opposition and persecution from their compatriots. It also left them free from any self-interested professionalism and from any formal ties with the great religious and political institutions of Israel.

The prophets stand out for their remarkably detailed knowledge of international affairs, and for their awareness of the policies and diplomacy of Jerusalem and Samarian courts. They displayed a political interest which assumed from the state that God was deeply concerned about the social and political realities of life in Israel. They argued that God was exercising a controlling influence upon international affairs, and that in encountering their political fate Israel and Judah were being brought face to face with God (cf. Amos 4.12). Disaster and defeat were his judgments, deliverance and victory were his salvation. Most prominently, however, it is the negative aspect of judgment which looms largest in the prophets' preaching, making their threat a continued rebuke against political pride and military arrogance, and sharply condemning Israel's religious complacency.

In giving their interpretation of events the prophets used various pictorial images to describe the historical situation in which Israel was placed. Most dramatically Hosea pictures Israel as the bride of God (Hos.2.1 ff.), who has wilfully become unfaithful by turning to other lovers, the Baal gods. The coming judgment will be God's divorce of his faithless wife (Hos.2.2 f.). This same marriage metaphor is taken up later by Jeremiah (Jer.2.2 ff.). Such pictorial language provided a vivid and dramatic interpretation of Israel's historical situation, and provided a sharp moral condemnation in explanation of the coming catastrophe.

Another popular metaphor is that of the law-suit in which the prophet pictures Israel as summoned to account for its behaviour in a court of law (Isa.1.2–20; Micah 6.1–5). Israel is accused of disloyalty to God, of having broken its pledges to him, and of countless acts of disobedience. The time has come for God to act, and to call his erring people to judgment. In this metaphor God is both the plaintiff and judge, while heaven and earth are called upon to act as witnesses of Israel's offences. In this lawsuit in which the prophet pictures Israel as similarities between God's case against Israel and the kind of ultimatum which a reigning emperor would deliver to a vassal ruler whom he suspected of treason and disloyalty. Thus the covenant between God and Israel shows certain similarities with treaties between imperial and vassal states.

In their descriptions of the coming divine judgments upon Israel the prophets naturally drew upon conventional knowledge of life and affairs. Their widely used imagery of battle and defeat was drawn from their knowledge of contemporary military practice. Essentially it was the certainty of judgment, rather than its precise details, which the prophets foretold. Nahum could describe the violent overthrow of Nineveh, although in the event the capture of the city by the Babylonian armies was virtually unopposed (612 BC). The moral significance was of far greater importance than the literal accuracy of the details of the fulfilment of prophecy, so that such a situation in no way lessens the religious 'truth' of what the prophets said. It was not simply their ability to predict the future, but their power to interpret it, which gave to the prophets their greatness. They related past, present and future in a consistent story of God's concern for his chosen people Israel, and they interpreted this story in accordance with the moral purpose for which Israel was called. They did not therefore exclude other nations from their field of vision. Jeremiah was specifically called to be a 'prophet to the nations' (Jer.1.5), and this was certainly also true of Amos and Isaiah. The prophets interpreted Israel's history in relation to a universal purpose of God for which Israel's election had meaning. The very notion that Israel should be judged received significance in the context of God's wider concern for the welfare of all nations, and Israel's responsibility to be a light and a witness to them.

Our ultimate evaluation of the prophets' message cannot therefore be reached simply by asking whether what the prophets threatened for Israel came 'true'. Rather their 'truth' lies deeper in the realm of spiritual and moral understanding. Is the prophets' interpretation of Israel's downfall more convincing than the arrogant religious claims of contemporary Assyrian and Babylonian nationalism, or than the suggestion that it was a purely meaningless historical accident ? The spiritual fruits of the prophetic interpretation in terms of humility in the face of suffering, spiritual sensitivity and a passionate concern for social justice, encourage us to believe that the prophets did preach 'truth'. This truth is not only applicable to Israel, and to the distinctive circumstances which prevailed in the eighth to the sixth centuries BC, but to a wider area of life. It concerns us also, since we also are faced with questions of nationalism, social injustice and widespread beliefs in the divinely given supremacy of certain nations and races. By their moral interpretation of the belief in Israel's national election, the prophets warned against any selfish or material conception of it. The 'truth' of prophecy can speak to us in our own situation, with our national hopes, our social needs and problems, and our personal responsibilities to one another. It is a truth which can give us insight into the meaning and purpose of life, and of the divine government of the world in which that life is lived.

R.E. CLEMENTS

12 Worship in Israel

Places of worship

While the territory of Israel contained many holy places, there was from the first a tendency to centralize the main festivals in one designated sanctuary. This followed from the nature of the religion as a union between God and the entire society. For a major festival it was appropriate that (in principle) the whole people should assemble as one in the place where God, in some mysterious way, would make his presence known to them. From far and near the worshippers would converge with cattle and harvest produce for their offerings; in orderly fashion they would take up temporary stations to spend perhaps a week or more in the vicinity of the sanctuary. Traditions about a tent-sanctuary suggest that in the early period the assembly may have been convened in a desert region, forming a great camp of tents. But during most of the era before the monarchy, the place of central assembly was by a town in the centre of the land. The choice varied from time to time – Shechem in the early days, Shiloh at the end; other places which had their turn included Bethel, Mizpah, and Gilgal near the Jordan crossing. Such important sanctuaries have often bequeathed to the Old Testament their own peculiar traditions reflecting stories of their origins and local customs. Sometimes these places returned to prominence in later periods; the oldest has proved the most enduring, for the Samaritans have continued to celebrate the Passover on Mount Gerizim above Shechem to this day.

Sacred buildings were relatively slight, since much of the proceedings took place in surrounding open courts, for example, the sacrifices burnt on altars. The ancient practice of setting up tall stones was continued; such pillars were said to be witnesses of Israel's pledges to God, reminders of her commitment in the covenant. But the most important symbol of the central sanctuary was the ark of the covenant, a portable chest which apparently contained tablets inscribed with the laws of the covenant and which was also imagined as a footstool before God's throne, a sign of his invisible but powerful presence.

The Philistines captured the ark in battle and proceeded to devastate its sanctuary at Shiloh. The stories about its return to Israel and how David eventually brought it to the newly conquered city of Jerusalem (c.1000 BC) seem to derive from the Jerusalem sanctuary's own account of its foundation; that this account was re-enacted at Jerusalem in regular services of reconsecration may be concluded also from Ps.132 (see below). As the new home of the ark, Jerusalem was now able to rise to predominance as Israel's place of worship. The ark made it the focus of the religion of all the tribes, while in addition it was the seat of David's dynasty, which claimed an everlasting commission to rule with and for divine right. A millennium of pre-Israelite tradition had already invested the place with a rich ideology (cf.Gen.14.18–20). The new circumstances brought a potent synthesis of ideas in which the old Israelite conception of God was decisive, though developed in new directions.

Some ceremonies used to be performed at the spring of Gihon in the valley below Jerusalem's east wall. From here one could ascend the hill which overlooked the city of David from the north. This may have been the 'high place' used for worship by the pre-Israelite population; at all events, it was chosen by David as the area for his sanctuary, though he did not himself erect important buildings on it. This latter step was taken by his son Solomon who constructed an impressive complex of temple and royal buildings set in spacious courts.

The temple itself was an oblong building consisting of three rooms in a line from east to west. The entrance was at the eastern end, and outside it were two great free-standing pillars. These were made of bronze and crowned with ornamented capitals; they were named 'Jachin' and 'Boaz', but their significance remains disputed. The entrance gave access to the first of the temple's three rooms, the porch or entrance hall. Passing through this, one entered the second and much the largest room, a kind of nave. Here were found a gold altar for incense, two sets of five candelabra, and a gold table bearing twelve loaves and more incense; the loaves were the 'shewbread', a sign of the covenant of the twelve tribes before the face of God. Beyond this room and approached up a flight of steps was the 'most holy place' or 'holy of holies'. Here in thick darkness were the symbols of God's presence: the ark and the two cherubs, human-headed animal figures with wings outstretched above the ark, representing the heavenly attendants and throne-bearers of God. It is likely that this third room centred over the ancient holy rock at the summit as does the Muslim Dome of the Rock today.

Against the outside of the north, west and south walls of the temple was built a series of quite small rooms in three low storeys. These were for the use of the temple staff and for storage. The main altar for sacrifices was probably situated in the open court to the east of the temple. Also in the court was a bronze platform from which the king led the prayers. Other items in the open included an enormous bronze basin of water resting on twelve figures of oxen, and ten smaller basins on wheeled stands. These may have served partly for ceremonial washing, partly in some ritual as a symbolic of the sources of rain.

While many details of the temple's construction and furnishing remain obscure, its significance as the 'house of God' is clear enough. Here God was said to dwell, an invisibly enthroned presence. It was as though this holy place became mysteriously identical with the heavenly abode, or as though God filled it with an extension of his own person (in biblical terms, 'putting his name there'). And so the place could be regarded poetically as the summit of all creation constructed by God himself, as the paradise-centre, or as a rocky nucleus of the cosmos standing firm amidst chaotic seas.

With these developments, Jerusalem's role as 'the city of God', the supreme 'joy of the whole earth' (Ps.48), was well established, and her royal festivals had great influence on the form of the people's devotion. When the northern provinces broke with Solomon's successor (*c*.931 BC), their rebel king, Jeroboam, gave the honour of principal sanctuary to Bethel near his southern border, supplemented in the north by Dan near the Jordan's springs. He timed their chief festival (in the autumn) a month later than Jerusalem's, as though not to risk direct competition. He appointed new priests and for signs of the divine presence he provided bull-images. In all this, as with David and his successors, we see how the kings had chief responsibility for the conduct of worship, the priests being generally subordinate.

Mention of the bull-images reminds us that the severe standards of the religion descended from Moses were often threatened by other religions in the environment, at whose sanctuaries might be found images of gods, male and female sacred prostitutes, and sacrifices of children. Sometimes Jerusalem itself succumbed to such influences, particularly when the area was dominated by Assyria and Babylonia. But there were also times of reformation, and the reforms of the Judaean kings Hezekiah and Josiah included the restriction of worship to the Jerusalem temple alone. Josiah's drastic suppression of other cults (*c.*622 BC) established Jerusalem's position as the sole sanctuary, a status further confirmed in the years following the exile. (The rival sister-religion of the Samaritans persisted at Shechem, however, and we know of two cases where Jews in Egypt had their own temple for a time, at Elephantine and Leontopolis.)

The centuries of Jerusalem's sole legitimacy also saw the growth of Jewish settlements abroad. Obviously the chances of making pilgrimage to her festivals would not be enough to sustain the religion of such a far-flung community. In addition to the central sacrificial cult, it was necessary to allow practices of prayer and instruction in local gatherings. We have a few glimpses of such gatherings in the exile, but the well-organized system of local synagogues is not clearly attested until towards New Testament times.

Solomon's temple was razed to the ground by the Babylonians in 587 BC. But their successors, the Persians, supported its refounding. The second temple, less splendid, was dedicated in 515 BC. Soon we hear of a period of stagnation and cynicism which affected many priests (Mal.1.6 f.). Notable reforms, however, were achieved under Nehemiah and Ezra some time after 445 BC. Under the Hellenistic empire of Antiochus Epiphanes (175–163 BC), the temple was for a few years forced into the style of the imperial religion and the laws of Moses were suppressed. With the triumph of the Maccabees, orthodoxy was restored. The temple prospered. Herod the Great, great certainly in his buildings, sought to please his Jewish subjects by undertaking a magnificent reconstruction (20 BC). One of the wonders of the world, it had scarcely been completed when it was destroyed in the war against Rome (AD 70). But the vast area of its courts and parts of their outer walls remain clearly in evidence today. The ancient memories seem to live on in the beautiful Muslim shrines and earnest worship which still adorn the courts; the summit of living rock is gracefully sheltered by the Dome of the Rock, as once it may have been by Solomon's 'most holy place'. Nearby, Jewish pilgrims still pray at the outer wall of the court, the 'Wailing Wall', and Christians of all races venerate the site of Jesus' sacrifice. Thus tangibly, but also in the realm of the human mind, Jerusalem lives on as the supreme place of worship, the 'city of God', the symbol of Paradise.

Seasons of worship

In spite of variations in emphasis through a long history, Israelite worship generally retained a pattern of three pilgrimage festivals a year, which were understood to have been directly ordained by God. They were anchored in the agricultural seasons, but were also interpreted as commemorative renewals of the great events in which the community's life and religion had originated.

The festival in March-April was really a combination of two observances, the night of *Passover* and the week of *Unleavened Bread*. The Passover may go back to a protective ceremony carried out by semi-nomadic shepherds before their annual migration from the desert towards the cultivated fringes; on a night of full-moon a lamb was consumed in each tent-family and the equipment smeared with the blood to ward off evil, before the camp was broken up in haste. For Israel it became a commemoration of the night when God brought death to the land of her oppressors and passed over the Israelite households marked with the sacrificial blood, who then departed in haste with their flocks (Ex.12). The passover in itself was an observance in the family circle rather than a pilgrimage festival, and it is accordingly not mentioned in early festival calendars. It comes into prominence towards the end of the monarchy, when it is linked with the pilgrimage festival of Unleavened Bread. This latter was a week originally in celebration of the earliest harvesting, that of the barley; the first cuttings, and first-born animals too, would be presented in the sanctuary, so that the rest could be taken for human use without arrogance. The week was marked by a ban on leaven, as though to avoid contaminating the new crop with the old. When the festival came to be interpreted as a commemoration of the exodus, the unleavened bread suggested the haste of the meal in Passover night.

In May–June fell the festival of *Weeks*, so called because it was counted seven weeks after the preceding festival. It is also called Harvest, and in fact it marked the harvest of wheat with offerings of the first cuttings. Originally a one-day observance, it was later expanded to a week. It was slower than the other festivals to be interpreted as a commemoration of Israel's early history, but eventually, before New Testament times, it was related to the making of the covenant.

In September–October fell the autumnal festival sometimes called *Ingathering* or *Tabernacles*. The late fruit harvest was completed and all produce had to be taken in and stored as the long summer drought might soon end. Ancient festivities included the dancing of maidens in the vineyards and the drinking of wine. The 'tabernacles' or booths, in which the pilgrims resided, originated in the temporary shelters of branches erected in the harvest fields and vineyards. But they came to be equated with the tents of the ancestors in the desert, as the festival was used to commemorate the Exodus and the revelation on Mount Sinai. Although this festival is listed third and its month eventually counted as the seventh (as in the Babylonian calendar), it fell at the time of the new agricultural year in Canaan. It is interesting that an inscription of about the twelfth century BC found at Gezer lists 'Ingathering' as the first of the activities of the agricultural year. A great concern of the festival, then, would be to pray that the imminent rainy season, the indispensable prelude to cultivation and growth, should not fail, as it sometimes did. (Note the reflection of this festal theme in Zech.14.16 f. The Mishnah, a commentary on the Jewish Law, tells us that water was brought up each day of the festival from the spring Gihon and poured over the altar – an acted

137

prayer for rain.) In general, then, this season was a time to look again at the foundations of life, to seek cleansing and renewed relationship with God, and the gifts of life that could then ensue.

The indications are that this festival was the most important of the three at least until the end of the monarchy. As celebrated by the league of tribes at Shechem, Shiloh, etc., it served especially to reinforce their commitment to the covenant. As celebrated at Jerusalem under the kings, it served in addition to show the place of the Davidic ruler and of Jerusalem in God's designs. The hymns of the Jerusalem festival represented God especially as the true king of all creation, subduing all harmful and turbulent forces and richly blessing the processes of life. Just as an element of drama was used (and still is) to re-create the experience of the Passover night, so too the special themes of the autumnal festival were dramatized in ceremonial movements and recitations. The malevolent forces were represented once more as overthrown, the purposes of God as the eternal king newly revealed. By such drama, the traditions of ancient salvation became a living part of the present joy of the festival. And because of the contrast with the actual sorry state of things, this festival experience of perfection had also a prophetic quality, pointing forward to a new era of salvation still to come.

In addition to the great pilgrimage festivals, there were many other regular observances. At the temple the priests presented offerings every morning and evening. There were additional offerings for the weekly rest-day, the *sabbath*, and for the first day of every month, the day of the new moon. Great events might be commemorated on their anniversaries, as was the Babylonians' destruction of the temple; two commemorations of the later period are still observed: *Hanukkah*, which celebrates the reconsecration of the temple in 164 BC under Judas Maccabaeus, and *Purim*, which remembers the deliverance described in rather embellished form in the book of Esther. In times of crisis (war, famine, etc.) a special day of prayer was decreed, and the people gathered at the sanctuary to implore divine intervention.

The observance of the *sabbath* was not specially bound to the rites at the sanctuary; it was a matter of resting in one's house 'to the Lord', giving rest also to servants and beasts of burden, and imitating God's rest in the creation story (Gen.2.2 f.). Such consecrated rest was a holding back of domineering tendencies and acquisitiveness; the one day devoted to God signified basically that all days belonged to him and were held in trust. This intention emerges clearly in other observances related to the sabbath – the sabbath year and the year of Jubilees. The *sabbath year* was practised probably in the early period, before agriculture had become such a central part of the tribal economy. Every seventh year the land was left uncultivated, its free growth being left for the poor; other acts of restoration were added, the annulling of debts, the freeing of slaves, and perhaps also some redistribution of land. Similar practices characterized the *year of Jubilees*, which was the fiftieth year, marking the completion of seven sabbath years. In the conditions of a complex economy, these sabbatical years fell into neglect, but they had represented a noble ideal; recognition of the sovereign rights of God, the checking of man's thrust to self-aggrandizement, a new deal for the poor and down-trodden, consideration for the other species of life on the planet.

Little is known about set times of individual prayer. Muslims observe three or five set times of prayer daily and bow down in the direction of Mecca. The Jews had similar observances, praying at morning, noon, and evening, and turning towards the 'most holy place' of the temple.

Leaders of worship

The Davidic kings held the chief authority over the affairs of the temple. They were supreme not only in material matters, but also in leading the national worship. After the end of the monarchy the senior priest of the temple, the 'high priest', gradually acquired much of the dignity that had belonged to the king.

All sanctuaries had a staff of sacred officials. Such offices were largely hereditary, and as various family guilds developed, there was a complicated history of rivalries. The original lay tribe of Levi was probably distinct from an ancient priestly order called 'Levites'; these Levites seem to have been priests among the invading Israelites and functioned around the ark. They could not always establish themselves against sanctuary staffs of other origins (descended from pre-Israelite worship, or appointed by Davidic or northern kings, etc.). The priestly clan of Zadok prevailed over them at Jerusalem, and in the north, too, they were ousted by men appointed by the rebel king Jeroboam. It is thought that they still continued to cherish their ancient traditions descended from Moses and were able to influence the reforms of Josiah. In post-exilic Jerusalem, however, they were firmly accorded an inferior status as guardians and musicians.

The priest was an expert authority on matters for which special sacred knowledge was required. He gave guidance and decisions both on matters of religious ceremony and also in hard cases of ordinary law; he was the exponent of the laws of God. His pronouncements might rest on the basis of priestly traditions or be reached by the casting of the sacred lot ('Urim and Thummim'), which in some way yielded an oracular decision on the question propounded. He was a father and counsellor to God's people. The proceedings at the sanctuary were his special care, including the sacrifices. He lived by receiving a share of the people's offerings. However, sacrifice was not the principal task of his office, and especially in early times certain sacrifices might be offered by any head of the family.

The authorities of the Jerusalem temple under the monarchy included prophets as well as priests. Moreover, the prophetic books contain much material related to worship (hymns, laments, etc.), just as the texts of worship in the psalms contain prophetic oracles. It is notable, too, that minor priestly orders of the later temple are often depicted as inspired prophets. All in all, it is clear that while prophecy was not restricted to service in the sanctuaries, it had an important role there. Prophets had a place there alongside the priests as ministers of God. Mediators of revelation like the priests, they were distinguished in that their very personalities were the means of inspiration; exalted states of consciousness gave them perceptions beyond the ordinary. Pilgrims to the sanctuaries would consult them and seek a word from God by them. Even in the formal ceremonies of worship they seem to have had a part, especially in bringing divine messages to the assembly through their sudden inspiration. Sometimes a great prophet might take the lead in renewing the covenant with God, in the manner of a Moses, Samuel or Elijah.

Another speciality among the servants of the sanctuary was that of music and chanting. There were hereditary guilds, connected closely with the priests and prophets, who composed and sang the poetic hymns and prayers and executed the carefully prescribed musical accompaniment. Our book of psalms is largely a deposit of their traditions.

Sacrifices in worship

A prominent feature of worship was the presentation of offerings from the produce of fields and flocks. It is difficult to win a clear picture of the types of offering and their significances, as a great variety of traditions and developments has been woven together in our present sources. The central idea is that of relationship; the presentation and acceptance of the offerings are a visible sign of the bond between God and his worshippers. In response to God's own direction, his people present their gifts in costly obedience. Their offerings mean in part a self-giving, an act of self-deprivation in honour of the God to whom all belongs. Thus they give themselves in their gifts and are accepted. Such gestures of relationship imply the removal of any barrier that might have existed; the idea of the removal of sin is thus present with all the offerings, although some are explicitly concerned with this.

Distinguishing the main types roughly, we may note first those which especially had the nature of gifts. These might be vegetable or animal, and were generally burnt on the altar, as it were sent up to heaven in the form of smoke. They were sometimes offered with intercessions or in fulfilment of a vow. They expressed dependence, reverence, gratitude.

With these we can consider the first-fruits of the crops and the first-born of animals, offered in acknowledgment of God's first claim as the true lord and disposer of all creation; only then was the way open for ordinary human use of these species. A primitive Canaanite custom of including also the first-born of human beings was replaced in Israel by the system of 'redemption': the child, like the whole race, belonged to God, but his life was spared and replaced by the sacrifice of an animal.

Then there were sacrifices which had the character of fellowship-meals. Originally all slaughter of animals was reserved for sacred ceremonies, a restriction which had to be abandoned when the numerous local shrines were abolished. Groups of worshippers would share in the meal at the sanctuary after the best parts of the beast had first been offered to God by fire. Such a sacred banquet signified the closest ties of trust between the deity and his worshippers, and between one worshipper and another. It is not surprising, then, that such sacrifices accompanied rites of covenant-making (Ex.24.3 f.; Ps.50.3). 'Sacrifices of thanksgiving' might have the character either of gifts or of communion meals, but they were specially designed as an occasion for testimony to some specific deliverance. Such offerings might be in fulfilment of promises made in the time of need.

Finally, we may note the sacrifices which were particularly related to purification and atonement: the sin-offering and the guilt-offering. With these the worshipper prayed for the removal of his sin and impurity. Such purification was especially the theme of the Day of Atonement, when expiatory sacrifices were made for sanctuary, leader and people. This was the occasion of the peculiar rite described in Lev.16.20–22, when a goat was driven into the wilderness, symbolically carrying into oblivion the year's burden of sin.

There were times when the worshippers distorted the purpose of sacrifices. They had to be warned not to suppose that God needed them as food, nor that abundant sacrifices could obscure God's moral requirements. Some prophets indeed yearned for the days before sacrifice, under Canannite influence, had come to such proportions. Nevertheless, the system represented much of value. Above all it demonstrated the costly basis of fellowship between God and man.

Glimpses of worship

The narratives of the Old Testament frequently give us valuable glimpses of worship. Some outstanding examples are noted in the following paragraphs.

The ancient sagas of Genesis acquired a rich multiplicity of meaning through their long history, and part of this meaning is often related to customs of worship. Thus the story of Cain and Abel (Gen.4.2–7) shows two types: the semi-nomadic shepherds who sacrifice their first-born animals, sending up the choicest portions in fire on the altar, and the settled cultivators whose offering is from the produce of their fields. The former proudly think of their simple mode of life as more pleasing to God. In some way an indication is given to the worshippers (through the word of the priest ?) whether the deity accepts or rejects their offering; it is fundamental that the acceptance depends on well-doing.

Again, in the profound story of Abraham's sacrifice (Gen.22), we can detect how the practice at some sanctuary of sparing the first-born child by offering instead a lamb was justified by reference to Abraham. The willingness to give all is thus still asserted, while it is recognized that child-sacrifice is not the will of God.

The story of Jacob's dream (Gen.28.10–22) contains elements from the traditions of the ancient sanctuary of Bethel, traditions which explained to worshippers its wonderful credentials. Its anointed stone was a sign of God's presence; the place was a gateway of heaven, a place of direct communication between heaven and earth, symbolized perhaps by some stairlike building suggestive of a ladder up to heaven. The story of Jacob's experience thus gave the worshipper at Bethel confidence that here his prayers would reach heaven; here God himself was near.

Several stories of Joshua reflect customs of worship. The crossing of the Jordan (Josh.3–4) is depicted as a religious ceremony ending at the sanctuary of Gilgal and commemorating the crossing of the Red Sea in the exodus. One can trace here a regular observance around Passover time (Josh.5.11), with a procession of the ark over the Jordan and ceremonies around the sacred pillars, the intention being to re-enact the exodus scene. Close to Gilgal were found the ruins of Jericho; the famous story of the capture of Jericho (Josh.6) may have developed out of similar festal processions, the priests bearing the ark round the ruined site in commemoration of the conquest of Canaan.

The story of the tribal assembly in Josh.24 seems to have been shaped by the proceedings of regular festivals in the tribal period. From it we can see how representatives of all the twelve tribes assembled at Shechem. There was a presiding figure who, in the tradition of Moses and Joshua, mediated between God and Israel in the renewing of the covenant. He relays words of God in the manner of a prophet. The assembly understands that God himself has come to confront them and speak through the mouth of the mediator. In this way God's speech begins by recalling his dealings with the fathers, calling, saving and establishing them in Canaan. The mediator adds his own exhortation, calling upon the assembled Israel to renounce all other cults and enter into God's exclusive covenant. The assembly expresses assent. The leader gives further exhortations, stressing the formidable nature of the undertaking, and the congregation further responds with assent: 'We will serve the Lord. He is our God.' Their decision is then solemnly attested like an oath. Some ceremony marks the putting away of other gods (burial or destruction of images?) and the covenant is formally concluded. The leader rehearses the covenant laws, and a sacred stone is regarded as a witness that the people have pledged themselves to keep them. The leader then dismisses the assembly, no doubt with a blessing.

A further glimpse of these ancient ceremonies is afforded by Deut.27. The scene again is Shechem and the leader in the tradition of Moses is again prominent with his exhortations. But a picturesque detail is added. The obligations of the law are underlined by the division of the assembly on to the over-looking mountain-sides. One party stands on Mount Gerizim to the south of Shechem's natural amphitheatre, while priests among them pronounce blessings to take effect on the obedient (cf. Deut.28.1–6). The other party stands on Mount Ebal to the north, where priests declare calamity for the unfaithful; the sins listed are especially those which easily escape human detection (27.15 f.). To each curse the congregation answers 'Amen'.

Valuable glimpses into the annual festivals are also given by the story of the birth of Samuel (I Sam.1–2). In particular we see the occasion from the angle of a pious family of pilgrims and their domestic problems. Once every year, probably in the autumn, they make pilgrimage to the festival at Shiloh, where the presence of God as 'the Lord of hosts' was marked by the ark. The head of the family sacrificed; the fat portion was to be presented by fire to the Lord, the rest boiled in a cauldron in preparation for a sacred meal. Parts would then be due to the priests, and the rest was to be carefully apportioned to each member of the family. As it happened, the sons of the chief priest were greedily disregarding the law, taking more than their share, and even before the part for God had been presented; their misconduct with the sacred women may reflect the influence of Canaanite religion, in which sacred prostitutes had a place. Significantly, however, the corruption of the authorities did not prevent the pious pilgrims from valuing the festival as a true encounter with God. As the autumnal festival was the time to pray for the new year of fertility and growth in fields and flocks, so also prayer was made for the blessing of the human family, and the childless wife would make an earnest plea. Hannah's prayer is strengthened by a vow (I Sam.1.11). The aged senior priest, seated in honour by the entrance of the temple, mistook her emotional praying for drunkenness, since much wine flowed at that festival. But realizing his error, he was able to give her an indication that God had accepted her prayer (1.17, translate 'will grant'). The story thus illustrates how a family, and indeed an individual, found place for personal needs within the framework of the national festival.

Soon judgment was to fall on the insolent priests; even the atoning power of sacrifice could not avail for so great an offence (3.14).

In I Sam.4–6 and II Sam.6 it seems that the historian has drawn on the sacred story which went with a regular ceremony celebrating and renewing the foundation of Jerusalem's sanctuary (see below on Ps.132). In II Sam.6 we see how the progress of the ark along its various stations was accompanied by dancing, music and sacrifice. The participants represent the entire people, and the king himself takes the leading priestly role, dressed in the priestly apron ('ephod'), dancing with all his might, sacrificing, pronouncing the benediction. The procession of the ark up to the sanctuary seems to symbolize the triumphant ascent of God, fresh from the rout of his foes, to his heavenly palace; the ark deposited under the wings of the cherubs points to the mysterious sanctuary-presence of the Lord of hosts enthroned in glory (6.2). The much later passage, I Chron.15–16, pictures the ceremonies with more interest in the psalms and music used on such occasions.

In II Chron.20 we have a good example of a holy convocation in face of a crisis. King Jehoshaphat (873–849 BC), hearing of an enemy advancing from the south, decreed a fast and a national assembly for worship and intercession at the temple. The king took the lead in offering persuasive prayer. One of the temple ministers was then inspired to deliver an oracle promising victory. The service ended with prostration 'before the Lord' and the loudest possible hymn-singing. As the army went out to battle next day, the king declared that if they believed the word of God given by the prophet, they would succeed, as in fact they did.

Shortly after 445 BC, a special service was held to dedicate the encompassing walls of Jerusalem which the new governor Nehemiah had built. As described in Neh.12.3 f., the arrangements for the service were ordered by the governor. Two parties of notables were formed, each headed by sacred choirs and musicians. After ceremonies of purification, the double procession was commenced from the middle of the western wall. One party proceeded along the top of the wall southwards, while the other likewise moved northwards. Eventually they met on the eastern side, turning into the temple there. Sacrifices were offered and hymns were sung with the greatest volume. One may see here how such an encompassing procession is meant to trace out an area of God's blessing; the city's rampart is made a wall of divine salvation.

Finally, we may note a vivid glimpse of worship around 200 BC. In the Apocrypha, Ecclus.50, we hear of a high priest, to whom falls the duty of the earlier kings to maintain the temple buildings. Not less than royal is the splendour of his appearance as he leads the ceremonies on the Day of Atonement, emerging from the innermost shrine like a luminary in the heavens. The glowing description reflects the author's joy in worship as much as the actual spectacle. We hear of the high priest robing afresh and mounting to the altar in the open court. Assisted by a company of priests, he burns sacrifices to the Lord on the altar and pours out a wine-offering at the base. The priests shout and blow trumpets. The presence of God is now most keenly sensed, and the people fall on their faces. The singers sing psalms. Prayers are raised. The people bow again as the high priest concludes with a benediction 'from the Most High'.

The psalms

The psalms deserve a special place in the present study. As poetic pieces generally intoned or chanted in worship, they often reflect ceremonies which they accompanied, and even more, the thoughts and beliefs which filled the minds of the worshippers. While the setting of many psalms in festal worship is clear, the exact contexts and sequences remain uncertain. In spite of many disputed points, however, it will be seen that the psalms do reveal the main ingredients of the festal experience; the grouping of the psalms below relates especially to the autumnal festival in royal Jerusalem.

The chief feature of the poetry of the psalms is called 'parallelism'; most verses fall into two (sometimes three) parts, which are parallel in thought and expression. In one type ('synonymous') the two parts are saying the same thing in different words: 'O come let us sing to the Lord/let us make a joyful noise to the rock of our salvation.' In the second type ('antithetic'), the duplication takes the form of a contrast: 'The Lord lifts up the downtrodden/he casts the wicked to the ground.' In a third type ('synthetic' or 'formal'), the twofold structure is maintained, but in fact there is only a single statement: 'I have set my king/on Zion my holy hill.' Yet another variety has been called 'stair-like'; the second part repeats some words from the first and then adds a fresh element: 'Ascribe to the Lord O heavenly beings/ascribe to the Lord glory and strength,' or 'The voice of the Lord breaks the cedars/the Lord breaks the cedars of Lebanon.' However, many other variations are possible, and the patterns can also be woven through groups of verses (e.g. Pss.114.1 f.; 124.1–5).

Little agreement has been reached on how the Hebrew poets used metre. Their use of parallelism, however, imposed a disciplined rhythm of thought, which produces, even in English translation, some balance and rhythm of sound. Each part of the Hebrew verse has about three principal words, and even in English the lines are still fairly brief: 'He gives snow like wool/he scatters hoar frost like ashes,' or 'The Lord is near to all who call upon him/to all who call upon him in truth.'

Parallelism enables the poet to achieve various effects. The repetition may express emphasis or excitement. It helps to clarify the thought. It gives variations of pace, the progress of thought being sometimes held back by sheer repetition, then hurried on with single statements. Sometimes the first part leaves you guessing, and satisfaction comes only at the very end: 'Than the thunders of the great waters/than the lordly breakers of the sea/more mighty on high is the Lord' (Ps.93.4).

The wording of Hebrew poetry is unpretentious. Qualifying adjectives in the original are rare; a genitive relation is preferred: 'king of glory', 'fountain of life', 'oil of gladness', 'beasts of the forest'. Traditional vocabulary is used again and again. Especially common are the apparently moral terms, which usually revolve around the notion of covenant or established bond of goodwill: 'steadfast-love', 'mercy', 'truth', 'peace', 'righteous(ness)', 'faithful(ness)', 'upright', 'saints', etc. Correct interpretation here depends on remembering the background of covenant thought (especially religion as a covenant of the king or nation with God) and on consideration of the context. Thus the various 'moral' qualities will usually refer to fidelity to covenantal promises or loyalty to the other partner. The words for states of happiness and well-being likewise refer to the harmony arising from a sound covenant relationship. Good passages for practice in such interpretation are Pss.18.20–25; 85.7–13 (including personification); 89.1–5, 14–16; 101.1 f.; 136. A difficulty of translation is that in themselves the verbs are ambiguous in time-reference; the choice of past, present or future in English depends on the interpretation of the whole context, and sometimes uncertainty persists (cf. below on Ps.101).

Most psalms have superscriptions. Since these are problematic in meaning and origin, they are best left aside in the present study.

1. The journey to the festival

Prominent in the experience of Israelite worshippers was the journey, often long, to the central sanctuary. Hardship was offset by the fellowship along the way and above all by the anticipation of a festival so rich in meaning. There are several psalms which some scholars think were sung on the journey. Although their place seems rather to have been within the festival, such psalms certainly tell us something about the pilgrimage and arrival.

Psalm 122

1–2. The keynote is gladness, the thrill of entering the presence of God by visiting 'the house of the Lord'. The singer expresses the typical feelings when the pilgrims from a particular area joined together to commence their journey. Translate: 'Our feet are now standing . . . '; this expresses the wonder of finding oneself at last within the holy city. (RSV here relates the psalm to the end of the festival.)

3–5. The psalm now addresses Jerusalem appreciatively. A stirring sight from the encompassing mountains, the compactly walled city seems to symbolize the fellowship of the worshippers. It is loved not for any outer grandeur, but as the place God has chosen as the centre for all Israel to converge and invoke his name(and hence his presence)in the festival; the place from which his healthful order ('judgment') should radiate, especially through the rule of the successors of David.

6–9. The worshippers are exhorted to pray for Jerusalem, for her safety and well-being. There is much play here on sounds and meaning, several words echoing 'Jerusalem', especially *šālōm*, 'peace'. The love of this particular city exceeds ordinary affection; it is cherished as the focus of communion between men and God.

Psalm 84

1–3. The singer expresses the emotion of pilgrims approaching the temple at Jerusalem. They come like men weak with thirst to a spring of living water, or like a bird which finds the perfect nesting-place.

4–7. As the preceding admiration of the temple is really a way of raising God, so now is the appreciation of the good fortune of the temple's ministers (v.4) and of the pilgrims (vv.5–7). The pilgrims' journey may be arduous, but the strength which will be given in the great meeting with God is already reaching them in advance. Their minds are set on the highways to Zion (= Jerusalem), probably the sacred route up the temple hill used by the festal processions. Whether there was an actual placed called 'Baca' is not sure, but in any case the reference is to a drought-stricken region. The belief was that where the pilgrims passed, God would soon give the blessing which was prayed for especially at this autumn festival, the 'early rain' which would begin the new year of growth. Toiling onward, 'they go from strength to strength' as they draw near to the place where God will be 'seen'. In the religions which used statues of the gods, the climax of the festival was the unveiling of the image. In Israel such images were forbidden; the divine presence was invisible to all but an inspired prophet (e.g. Isa.6). But the sense of God's nearness in the worship was still so strong, that the old concrete language of 'seeing' (him, his face, his beauty, etc.) was still used.

8–9. Prayer is offered that God should look favourably upon the king ('our shield', 'thine anointed'). The phrase 'God of Jacob' emphasizes the tradition of the old association of the twelve tribes, which David carefully carried over into Jerusalem's worship.

10–12. The conclusion returns to praise of God, partly again by way of admiring the happiness of those close to him. The contrast is better if 'doorkeeper' is not a reference to the high sacred office, but to some lowly station, perhaps even to beggars by the temple gate. The blessings which God bestows in his temple, however, are only for those who 'walk uprightly' – in integrity. The basic requirement is 'trust', a deep committal to God. All in all, the psalm gives an excellent conspectus of the features of the autumnal festival under the Davidic kings: the great central shrine, heir of the old covenant traditions; praise of God as king; his self-disclosure; his rich gifts, especially rain; prayer for the dynasty.

Psalm 15

1. Ancient sanctuaries had rules about fitness for admission. In this psalm, which may be connected with ceremonies of entry, some of the requirements for taking part in temple worship are rehearsed, the emphasis being on a sincere and fair way of living. A direct question

on the matter is put to God; his answer will be given back through his ministers (for this procedure cf. Mal.2.5–7; Zech.7.1 f.; II Sam.21.1; Micah 6.6–8).

2–5. The answer is in ten parts, like the Ten Commandments. (i) God's worshipper must live in whole-hearted loyalty to God, doing his will. (ii) His words must be sincere. (iii) He does not spread slander. (iv) He does no harm to his fellow. (v) He does not throw cruel words at him. (vi) He does not 'go along with' evil men (or translate v.4a 'In his own eyes he is small and of no reputation'). (vii) He honours true followers of God. (viii) He keeps his promises, even to his own disadvantage. (ix) He does not exact interest on a loan he has made to an impoverished family. (x) No bribe can buy his assistance in condemning the innocent. God's answer concludes that one who so lives will not only be welcome to the temple; he will never be 'moved' – cast down to destruction. As when his feet stand on the rock of the temple hill, so his whole life will be lived on an unshakable basis. Such then were the teachings put before those who would come to the festival as guests in God's 'tent' or 'house'.

2. Acts of penitence and purification

We have seen that the worshippers had a vivid belief that they were coming before the face of God, and also that his standards for human conduct were high. They could not come without trepidation because of their unworthiness. Confession of sin and prayer for forgiveness were therefore among the early proceedings of the festival. There were ceremonies which expressed the divine grace of purification and atonement.

Psalm 130

1–6. A leading voice prays for all the people, crying to the Lord from 'the depths', the underworld which in the imagination stands for the lowest condition – corruption, darkness and death. The appeal is for the divine forgiveness, which alone enables sinful man to stand and to worship. All concentrate in faith and yearning for the coming of God with his word of reconciliation, which was perhaps to be expressed in the ceremonies as dawn broke. 'Watchmen' were posted to signal the rise of the sun above the eastern mountains, the moment for the dawn sacrifice.

7–8. The singer now addresses the worshippers, who represent the entire society. He urges them to wait trustingly for the Lord. The long vigil in the festival is a model of the religious life: men endure long ordeals of suffering, holding to the hope in the faithfulness of God as redeemer. He will at last deliver them from the slavery of sin.

Psalm 51

1–2. In asking for his own cleansing, the representative leader has in mind the healing of all the community (v.18). He believes that God alone can wash away the stain of his sins.

3–5. He confesses his sinfulness in the general terms suitable for public prayer repeated regularly. He faces it squarely and recognizes it as in essence a breaking of faith with God. That he was born in sin (v. 5) means that he feels his whole existence to be marked by it; he is sinful in the roots of his being, so that only a miracle can redeem him.

6–9. He resumes his prayer for forgiveness and purification. Verse 7 refers to a ceremony of purification in which water was sprinkled from sprigs of the hyssop; under such outward gestures were signified the will and power of God to purify and restore his people. The 'broken bones' mean the state of sorrow and punishment which is to be transformed.

10–12. Corresponding to his earlier recognition of the deep pervasiveness of his sin, he describes the restoration for which he continues to pray as virtually a new creation. The inner man, all the inner forces of his being, must be made new. The reference to God's 'holy Spirit' and 'presence' refer to the divine presence in the temple and so in the centre of God's covenanted people; a continuing union with his world, which draws it into his own perfection. Israel's leader prays that he may be made fit for this union and not cast out; may divine aid direct and sustain him, ennobling his soul (v. 12b).

13–15. He promises that when he is restored and cleansed of his guilt ('bloodguiltiness'), he will testify openly to God's saving power, leading many to follow the same way to healing.

16–19. Some scholars think that these verses reflect the exilic period when the usual sacrifices were suspended; a service of lamentation is offered instead, until the rebuilding of the temple will permit a return to normal. We can, however, give an explanation which fits the usual services. The singer asserts that the sacrifice of animals is not enough in itself to make atonement for sin (only for accidental errors, according to Num.15.22–31). The people must also offer true repentance, a readiness to be remade according to God's will. If God accepts them and gives them joy, they will offer many sacrifices in glad testimony, a service pleasing to him (v. 18 'rebuild': rather 'build up', make prosperous').

3. The resanctification of the temple

The rites of purification were applied to the

147

temple as well as the people. As the festival progressed, they could sing again: 'Holiness adorns thy house' (Ps.93.5). The ground of communion with God was thus re-established; he had made firm again the foundations of happy life. The temple and 'Zion' (the holy city) could again be described as clothed in holy splendour.

Psalm 132

1–5. Part of the ceremonies renewing the sanctuary was, it seems, a re-enactment of David's bringing the ark to Jerusalem (II Sam.6). This psalm goes with the re-enactment. It begins by praying that in favour of David's dynasty may be counted the self-denying zeal with which David had set himself to secure a sanctuary fit for the ark and the presence of God.

6–7. The voices here seem to take the role of David's men who had been sent to find the ark. They report back how they heard of it in 'Ephrathah' and found it in 'the fields of Jaar'. Ephrathah may be a name of David's home-town, Bethlehem; or, like the fields of Jaar, it may be in the area of Kiriath-jearim, where the ark had been residing (I Sam.7.2). In response to this news, the cry goes up to hurry to the place and make obeisance before this symbol of the divine presence.

8–10. Having now come before the ark in an outlying place, the company begins the procession with sacrifices, singing and dancing into Jerusalem. As the priests lift the ark, they echo the ancient prayer, 'Arise O Lord!' (Num. 10.35). Prayer is made for the priests, for the whole covenanted society (RSV 'saints') and for the present heir on David's throne.

11–18. In answer to the prayer, the prophetic ministers declare the oracle of God. As he has chosen David's dynasty, so also he has chosen Zion. This is where the ark must be taken; this is to be the pre-eminent place of the divine presence, the centre of communion and blessing. The metaphors of the bull's horn and the lamp in v. 17 denote the victorious strength and salvation which God will send through the house of David.

Psalm 87

1–3. The temple is again pure and beautiful, founded by God and chosen by him above all other Israelite sanctuaries. And now to this 'city of God', an oracle is to be spoken, 'glorious things', divine words heavy with meaning for her destiny.

4–7. God is envisaged as writing up the roll of the citizens of his kingdom, recording for each one the name and home-city. The 'citizens' mentioned are personified peoples, and they include some who had once been enemies, such as 'Rahab' (=Egypt). Representing all peoples, they are all recorded in God's register as natives of Zion ! Thus the psalm declares that Jerusalem is the nucleus of God's universal society, into which are to be gathered all peoples, even former foes. The singing and dancing of the present festival will then be taken up by them all, praising Zion as the fountain of divine life, the spring of Paradise (cf. Gen.2.10).

4. God's battle

Underlying all the joyful songs which were sung in God's honour at the festival is the thought that he appears fresh from a victory. The battle he has waged is a poetic construction, serving to commemorate and renew God's mighty work of creation and ancient salvation.

The poetic drama of the festival imagines that all the forces which would harm life have even now risen up together to make chaos and misery prevail, but God has routed them. This poetic vision embraces both what we should call 'Nature' and 'History'. It understands the battle as the mighty deeds of the Creator against a dragon-like chaos, a dark and raging ocean; but also as God's victory over raging nations. Thus year by year, the worshippers dramatically reassert the basis of their hope in all aspects of life – the power and goodness of God, the king of all. In addition to the following psalms, we may note the theme of the battle underlying creation in 74.12–17; 89.5–18; 93.3 f.; 104.7–9.

Psalm 46

1–3. The chaos-powers are imagined as beating upon the world of life. The earth rocks (RSV 'change'), the mountains tremble, as the ocean rises with demonic rage. The worshippers declare their faith in the victory of God who is 'very present' in Zion.

4–7. Zion stands firm in the midst of all these assaults; she is pictured as the source of the Paradise river, the centre of the holy power of life, because God is in her. The kingdoms of the world are imagined as joining to attack her, but at the break of morning God will save her (v.5). At his mighty word of rebuke, the enemies collapse.

8–11. The singer surveys the scene after the battle. He has a vision of the whole earth at peace, all weapons smashed and burnt. He sees the Lord exalted in victory and hears his word 'Be still and know that I am God'. The people of God's city triumphantly proclaim the confidence they have through him.

Psalm 48

1–3. Praise is offered for the deliverance signified in the dramatic ceremonies. The fortress-sanctuary of Zion stands once more serene and beautiful, the dwelling of God, the fount of joy for all the living order. ('In the far north': originally a term denoting a Phoenician sacred mountain, but applied now to Jerusalem.)

4–7. It had been imagined how the kings of the nations had swept up to assault God's city, but were overwhelmed by the sight of his glory. His desert wind had smashed their fleets of massive ships. (This image seems to be another adaptation from Phoenicia. 'Ships of Tarshish' may be large vessels developed for the mining trade.)

8–9. The ceremonies have somehow represented this model of deliverance to the ears and eyes of the worshippers. In the temple there has been an acted parable of God's fidelity to his undertakings in the covenant ('we have thought on': rather 'we have made a likeness of').

10–11. The salvation of Zion is thought of as decisive for that of the whole world. The glory of the victorious God shines out far and wide, and his right hand holds the sceptre of victory over all the cosmos.

12–14. The lesson is to be further weighed as a procession winds about the city's unharmed ramparts. Its message is to be recounted through succeeding generations. The God with whom they are covenanted is worthy of all trust; he will lead them to victory over all evil. (Very similar is Ps. 76.)

5. *God's procession of victory*

The symbolic victory just treated was further celebrated by a procession up the hill and into the temple like the victory march of a warrior king leading captives and spoil, heralded by messengers, and greeted by dancing and singing women (cf. Ps. 68).

Psalm 24

1–2. The procession approaches the temple gates, dramatically representing the victory-march of God the triumphant king. The victory is here seen in terms of creation: having subdued the primaeval ocean and made it serviceable to life, he has made firm in its midst the inhabited world. Accordingly, he alone is the Lord and Owner of all life.

3–6. At the gates there are exchanges between the procession and the guardians of the threshold. As in Ps. 15, conditions for entry are declared. In v. 3 the inquiry seems to be put from the procession. The guardians answer in vv. 4 f., and perhaps v. 6: worshippers will receive the blessing in the festival if they are doers of right, not worshipping false gods, honouring their commitments. Verse 6, however, may be a confirmatory response from the procession.

7–10. The leader of the procession now calls for the opening of the gates to admit 'the King of glory', the invisible presence being indicated by the ark. The doors are called 'eternal' (RSV 'ancient') because they correspond to the gates of the heavenly palace. 'Who is the King of glory?' ask the guardians, and are answered by the citation of the special Israelite name for God ('Yahweh') and his titles as supreme conqueror (v. 8). The repetition of this dialogue in vv. 9 f. gives opportunity for still greater emphasis: God as revealed in Israel, he alone is the Creator and Monarch of the cosmos.

6. *The proclamation of God's kingship*

With the ark installed once more on Zion, the worshippers' minds are held by the conception of the invisible Lord enthroned above this 'footstool'. By the mighty deeds commemorated earlier, he has established his kingdom; the enemies of life have been put to flight. His victory march was already in celebration of his kingship, but now there is a special proclamation of it, as he is imagined as taking the throne in his temple-palace, manifest to his acclaiming subjects in his robes of glory. Trumpet blasts, prostration, and concerted shouts of homage mark the great moment. The psalms proclaim, 'The Lord now reigns!' or 'has commenced his reign!' It is the experience of God's kingdom as newly begun, a new era, a new world. (In addition to the following psalms, one may connect 29 and 96–100, and more generally 33; 103–4; 145–150.)

Psalm 93

1–2. The formula of proclamation resounds at the outset. The heavenly king is portrayed as radiant in the power which has secured the creation. The drama of worship is presenting eternal realities, established before time itself (v. 2).

3–5. The battle presupposed by the present scene is recalled – the quelling of the waves of chaos, the victory underlying creation. His supremacy asserted, the Creator-king issues 'decrees' which direct and control the elements of the cosmos. The temple is beautiful again with 'holiness', the divine life-power.

Psalm 47

1–5. God has gone up to his temple-throne amid acclamation and the sound of trumpets. All peoples are invited to join in the clapping and cheering. He has exerted his tremendous power (RSV 'is terrible'), establishing his supreme sovereignty. The preceding battle is here linked with the Israelite conquest of Canaan, but this is seen as part of God's good design for all men.

6–9. Again the call to praise goes out, ecstatically repetitive. The proclamation of the enthronement insists also on God's universal supremacy. Accordingly the worshippers who now give him homage are understood as representative not just of one nation, but of all peoples and rulers ('shields').

7. *The speech of God*

The enthroned Creator-king now speaks words vibrant with power to effect his will. As we have seen (Ps. 93.5), his creative decrees direct the elements of the cosmos. He also speaks words of promise, warning and judgment to all his subjects (cf. Pss. 75 and 82). Especially does he speak to his covenanted people Israel, as he did on Mount Sinai; and the covenant is thus renewed.

Psalm 95

1–7a. The situation here is as in the previous section. Acclaim is given to God revealed as enthroned Creator. All other powers have been subjugated (v. 3). The worshippers prostrate themselves before the symbols of his throne, conscious of being covenanted under his shepherd-like reign.

7b–11. The prophet who is to utter God's own words introduces them with an earnest, though hardly optimistic wish that the worshippers will take them to heart. The speech of God begins at v. 8. It is a warning that the people should not be insensitive to his will and quick to rebel and disbelieve as was the generation of Moses' time. Strong language (v. 10) expresses how that conduct had brought judgment, exclusion from the promised land.

(Meribah and Massah were halting-places in the desert; there are various traditions about what happened there, Ex.15.25; 17.1–7; Num.20.1–13: Deut. 32.51.)

Psalm 81

1–5a. Again the manifest God is acclaimed by the festal throng with shouts and songs and instruments. (According to the calendar of later times, v. 3 would refer to fanfares first on New Year's Day and then at the beginning of Tabernacles a fortnight later; there have been various attempts to explain the Hebrew as referring to only one of these days.) The psalm stresses that the festival is ordained by God. The prominence of the traditions of the exodus and covenant suggests that the psalm has descended from the days before the monarchy.

5b–16. The prophet first indicates his inspiration, whereby he has heard a mysterious heavenly voice. From v. 6 he delivers God's own speech. God recalls his salvation of the people from slavery ('Meribah': see Ps. 95.8, previous column). On the basis of this salvation, he has become their covenanted Lord. He forbids them other gods. He promises them all good things. He yearns that they would walk in his ways and not become estranged like the first generation. The echoing of the words of the revelation on Mount Sinai (especially vv. 9 f.) indicates how this festival renews for the worshippers the original event. Today they also stand before God and can choose to follow him in the way of true life. (A similar psalm is Ps. 50.)

8. *The new year of growth*

In the land of Canaan a summer drought extends from about May till October. If the following year is to yield crops and pasturage, the winter rains must fall abundantly and in good time. To the ancient inhabitants it seemed that the autumn and winter storms were indeed a war of deliverance waged from heaven. Hence the autumnal festival's themes of God's appearing in triumph were linked with the need for rains and fertility. The worshippers pray that God, who in the service has shown himself king over all the elements, will once again command the rains and give growth and fertility.

Psalm 65

1–4. The opening hymn shows how the festal worship is marked by praise, fulfilment of sacrificial vows, forgiveness of sins, and a drawing close to God to receive blessings.

5–8. The psalm acknowledges the mighty deeds of God as Creator-king, the victory over chaos-seas and raging nations which establishes a joyful cosmos. This is the saving event which the festival has already represented.

9–13. The coming of God now experienced in the festival is seen as the time when he determines the course of the new year and makes preparation for its growth (v. 9). Verse 10 is better translated as a prayer: 'Water its furrows . . . .' The New year is now inaugurated ('crowned') as one to be characterized by God's bounty. The processions with the ark are like the riding of God's storm-chariot through the skies; in its wake will follow a lush growth. Verses 12 f. give a future prospect: soon the parched hills will flow with rain, and a wonderful verdure will quickly appear.

Psalm 126

1–3. The theme is miraculous transformation from national misery to joyful life. The reference here may be primarily to political events.

The psalm prepares persuasively for its later petition by recalling how the earlier deliverance spread the fame of Israel's God among the nations.

4–6. The prayer for a new transformation is marked by thoughts of the change in the seasons. The people ask for their circumstances to be transformed as marvellously as the dry desert gullies when they run with winter floods and spring with grass and flowers. Verses 5 f. are perhaps a prophetic speech of assurance: 'Those who sow . . . shall reap . . . .' As harvesting was celebrated with rites of rejoicing, so in ancient times rites of lamentation accompanied the burial of the seed.

Psalm 127

1–2. The worshippers are instructed that only as God is in their work can it prosper. The references to daily tasks may also allude to festal themes: the welfare of this 'house' of the temple, of the city of Ziion, and of the fields. (In v. 2 we may render: 'in their sleep'.)

3–5. The pilgrims desire the gift of children, especially sons, who gave much prestige and family strength. They are taught that these are in the gift of the Lord.

Psalm 128

1–4. Blessings are pronounced over worshippers who follow God's teachings. Their fields will yield well. Their wives, too, will bear many children.

5–6. Such are the blessings that go out from the divine presence in Zion, bestowing upon a faithful community long and fruitful life.

9. God confirms the dynasty of David

If the festival saw the renewal of fundamental things, the office of the Davidic kings could not be left out. For the royal office had become one of the great elements in Israelite religious thought; the king was said to have been raised up over mankind to be God's viceroy on earth, equipped with holy wisdom and insight; God's covenant with David had entered the foundations of the faith of the community worshipping at Jerusalem. Accordingly, a number of psalms seem to have belonged to festal ceremonies which set forth the nature of the king's office. Such annual ceremonies probably repeated elements from the king's first coronation and so renewed the efficacy of his reign. Like the other parts of the festival, they seem to have had a dramatic character. A preliminary statement of God's covenant with his king is followed by a time of testing and humiliation. The drama shows the king at the mercy of evil forces, until God, being satisfied with his humility, trust and obedience, thunders to his rescue and then confirms him in glory on his throne. Such a ritual drama can be traced through Pss.2; 89; 101; 18; 21; 72 and 110, and others, such as 22 and 144, may have been used in similar rites.

Psalm 2

1–3. The scene is of a general rejection of the kingship of God and of 'his anointed', the Davidic king whom he deputes to rule on earth. Just as the sacred drama had represented a general assault by wicked kings on Zion (Pss.46 and 48 above), so now it portrays a similar insurrection against God's ruler.

4–6. But the prophetic speaker, perhaps the king himself, declares that God mocks their presumption and speaks a word of power to confound them. This word is simply a statement that God himself has installed the Davidic ruler; he is God's king set on God's holy mountain. The implication is that no powers will therefore prevail against him.

7–9. The king gives further evidence of the strength of his position. He quotes from the 'decree', a document presented at his installation. It records an oracle to the effect that this king is adopted by God as his 'son', the unique representative of God's kingdom on earth. The oracle confers on him a privilege of effective prayer; the very ends of the earth will be granted to him; he will be able to break rebellion with his royal sceptre as a man might smash jars of earthenware. (In Egypt, jars inscribed with the names of potential rebels were smashed or buried to signify the Pharaoh's supremacy.)

10–11. He warns the rebels and advises them to make their submission while there is still time.

Psalm 101

1–2a. The ceremonies will have shown the king brought low before his foes. Before God delivers him, he is required to make a statement about the righteousness of his rule. According to RSV, he has to vow to rule justly. We could otherwise translate the psalm as a statement that he has so ruled in the past year, altering the tenses from vv. 2b–8 to the past. Either way, he is pleading that God should come to deliver him from his ordeal: 'Oh when wilt thou come to me ?'

2b–8. The king must especially be concerned to have as his ministers worthy men. Corrupt officials must be banished from his palace. He is pictured like the Arabian rulers who sit to dispense justice early every morning.

Psalm 21

1–7. The continuing drama has portrayed

God's approval of the king. He has rescued him
and now causes him to be enthroned and
crowned. The singer thanks God for all that the
preceding acts have signified – the answering of
the king's prayer of distress, the confirmation
in power of life and majesty by virtue of his
reliance on God.

8–13. A prophet speaks over the king the
divine promise of success. In v. 13 a concluding
prayer asks God to manifest his sovereignty in
the days ahead, acknowledging that all power is
his alone.

Epilogue

Our study of the psalms will have suggested
how many great themes of later theology were
first fashioned in Israelite worship. It is amazing how the psalms are prophetic of later
developments. The festivals not only commemorated and represented the great moment of
salvation from the past. With prophetic vision
they looked deep into the nature of things and
so into the ultimate destiny of the cosmos under
God. Their declarations about the kingdom of
God and his 'Anointed' (Hebrew 'Messiah',
Greek 'Christ') live on in later Jewish teachings
and in the Christian gospel.

J.H. EATON

13 Wisdom in Israel

Wisdom in Israel and the ancient Near East

The Old Testament wisdom tradition is a larger subject than the wisdom literature of the Old Testament. This is because the wise men were statesmen and administrators as well as men of letters and exerted great influence on the affairs of Judah from the time of David to the fall of the Judaean state. These wise men are also called 'scribes', and they belong to an educated class which was international in character and was recognizable in terms of its ethos and its role throughout the ancient Near East. They are the products of a higher education whose aim was to inculcate a rigorous mental discipline and to provide hard-headed and clear-thinking men to fill important diplomatic and administrative offices in the state.

The title of 'scribe' was given to such high officials in Egypt and that of 'scribe' or 'secretary' to their counterparts in Babylonia and Assyria. For instance, we read in an Aramaic papyrus of a man named Ahikar, who is represented as an Assyrian official, who is called 'a sagacious and keen-witted secretary', and is also counsellor of all Assyria and bearer of the seal, on whose advice Sennacherib, king of Assyria, leans. The title 'scribe' or 'secretary' does not, in these circumstances, simply mean that the person so entitled is a 'writer', nor does it show that the office which he discharges is one which calls principally for linguistic skills. It does, however, indicate that without these skills a man did not have what were regarded as essential qualifications for office, and it is a reminder that the mastery of the Egyptian hieroglyphic and the Sumerian-Babylonian cuneiform scripts required intellectual concentration of a high order. The same technical sense of 'scribe' is attested for the Old Testament as the following passages show.

In II Sam.8.16–18 and 20.23–25 there are official lists of the leading members of David's establishment, ecclesiastical, civil and military. Of the two political officials named, one Seraiah has the title 'scribe' or 'secretary', and there is no doubt that, like Ahikar, he is a secretary of state, and that both he and Jehoshaphat ('the recorder') are of the highest rank. Further information about other high officials of David is given by I Chron.27.32–34. Jonathan, David's uncle, and Ahithophel have the title 'counsellor'; Ahithophel is the 'king's counsellor', whereas Jonathan along with Jehiel is a counsellor to the king's sons. Jonathan has one of the fundamental intellectual virtues of the professional political adviser in that he is perceptive and lucid. He was also a 'scribe', and this should be taken in the general sense that he belonged to the educated class of officials rather than as a reference to his tenure of a particular, high, political office. Hushai is also mentioned in the Chronicles passage as occupying the advisory office of 'king's friend', the post held by Zabud in Solomon's reign (I Kings 4.5). The testimony of this passage that Ahithophel and Hushai were leading statesmen in the reign of David is supported by the influence of both as policy-makers in the Ahithophel-Absalom story (II Sam.15–17).

Solomon's principal officials, civil, military and ecclesiastical, are called 'statesmen' and the hereditary principle is seen to apply in both civil and ecclesiastical spheres. The office of secretary which had been occupied by Seraiah appears to be held jointly by his two sons (I Kings 4.1–6). The list is larger than those coming from David's reign, and this reflects the more complicated organization of Solomon's state. Azariah, the son of Nathan, is said to have control of 'the officials'. These are probably the twelve officials appointed by Solomon over all Israel (I Kings 4.7), each of whom was responsible for the provisioning of the royal household for one month of the year. Ahishar who is 'over the house' holds an office which still existed in the reign of Hezekiah (II Kings 18.18; Isa.36.3). The degree of centralized control which was exercised by Solomon brought into existence a cadre of officials who had close associations with Jerusalem and the court and to whom administration and diplomacy were entrusted. These correspond to the 'scribes' who filled comparable offices in Egypt and elsewhere in the ancient Near East. They were a class specially educated for the responsibility of high office, and it may be that a school for 'scribes' had been founded by Solomon in Jerusalem with a view to meeting the demands for able officials created by the structure of his state.

In II Kings 12.4–16 a 'royal secretary' acts with the high priest in counting and removing money which has been collected in a box for the fabric of the temple. This royal secretary should be equated with the secretary of David's administration (II Sam.8.17 and 20.25). This is indicated by the circumstance that later, in the reign of Josiah, Shaphan, who was certainly a secretary of state, was sent to Hilkiah, the high priest, in order to find out how much money was in this box (II Kings 22.3 ff.). The offices mentioned in II Kings 18.18(Isa.36.3) are familiar from the previous lists. Shebna is 'secretary', Joah is 'recorder', and Eliakim is 'over the house' ('house' referring to palace and not temple). These three were apparently the king's leading advisers and made up the inner circle of government. The 'secretary' of Jer.36.11 f. is one of the statemen, and the cabinet meeting takes place in his room. He is to be identified with the 'secretary' of the lists and he acts here as the king's first minister. The 'secretary' in Jer.37.15 f. (Jonathan) is also associated with the statesmen, and it is reasonable to conclude that he is the holder of the same office which has changed hands in the interval (in 36.11 f., Elishama is 'secretary').

These 'scribes' or statesmen were at the centre of government and affairs in Israel and Judah from the time of David to the end of the monarchy. Their prestige and reputation as weighty counsellors is reflected in the story of Ahithophel, whose judgment was so impeccable that his words were placed on the same level as the word of God (II Sam.16.23). David is convinced that Ahithophel will give Absalom the very best advice and that he himself has no hope of retrieving his position unless he can confound the wisdom of Ahithophel. This David does by planting Hushai in Absalom's war cabinet. Hushai's deliberately bad advice, and the unperceptiveness of the elders of Israel bring about the rejection of Ahithophel's advice, which was the best that Absalom could have had (II Sam.17). Diplomacy and administration had become a profession in Judah and were in the hands of a class of men who understood international protocol, and had their own standards of efficiency and integrity.

Statesmen versus prophets

This, however, posed profound problems for those who still claimed the totality of Judah's life for God and who believed that God's word still offered comprehensive guidance for its direction. The scribes or statesmen or wise men claimed that it was their business to direct the internal and external affairs of Judah, that this was within the sphere of their professional competence and responsibility, and that they alone were equipped by education and expertise to take decisions on which the well-being and even survival of the nation depended. But the prophets, who were bearers of the word of God, could not concede a monopoly of policy to the wise men on those issues which affected the future of the community most crucially. Otherwise they would seem to be condemned to ineffectiveness. Their authoritative word was to be ruled out of order wherever the issues were important. They were to be left with a narrow and insignificant sphere of operations. Yet Judah was God's community and they were his accredited spokesmen, and who better than they to issue directives to the nation in relation to the great matters of the moment ?

The conflict between political wisdom and prophetic authority is best attested in the books of Isaiah and Jeremiah. Isaiah's demand to Ahaz in the face of the threat to Jerusalem offered by a Syro-Ephraimite coalition was the negation of orthodox political wisdom (Isa.7); yet it is in accord with the consistent attitude of Isaiah and Jeremiah in so far as it involves a repudiation of diplomacy and foreign alliances. Judah must do nothing at all at this moment when her existence is threatened. It is not a time for diplomatic initiatives or for military bargains; it is a time to wait on God and depend absolutely on him. Here is a policy to shock the professionals; a radical concept of faith in God which leaves no room for self-help. It is not to be wondered at that Ahaz and his advisers would not take the risk. Jeremiah, too, was deeply concerned to influence the foreign policy of Judah, and the extent and seriousness of his implication in these matters may be judged by the hostility which he encountered from kings and statesmen (Jer.36–39). He was regarded as a serious political threat, a dangerous enemy of the state who had to be restrained by imprisonment and threatened by death. His opposition to all intrigues with Egypt and his counsel that submission should be made to Babylon finally brought him to a place of loneliness and disrepute, where he was under suspicion as a deserter and was thought to have undermined the morale of the community in the face of the enemy.

This conflict has to be described from the side of these professional statesmen no less than from the prophetic side. The explanation is not that the wise men were irreligious or anti-religious, any more than Ahaz was irreligious because he was unable to identify himself with Isaiah's radical concept of faith in God. The wise men were loyal to religion according to their understanding, but they were not prepared to give credence to the revealed word of a prophet in relation to affairs which they believed to be within the province of their professional competence and political judgment. They had their own canons of conscientiousness and integrity and they would not surrender these to a word of God spoken by a prophet.

The book of Proverbs

There are different kinds of material in the

book of Proverbs and these can be correlated with genres of wisdom literature in Egypt and Babylonia. The form of Prov.1–9; 22.17–24.22 and 31.1–9 is that of the *Instruction* of which there are a number of Egyptian examples. In the case of Prov.22.17–23.11, there would appear to be a literary dependence on the Egyptian Teaching (or *Instruction*) of Amenemope. In Egypt, the *Instruction*, as its name suggests, was concerned to cultivate in apprentice officials the mental attitudes and manners which made for effectiveness and success in the service of the state. Its home was the school, where it was the instrument of an education whose goal was intellectual rigour and nicety of judgment and discrimination. It is an attractive conjecture that the genre found its way into Israel in the reign of Solomon in order to fulfil a similar educational function, and that in Jerusalem as well as Egypt it was an instrument for the education of 'scribes'.

There is, however, only a little evidence of this in the contents of Proverbs. On the whole the Israelite *Instruction* is not concerned with the education of officials, but with the instruction of the community and especially of the young men. There is a prudential emphasis in the teaching and the dangers of sexual indiscipline are a great matter. The foreign woman, strange, alluring and freed from all restraints, is regarded as a particular menace and her house is represented as the gateway to the underworld (2.18). The 'my son' address is an indication of the fundamental place of parental wisdom, but also of the kind of relation existing between teacher and pupil in the classroom, where the teacher claims a quasi-parental authority. In certain passages in Prov.1–9, however, the parent or teacher is replaced as spokesman by a personified wisdom.

1. *The character of wisdom*

Wisdom – thought of as feminine – is portrayed with the characteristics and speech of a wisdom teacher or a prophet (Prov.1.20 ff.). Elsewhere there is the possibility that she has been created as a rival to the seductive queen of a fertility cult (especially ch.9). In Prov.8 the personification of wisdom embraces both the concerns of political wisdom and the wisdom whose subject is the wonders of God's created works. On the one hand, wisdom asserts that through her God effectively formulates and executes his plans for the nations (Prov.8.14–16), and this is comparable to the claim which the prophets make for God as counsellor and executive. On the other hand, she establishes for herself a special place in the counsels of God in connection with the creation of the world. Wisdom was beside God as his confidant (?) before the world was created. This is a further development of a recognizable trend in the wisdom tradition to regard the mystery and incomprehensibility of God's created works as the supreme manifestation of his wisdom. It is here that man is left far behind and feels his mystification and impotence. Although Proverbs, for the most part, represents an earlier stage of the wisdom tradition than Job and Ecclesiastes, this personification of wisdom in Prov.8 in relation to the creation of the world has the appearance of lateness. It is a step beyond the assertion that God's creative works are the supreme manifestation of his wisdom. It is the making of wisdom into a person and the assertion that she is with God before the creation of the world. How this is to be evaluated is a matter of great difficulty and uncertainty, but it would seem to be more than a mere literary device. Wisdom does not now consist in the demonstration of the divine intelligence and power in the creation of the world. The mystery of wisdom deepens and her distance from the world and from men is increased. Already before the world was made wisdom was the companion and confidant of God.

2. *Proverbial maxims*

Apart from the longer poems in Prov.30 and 31.10–31, the remainder of the book is, for the most part, made up of wisdom sentences. Three main divisions of the material can be made.

(i) There are those sentences which embody a this-worldy, hard-headed wisdom from which any trace of moralism or piety is absent. They are addressed to the individual, and it is his success, prosperity and well-being which they seek to safeguard. They define mental attitudes and a prudential morality which the individual had better cultivate, because they are the marks of the wise man and will bring him success and safety as a member of a community.

(ii) Other sentences also discourse on the individual but they have social implications. They are about the anti-social, malevolent man whose activities are deliberately destructive of his community and injurious to relations between man and man. They discuss this behaviour both in respect of its bad effects on the community and the threat which it poses to its existence, and also its destructive consequences for the misanthropic man himself. Man is made for society and for constructive, beneficent relationships with his neighbour, and if he dedicates himself to hate and malice he is a man with a sick mind. The health of the mind is conditional on creative social intercourse. This is a condition of integration, but the effect of deliberate and systematic misanthropy is disintegration.

(iii) The third group differs from the other two in that it admits the language of piety and moralism. These are the sentences in which a doctrine of theodicy comes to expression, in which it is asserted that God rewards the righteous man and punishes the wicked man, and that righteousness is therefore an infallible guarantee of well-being and prosperity. The word 'theodicy' means that God enforces justice effectively so that the righteous man gets his reward and the wicked man his punishment. In association with this there is a moralistic vocabulary, righteous and wicked, upright and devious, good and bad, reliable and treacherous. Here the wisdom sentence in its antithetic form expresses the tidiness and barren finality of a doctrine which has settled all the problems of human existence.

It has been customary for criticism to arrange these wisdom sentences into collections and to discover a relative chronology for the collections. The value of this exercise is limited. A more profitable way of looking at these sentences is to regard them as a deposit of Israelite wisdom and to examine them with a view to discovering what they tell us about the history of the wisdom tradition.

The wisdom sentence is a literary product, characterized by finish and polish. It is an attempt to make an observation or state a general truth in a memorable, concise way. The popular proverb, on the other hand, need not have a high degree of formal organization. This is true, for example, of the popular proverb, 'Is Saul also among the prophets ?' (I Sam.10.11 f. [19.24]). Such a proverb is applicable and apt in any situation where there seems to be a lack of accord between a person and the situation in which he appears, where there is a strong incongruity in his behaviour. All that is required to preserve its contemporaneity and freshness is the ability to discern that a particular situation is right for the comment, 'Is Saul also among the prophets ?' Other examples of popular proverbs in the Old Testament are Gen.10.9; I Sam.24.14; I Kings 20.11; Jer.31.29; Ezek.12.22; (Ezek.18.2;) 16.44. Only a few wisdom sentences in the book of Proverbs have this proverbial quality (10.5; 13.4,7; 16.26; 20.4; 24.27; 26.13, 15, 27; 27.7).

The book of Job

The book of Job consists of a prologue (chs. 1–2), cycles of speeches involving Job, and his three friends Eliphaz, Bildad and Zophar (chs. 3–31), the speeches of Elihu (32–37), the speeches of Yahweh, Israel's God (chs. 38–41), Job's repentance (42.1–6) and his restoration (the epilogue, 42.7–17). There are formidable critical problems, but Job gives more evidence than any other book in the Old Testament of creative literary endeavour and artistic management. It is clear, for example, that a deliberate attempt is being made to carry forward the discussion of a difficult theological problem (the unmerited suffering of a righteous man) by means of an arrangement whereby Job and his so-called friends engage in a kind of conversation or debate. The debate may on examination not prove to be particularly convincing. One gets the impression that all of the speakers are bad listeners. Certainly the friends appear to be incapable of taking the point which Job is making. Job's settled conviction that they, on their part, have nothing to say to him is more understandable. This inability of Job and his friends to speak to one another may not be an artistic defect, but rather part of the effect which is striven after. Given the circums-

tances of these conversations and the character of the participants, these are exactly the kind of desultory exchanges for which we may look. The fact is that they cannot speak to one another; they are not on speaking terms. Instead, they lecture one another, but that is a different matter.

The most pressing critical problem, given this evidence of a work of art in the main part of the book, is how to reconcile this attempt to devise a literary mode for a serious treatment of a theological problem with the presuppositions of the prologue and the epilogue. The speeches of Elihu, whether they are original to the body of the work or subsequent, do not constitute so formidable a problem. The speeches of Yahweh and the account of Job's repentance are more troublesome. It is, however, in the prologue and the epilogue that the difficulties are sharpest. The representation of the prologue, that Job's sufferings are attributable to the licence given by God to Satan in a heavenly court to test Job's motives, destroys the seriousness of the debate in the body of the work, and the effects of the epilogue, with its account of Job's restoration to reputation and wealth, are even more devastating. The epilogue does not have a heavenly setting and is not clearly a resumption of the prologue. Job's eventual good fortune is in fact in accord with the orthodox prognostications of Eliphaz, Bildad and Zophar (8.5–7; 11.13–19; 22.21–30).

Then again the Job of the prologue is a different person from the tragic character in the body of the work. He does not rail against the day of his birth, nor long for death, nor charge God with relentless persecution, nor deny that God is a righteous judge. When he loses possessions and family he exclaims: 'Naked I came out of my mother's womb, and naked shall I return; The Lord gave, and the Lord has taken away; blessed be the name of the Lord.' When he becomes a diseased wretch and his wife invites him to curse God he replies: 'If we accept good from God, shall we not also accept evil ?' Here there is no hint of rebellion or despair. There is only the serene resignation of the pious man.

1. *The speeches of Elihu*

Although Elihu is himself convinced of the originality of his contribution and makes a point of dissociating himself both from Job and from the friends, he does not have very much to add. He is a younger man who relies on inspiration rather than on experience. He does not, however, thereby distinguish himself completely from the other three, for Eliphaz, too, had claimed to be a visionary (4.12 f.). Elihu, like the friends, maintains that God is a righteous judge who rewards virtue and punishes wickedness (36.5 f.). He repudiates Job's claim to be righteous and denies that God is a persecutor who has relentlessly harried Job. His most original contribution is his allegation that Job's attitude to God has engendered a kind of deafness. Awareness of sin is only given in a moment of revelation, and Job, because of his determination to take God to task, has no hope of hearing the God whose silence he condemns. He has abandoned himself to anguished protest and eloquent denunciation and, if so, he must not complain that God does not speak to him. The resounding protest that God does not answer is the reason why God does not answer. The fault is with Job and not with God (35.12 f.). Elihu, like the friends, appeals to the staggering dimensions of God's creative works, to the complexity and terror of the world which is the supreme expression of his wisdom, in order to crush Job with this account of intelligence and power, and to induce in him behaviour towards God proportionate to his creaturehood.

This is not an appeal which is peculiar to Elihu. It is a strain of thought which runs through the speeches of the friends, which is developed in the poem of ch. 28, and which receives lengthy and involved treatment in the divine speeches. These speeches add nothing new. God dwells on modes of wisdom which the friends and Elihu regard as the final answer to Job's pretensions. God, too, would make Job's mind reel as he recounts the vast operations of his intelligence, and describes the terrible and mysterious creatures whom he has made. But Job as conceded this all the way through. He has not doubted that he is impotent, that the totality of God's creation and creatures defeats his efforts at comprehension. This indeed is part of what he has asserted. He has always been puzzled and tortured and despairing.

2. *The three friends*

It is unwise to assume that the sympathies of the author are totally identified with his principal character and that he has created Eliphaz, Bildad and Zophar as wooden and pompous spokesmen of an empty orthodoxy. A close examination of the lines which he has given them does not bear this out. Their thought may be very ordinary, they may offer Job a stone when he asks for bread, but there is nothing ordinary or prosaic about the language in which their thoughts find expression. The poet whose imaginative power is discernible in the language of Job has not denied to Job's protagonists the same recourse to striking imagery and proverbial power. Is there not perhaps something to be said for Job's opponents ? Less, no doubt, than is to be said for Job, yet their words are not simply empty. Is it not perhaps the ambiguity of the problem and the desire to explore this ambiguity which has commended the pattern of speech and reply to the author ? Job and the other three are not in complete disagreement, but the defenders of orthodoxy are so earnest and anxious that they do not appear to be aware that this is so. In so far as the three friends are concerned to emphasize the unsearchable character of God and of his creative works, in so far as they ascribe to him in connexion with his ordering of created things and creatures an intelligence and power which man cannot match, they are not at odds with Job.

3. *The majesty of God*

Job, too, is struck with terror and bewilderment. Thus in ch.9 Job observes that there is no need for Eliphaz and Bildad to recite to him the majesty and mystery of God the Creator. He knows this and acknowledges it. Again when Zophar (11.7 f.) describes the transcendent, unsearchable God, Job replies that he accepts this (11.7 f.), and that it is because he accepts it that he cannot believe in God as one who sees that man gets justice, that the righteous man is rewarded and the wicked man punished. It is because he agrees with them and they seem incapable of grasping this or appreciating what its implications are for Job in his personal agony, that he loses all patience with them and denounces them as liars and quacks (13.4). Again he is in accord with them in their understanding of the marks of a man who has fulfilled himself, on whom God's blessing rests. Bildad's description of the fate of the wicked man implies that the righteous man may expect a stable home, reputation, long life and post-

erity (18.14–19), and it is this reputation and esteem of whose loss Job complains (19.14 f.). He, too, appeared to be well-set for a climax of attainment, his weight and influence in the community matched by his material prosperity, but now he is the object of contempt and ridicule (chs. 30–31).

4. *Is God just ?*

The three friends are unanimous that God is a just judge and that he metes out to every man his deserts. If this is so, Job's reversal of fortune can only be explained in terms of his sinfulness. God punishes sin and Job has got what he deserved. This is the main emphasis, but along with it there is the subsidiary thought that Job's suffering may be a corrective discipline (so Eliphaz, 5.17 f.). This is no more acceptable to Job than the main contention; nor will he accept the proposition that the apparent prosperity of the wicked can be explained by the circumstance that retribution may be delayed (21.19). Against the main charge, Job vigorously maintains that he is a just, merciful and compassionate man who has always acted out of a deep sense of social concern, with a tender conscience for the poor and weak, not vindictive nor an idolator (ch. 31). When Eliphaz makes specific charges against Job (22.6 f.), he counters these by giving a firm and convincing account of his social morality. However distraught and despairing and tortured he may be, he has no doubt at all that he is a righteous man according to the definition of social morality which is accepted by Eliphaz, Bildad and Zophar. What Job can no longer believe and what they insist that he must go on believing is that such righteousness is a guarantee of well-being and prosperity, because it is God's order which he enforces by rewarding those who live by it and punishing those who break it. This is contradicted by Job's experience; it is disproved by his suffering and anguish. In these circumstances, the defence of orthodoxy undertaken by the three can mean nothing to him, and this is what he keeps on saying. The three theorize, but he is the one who suffers and their nicely calculated theology does not touch him in his pain and despair. The reality for him is that God is a relentless persecutor who harries him without respite (6.1 f.; 7.11 f.; 10; 13.24 f.; 16.12). Why should God whose power and majesty Job freely acknowledges take it upon himself to hound a frail man such as himself ? For man's life is fleeting, and unlike nature he is not renewed (14.1 f.). The depths of his despair cannot be plumbed. He wishes that he had never been born, that he had been an abortion rather than a live-birth (3.1 f.). He longs for the swift release of death (17.1 f.).

The problem which comes alive in Job's suffering and tragic perplexity is constituted by two poles of the Old Testament wisdom tradition. There is the this-worldliness and earthiness of wisdom well-represented in the book of Proverbs, and the theodicy by which God's imprimatur is stamped on it. The theodicy states that God sees to it that the righteous prosper and the wicked are punished. It is the best of all possible worlds for the righteous man. The other pole is constituted by the recital of God's creative works as evidence of his wisdom and power (cf. Isa.40.12 f.; Job 28), where the emphasis is on God's transcendence, on the area of mystery in which he is shrouded and on the awe and terror which is evoked by the disparity of powers as between God and man. The transcendent God is the unsearchable God and the God whom man cannot bring to account, and the question may then be raised whether the tidy scheme of theodicy which implies so transparent an understanding of God's ways with man and with the world is not in jeopardy. For Job, this question is inescapable. He can believe in the transcendent, mysterious God whose ways with men are past finding out, but he can no longer believe in the God who takes a personal interest in every man and sees to it that he suffers no injustice.

This is the burden of his complaint against the three friends and this is the gravamen of his charge against God. Hence he says of God: 'The truth is that he is not a man like myself that I might answer him, that we might go to law together ' (9.32 f.). Again, addressing God, he says: 'Remove thy hand from upon me, and may thy terror not crush me. Then call and I will answer, or else I will speak and thou shalt reply. How many are my iniquities and sins ? Make me to know my transgression and my sin' (13.21–23). Is God a dark Power which terrorizes Job into abject hopelessness, or is the model of a Judge a meaningful one ? Job can no longer believe that it is meaningful. He knows how judicial proceedings are ordered and how a judge may be expected to behave. He would have access to a judge and would be able to put his case to him, to engage in argument and to persuade him to the best of his ability of the justice of his case. But God is not accessible and so not amenable to argument. Job can no longer believe that God is both far and near as his orthodox friends maintain. If his remoteness and mystery are to be extolled, the pedestrian clarity of the doctrine of theodicy must be given up, and men must resign themselves to the conclusion that they know much less about God's ways than they had supposed. No longer can they maintain that the morality of their society is Yahweh's moral order and that righteousness, as they define it, is a guarantee of well-being and prosperity.

The other way in which Job proceeds in his argument with the three is to say to them: Very well, I shall take the model of God as the righteous judge seriously, and, in that case, I have not the slightest doubt that my arguments are irrefutable and that I would be acquitted if I were given a hearing (ch. 23). If God is indeed a judge, he has shown no regard for justice in his dealings with Job and must be indicted: 'Know, then, that it is God who has done me wrong and who has encompassed me with his net. If I cry out "Violence", I receive no reply, in vain do I cry for help; there is no justice. He has blocked my path so that I cannot get through, and upon my paths he has set darkness. Of my glory he has stripped me and the crown he has removed from my head' (19.6–9). 'By God who has set aside my right and by the Almighty who has embittered my soul! So long as my spirit remains inviolate in me and the breath of God is in my nostrils, my lips shall not speak any falsehood, nor my tongue utter a lie. Far be it from me to admit that you are right; until I die I will not renounce my integrity' (27.2–5).

The book of Ecclesiastes

'God is great,' says Elihu, 'and we do not know how great, the number of his years is unsearchable' (Job.36.26). This is not so far removed from the theme of the book of Ecclesiastes, in which the consequences of having to do with a God who is ultimately unknowable and inscrutable are explored.

Ecclesiastes is a different kind of book from Job, because there is not a suffering, despairing man crying out for an explanation at its centre. In the book of Job the integrity of an individual

is at stake, but Ecclesiastes has nothing of this personal drama, and is rather a colder, more deliberate essay in scepticism in which the author is sufficiently composed and settled in his conclusions to appear in the role of a teacher – to give advice to others on what they may expect from life. Job does not have the leisure or the composure to instruct. He is too immersed in his own anguish to undertake the tasks of a teacher. Everything that he says emerges from the fires of his suffering. He does not transcend, nor has he any interest in transcending, the circumstances of perplexity and outrage in which he is engulfed.

Yet the affinity between the two books is not far to seek. Both indicate that a 'crisis of wisdom' had been reached in the Old Testament, just as it had manifested itself in the wisdom literature of the ancient Near East in Egypt and Babylonia. Two Babylonian compositions, *The Babylonian Theodicy* and *I Will Praise the Lord of Wisdom*, throw doubt in different ways on the existence of a moral order, and even the possibility of intuiting moral values, and pessimism comes to the surface in Egypt in the *Instruction* of Amenemhet. Both Job and Ecclesiastes are late representatives of the Old Testament wisdom tradition, and it is more important to establish this than to allocate dates to them. Even if the figure of the patriarch Job in the prologue is based on an old folk-tale, the folk-tale itself has little bearing on the evaluation of the book of Job. For it is the body of the book which is decisive and the Job who speaks to the friends is not the Job of the prologue. His reaction to personal disaster and suffering is different, and the mode of life which he indicates when he discusses his loss of status and esteem reflects the role of a senior citizen and counsellor in a municipality and not the antique and rustic grandeur of a patriarchal way of life. What can be said with some certainty is that Job and Ecclesiastes are later than Proverbs, because what appears in Proverbs as premisses which may not be questioned or conclusions which are finally settled emerge in Job and Ecclesiastes as problems around which discussion rages.

There are sentences in Proverbs in which the dogma that God rewards the righteous man and punishes the wicked man are repeated again and again with a pedestrian precision. But it is this doctrine of theodicy to which Job will not bow. As we have seen, it is the validity and the meaningfulness of conceiving God as a judge which is called in question by Job and Ecclesiastes. Does it make sense to speak about God as a righteous judge? Can I in truth have access to him as a judge? Can I argue my case with him if I seem to be the victim of injustice? It makes sense to talk about a judge and judicial proceedings when one is describing the legal machinery which exists in a community for the trying of cases and the redress of grievances. Here, indeed, there is a judge to whom one has access and whom one can address; here conversation, speaking and listening, is a possibility and there are intelligible principles which guide a judge towards his decision. What is meant by judge and justice is understood in this context, but can this be transferred to God and elevated into theology? The answer of Job is a passionate negative and the answer of Ecclesiastes is a cool, sceptical negative.

The dating of Job in the fifth or fourth century and of Ecclesiastes in the third century accords with these indications. The ascription of authorship to Solomon in the case of Ecclesiastes has probably the same significance as in the book of Proverbs. It is not an indication of authorship, but a pointer to the type of literature contained in these books and the close relationship between those who produced this literature and the court.

'Vanity of vanities'

God is brought very near by the doctrine of theodicy, for the community's morality is his morality; the man who deserves well-being enjoys well-being. But is it true that this is the best of all possible worlds for the righteous man? Is this a dogma which is detached from the confusion and the ambiguities and the injustices of our human situation? Job out of his own bewilderment and outrage is persuaded that this must be so. It is not then surprising that a Job or an Ecclesiastes should focus attention on the God who is far away, who is other than man and who is regarded with wonder, awe and terror, in order to undermine the trite and empty tidiness of the doctrine of theodicy. Man is left behind in his attempt to comprehend the ways of this God, the creator of heaven and earth, and the maker of the dread Behemoth (Job 40.15 f.). Ecclesiastes can be understood as taking its departure from what is a well-established feature of the wisdom tradition and probing its implications so as to call in question or demolish the structures of orthodoxy.

Everything, according to Ecclesiastes, is vanity or emptiness, and sustained human effort does not produce enduring results and is not consolidated into lasting achievement and gain. Man's frailty and fleeting life is mocked by the cyclic character of nature and the monotonously regular repetition of its processes which is infallibly maintained. All this underlines the futility of man's existence, for he can do nothing to modify or change its natural setting. The rhythms cannot be checked or disturbed; the processes are irreversible and they take no account of man's aspirations. The circular processes of nature have always operated and they are unaffected by the brief life-span of a man.

The writer of Ecclesiastes, unlike Job, does not speak out of the anguish of a personal tragedy. His tones are not those of a personal protest and repudiation. He is able to offer a cold, coherent analysis of how he has reached his conclusion that human life is emptied of permanent values and achievements. He had himself used the tools of a wise man in order to explore the character of historical existence ('all that is done under the sun') and he had found it a vexatious and profitless enterprise. His discovery had been that all the events and experiences in which man participates are nothingness and a striving after wind (i.e., empty pursuits). Even wisdom is impotent and ineffective, because vexation grows in proportion to wisdom and increased knowledge produces an increase in pain (1.12–18).

No relief is to be had from a feverish search for pleasure; a deliberate cultivation of gaiety or the adoption of a reveller's way of life will not even be a palliative. This, too, is emptiness. Nevertheless, pleasure is the only experience accessible to man which can be turned to gain, and it only can rescue his existence from total emptiness. The author had carried out an experiment of seeking pleasure and permitting himself indiscretion without abandoning prudence. Hence he acquired a sufficient fortune, built houses, laid out gardens, was waited on by servants and maintained singers for his diversion and entertainment. The only gain which he had from the entire undertaking was the pleasure which it gave him: 'For my heart found pleasure in all my toil and this was my reward for all my toil' (2.1–11).

The wise man appears to have a great advantage over the fool, and yet one fate is reserved for both, and death destroys the disparity between wise man and fool, effectively nullifying whatever advantages obtained to wisdom. Both wise man and fool are destined for oblivion, and the fruits of a man's toil may be frittered away by a fool who inherits from him. Hence there is no escaping despair, and the best course open to a man is to eat and drink and take pleasure from his toil (i.e., 'in return for his toil' not 'in his toil' as RSV translates in 2.24; 3.13; 5.18 f.; 8.15). But then not every man is capable of enjoying himself. Some are constitutionally incapable of experiencing pleasure and for them life is entirely empty (2.12–26).

There is the accent of predestination in the teaching of Ecclesiastes. Human activity has the same fixed and pre-ordained pattern as has nature (3.1–8). Whatever God has made is unalterable, and no new factor can emerge to give a different direction to existence. The vexatiousness of man's postion is constituted by the fact that God has put eternity in his heart. That is to say, man is dissatisfied with a fragmentary understanding of this world, but he has been denied the capacity for comprehension and is doomed to perplexity and futility. A feature of the world in which man lives is the confusion of moral values inherent in it. There is a total lack of definition, a blurring or obscuring of moral distinctions, a confounding of all moral judgments. Good and bad are entangled and cannot be extricated from each other (3.1–16). Life does not have the order presupposed by the orthodox account of the operations of God's justice. If God imposes a test on men, it is not a moral test. It is to show them that they are indistinguishable from the beasts, that both die the same death, both come from the dust and return to dust (3.19–22).

When the actual conditions of life are examined, it is disclosed that there is no moral order and that it is power and not righteousness which counts. The oppressed may have righteousness on their side, but there is no redress for them because the oppressor has the power. Hence (cf. Job 3), since life is dominated by force, the dead are better off than the living, but better than both is he who was never born (4.1–3). This, however, is contradicted by 9.4 f., which declares that death is worse than life. The living are at least aware that they will die, but the dead have no awareness or emotions. At this point the structure of the author's thinking is more or less complete, and what follows consists of further illustrations of the futility of life. Thus in 6.3–6 he observes that if a man lives to a great age and has one hundred children (long life and posterity are the accepted marks of the man who enjoys God's blessing), but is incapable of experiencing pleasure, he is worse off than a miscarriage (cf. Job 3.16) which never emerged alive from the darkness of the womb (6.3–6).

In ch. 7 and the succeeding chapters there is discussion about the inequities of human existence and the lack of a moral order. The righteous man perishes with his righteousness, but the wicked man enjoys a long life for the practice of wickedness (7.15). There is no point in striving too intently to be either righteous or wise, but, on the other hand, a man should not go out of his way to commit evil or play the fool, since this may bring about an untimely death.

'Untimely' relates to the predestinarianism of the book, that is, the assertion that every life has a term fixed by God (7.16 f.). Further reflections on the problem of justice include the remark that the wicked go in and out of the (Jerusalem) temple and pass as worthy citizens in the city where they have practised their wickedness. In the end they are safely and honourably buried. When it is seen that a swift retribution does not operate against such men, evil-doers are encouraged to persist in their evil (8.10 f.).

Chapter 12 is a recapitulation of the main findings of the book. 'Remember your Creator in the days of your youth' (v.1) is a doubtful rendering, since the command does not seem to be consistent with what follows which is more in keeping with the scepticism of Ecclesiastes. There is something to be said for the translation: 'Remember your vigour in the days of your youth', which means, make the most of your youth and vigour, for youth quickly departs and then there is only the sadness of growing old. This involves no alteration of the text. There follows a poetic account of a man's melancholy fate, a dwelling on the sad inevitability of death which brings with it cessation and oblivion (vv.2–6). Therefore take as much enjoyment as you can from life before 'the silver cord is snapped or the golden bowl is crushed to pulp, or the pitcher is shattered at the fountain, or the wheel crushed at the cistern, and the dust returns to the earth where it was, and the spirit returns to God who gave it. Vanities of vanity, says the Preacher, all is vanity' (vv.6–8).

The foregoing account has ignored the presence in the book of verses which give expression to traditional formulations of wisdom. It has been argued that these are evidences of tension or conflict in the mind of the author, and that his mind moved between acceptance and rejection of conventional forms of belief and piety. In the case, however, of such verses as 3.17; 7.18b; 8.5; 11.9b; 12.12–14, the view that these are pious attempts to correct heretical tendencies in the author would seem to be correct. Thus 12.13 urges fear of Yahweh and obedience to his commandments, and would appear to discourage the kind of speculation for which the author has shown a fondness, and v. 14, 'God will bring every deed into judgment', reintroduces a doctrine of reward and retribution which the author has categorically denied. Similarly, 8.12 f. looks like a pious rejoinder to the attack on the doctrine of theodicy in 8.10 f.

Job and Ecclesiastes

Thus the resemblances and the differences between Job and Ecclesiastes emerge. In both there is a rejection of a doctrine of theodicy and in both there is an acceptance that God is shrouded in mystery and is past finding out. The scepticism of Ecclesiastes is the more general, the more cerebral, but that of Job is the more human and the more compelling. Ecclesiastes' scepticism is more desolating in its comprehensiveness and in the weariness of its tone. It does not come out of a crisis situation in which a sympathetic human being is driven towards disintegration and despair. It betrays rather the tired accents of one who has not suffered greatly but whose world is filled with an unbearable grayness and lack of definition. Nor is his mysterious God described in the same way. Job's description of the unsearchable God whose wisdom is shown in his creative works is also part of the conception of God shared by Eliphaz, Bildad and Zophar, and appears in the speeches of Yahweh himself. But these stirring descriptions, which are a well-established emphasis of Old Testament wisdom, do not contribute to Ecclesiastes' portrait of the inscrutable God. His God is more desiccated, more abstract and more unbearable. Nature in its regularity is a witness to the fixed and unalterable patterns of existence to which man is also subject. A man cannot know why God has ordered his existence in just this way. He can know only that he has done it and that no escape or deviation is possible. As for the world in which he lives, it is one in which no moral judgments are possible, where wisdom can achieve little and where pleasure is the only positive experience, always provided that you are one of those to whom God has given the capacity for pleasure.

It is in the sadness evoked by death that the difference between Ecclesiastes and Job is most marked. Job still associates himself with the this-worldly concept of fulfilment and there is no evidence that he regards this as defective or hollow. The man who has achieved honour, reputation, wealth, children, a long life is not haunted by death. Death does not threaten the fulfilment and maturity of his existence. It is part of the blessedness that after the summit has been reached there should be this gentle descent into Sheol. It is part of the joy and contentment of a full life. In contrast, death has become a source of anxiety and proof of futility in the book of Ecclesiastes and this is a great change. The older religion with its this-worldly character and its acceptance of the boundary of death satisfied the individual only if he had the support of a community in which the worship and service of God came to effective expression. It may be that this condi-

fulfilled in the time when Ecclesiastes was written, and that the individual could no longer find a fulfilment which gave him communal tion was no longer fulfilled in the time when Ecclesiastes was written, and that the individual could no longer find a fulfilment which gave him communal support and permitted him to die without the fear of futility and emptiness. It is thus consonant with a date in the latter half of the third century, when religion and corporate values were challenged by Hellenism, before the revival of Jewish nationalism under the Maccabees.

WILLIAM MCKANE

14 The Exile

The evidence

1. Biblical references

II Kings 25 describes the revolt of Zedekiah and its results. It includes a brief account of the murder of Gedaliah, the Jewish governor whom the Babylonians had set in authority after the fall of Jerusalem, and of the subsequent flight to Egypt of the members of his court (including a reluctant Jeremiah). It ends with Jehoiachin's release from prison in Babylonia.

Jeremiah 39–44 is a longer account of the same, except that it omits any reference to the release of Jehoiachin and adds more prophecies uttered by Jeremiah in Egypt.

Jeremiah 24, the parable of the figs, and *Jeremiah 29*, the prophet's letter to the exiles, actually come from the period before 586, but are important for four reasons; (i) the parable of the figs expresses an attitude that became standard in Jewish interpretations of the exile: that the exiled fraction of the people were the faithful and the Palestinian remainder the worthless; (ii) they mention the prophecy of restoration after seventy years, which was a very potent one; (iii) they show something of what conditions were like in exile; (iv) they illustrate again the prophetic interpretation of the event of the exile.

Lamentations. Though traditionally known as the Lamentations of Jeremiah, the book has no genuine connection with that prophet. It is a set of five poems (corresponding to the five chapters) lamenting the fall of Jerusalem and mostly composed when the memory of the disaster was still fresh. All but the last are alphabetic acrostics.

Deutero-Isaiah and Ezekiel. Deutero-Isaiah means Isaiah chs. 40–55. For selected passages from these prophets see below.

2. Archaeological evidence

Excavated sites in Palestine produce no dramatic revelations bearing on the period of the exile itself. They simply confirm the general picture of a poor and under-populated land.

Excavations of Mesopotamian cities, especially Babylon, have given us a fairly full picture of life there, and have provided texts of various sorts with information about the background events of the period.

The Weidner Tablets, dug up in the royal palace at Babylon, are administrative documents which record, among other things, the allowances paid to Jehoiachin, king of Judah in exile.

There are two important accounts of the reign of Nabonidus, ending in Cyrus' rise to power; these are the Nabonidus Chronicle and the Verse Account of Nabonidus. These were both written after the accession of Cyrus and by Cyrus' supporters. We do not expect their picture of Nabonidus, therefore, to be sympathetic.

On Cyrus himself we have information in plenty. There is the Cyrus Cylinder, a kind of clay barrel found in Babylon, and as secondary sources the works of Xenophon (*Cyropaedia*), Herodotus, and other Greek historians, such as Diodorus Siculus, Ctesias and Arrian. To these we may add Josephus, *Antiquities* 10.8; 10.9; and 10.11,1–2.

We have information about the Jews in Egypt in the Elephantine Papyri, described below.

Why this period is important

The exile, dated from 586–538 BC, marks a dramatic upheaval in Israel's fortunes and a radical change in her constitution and status. Israel's history revolves round the two events of exodus and exile. In the exodus and subsequent events she was constituted a nation. At the exile she ceased to be one in the accepted sense. She lost her political independence, and apart from a brief period under the Maccabees, she did not regain it until AD 1947. The exile, too, marks the beginning of the dispersion of much of her population (the diaspora). Her people were scattered, and not only to Babylon.

The astonishing thing is that she did not lose her identity. Israel had developed, or developed in exile, a culture which proved resistant to the most powerful erosive forces. Her peculiar religion played a major part in this. Israel's unique conception of God goes hand in hand with a unique conception of her national identity.

According to the way in which ancient peoples thought, the defeat and break up of the state ought to havs been accepted as conclusive evidence of the failure of the national deity and to have led to the collapse of the national culture. Assyria's identity and culture did not survive her defeat at Carchemish in 605.

Israel refused to accept this as the logic of events. The fact that she did so is to be laid largely to the credit of the prophets. They had prepared her for the catastrophe not only by predicting it, but by interpreting it, before the event. They had asserted *ad nauseam* that it would take place not in spite of the efforts of the national God, but precisely because he would himself bring it about. They interpreted it in advance as a punishment for sin. Instead, therefore, of regarding the exile as evidence for the failure of Yahweh, Israel was able to see it as a vindication of the prophets' view of his character.

It must be appreciated that the religious structures which bound Israel together, and which showed themselves in subsequent ages to be so resistant to erosion, are not, in the form in which they are familiar to us, older than the exile itself. They were largely created at this very period, to meet the need of holding together the depressed and scattered people. Institutions like the law, the ritual of circumcision, sabbath-keeping, and many of the others that make up what we recognize as Jewish culture, either came into being at this point, or came into prominence only now. Circumcision, for example, though it had been practised from remote antiquity, had not previously been thought of as *distinctive*. And if the Old Testament as we now have it presents all these things as part of the normative religion of Israel, that is because the Old Testament itself is substantially a product of the exilic age.

The Neo-Babylonians

The Neo-Babylonian Empire arose at the end of the seventh century. (It is called *Neo-Babylonian* to distinguish it from Babylon's earlier period of empire in the eighteenth to sixteenth centuries BC, inaugurated by the famous Hammurabi). In alliance with the Medes, the Babylonians overthrew the reigning world power, Assyria. Under king Nabopolassar they took the Assyrian capital, Nineveh, in 612 BC, and finished the job in 605, at the battle

173

of Carchemish, when Nebuchadnezzar convincingly defeated an Assyrian-Egyptian alliance.

Nebuchadnezzar was the principal ruler of the Neo-Babylonian dynasty, reigning for over forty years. It was he who destroyed Jerusalem and deported the Jews in 597 and 586. His attempt to include Egypt in his empire, however, eventually failed.

His chief work was the rebuilding of Babylon. He restored the temple of Marduk, Babylon's patron deity, built a magnificent palace for himself, and also constructed the famous 'hanging gardens', which were reckoned as one of the 'seven wonders of the world'.

The achievements of his two immediate successors were modest. The third, and last, was Nabonidus, about whom so many contradictory things are said that it is impossible to do more than guess his true character or the real reasons for his policies.

Babylonian religion was an impressive affair, full of splendid and rich ceremonial, and festivals in which the gods were carried in procession along raised processional highways, and along the canals in ships. The New Year festival, in spring, when the king 'took the hand of Marduk' and led him in procession, was of great importance. The ritual of this feast seems to have included an enactment of the drama of creation, in which the god Marduk fights the chaos monster; a death and resurrection of the god; a sacred marriage between god and goddess (enacted by the king and a priestess) and a ritual abasement of the king, followed by his restoration to dignity. Babylonian religion was also much concerned with the procuring of oracles and foretelling the future.

All these features may profitably be borne in mind when reading biblical texts written during the exile, especially Deutero-Isaiah.

The life and thought of the Jews

1. In Babylon

The old phrase 'Babylonian captivity' is a misnomer. The Jewish exiles were not captives in the accepted sense of that word. They had freedom of association and considerable freedom of movement, as Ezekiel makes clear (e.g., 8.1; 14.1; 20.1 ff.). They were allowed to communicate with their homeland and receive communications from there (Jer.29). They must have been free to take jobs and make money and own property, for when the opportunity came to return, many of them had adjusted themselves only too well to Babylonian life and had no desire to leave. They seem to have been free to practise their own religion, in so far as it could be practised at such a remote distance from their only legitimate sanctuary. The existence of 'elders' suggests not only that they were gathered in separate Jewish communities, but also that these communities may have had a measure of self-government.

The numbers involved were not large. Jeremiah 52.28 ff. gives a total for all the deportations of 4600. II Kings 24.14,16 mentions figures of 10,000 and 8000 for the deportation in 597. Even if we accept the higher figure, the Babylonian exiles cannot have been more than a tiny fraction of the population of the country.

The exiles did, however, include most of the nation's leaders, and they themselves were acutely conscious of their status as 'the good figs' (Jer.24). They saw themselves as the true inheritors and guardians of Israel's traditions. They therefore felt themselves competent to work out a new and reformed system of religious faith and practice, and eventually to force this new order on the Palestinians. All this, however, came later, and really falls within the compass of the next section.

There was a new seriousness about religion. The prophetic criticisms of pre-exilic religion were accepted and assimilated. A new orthodoxy was created. Cut off from the temple cultus, the exiles reacted in two ways: they concocted idealistic schemes for the reform and re-establishment of the cult (this is the motive not only behind Ezek.40–48 but behind much of the Priestly writing also). At the same time they evolved institutions which made them less dependent on the cult in practice. It is interesting to note that after the final destruction of the temple in AD 70, the Rabbis reacted in a similar way, regulating the temple ritual in minute detail, but at the same time working out the means which enabled Judaism to do without it.

The Deuteronomic reform had partly prepared the exiles for this adjustment. In restricting sacrificial worship to Jerusalem it effectively cut off many Jews from the cultus for the greater part of the year. Deuteronomy itself therefore had already tried to fill the religious gap by encouraging the study of sacred law in the context of family life (Deut.11.18–20, cf. 6.6–9).

In order that their corporate religious life should have some way of expressing itself, the exiles seem to have created the synagogue. We have no direct evidence of its existence during the exile, but all the circumstantial evidence points to its origin in this period.

2. In Egypt

That there were substantial communities of Jews in Egypt is clear from Jer.44, and also from the Elephantiné Papyri. The Elephantiné Papyri are a cache of letters and legal docu-ments discovered at Yeb in Upper Egypt. They emanate from a Jewish military colony. The documents date from the fifth century but the community was older.

When did these colonies in Egypt originate ? Many of the Egyptian exiles probably went there after 597 and 586. Jeremiah himself was part of an even later wave of refugees. But it is possible that some may have fled there as early as 722, when Samaria fell to theAssyrians. The religious practices of the Elephantiné Jews suggest that they knew nothing of the Deuteronomic reform. They had a temple there, and offered sacrifice, and they worshipped other gods besides Yahweh, including a feminine consort of his. We have no evidence about whether the other Jewish colonies in Egypt adhered to this unreformed religion.

However large their numbers may have been (and we cannot even guess them), the Egyptian exiles were not influential in the way the Babylonian ones became, not, at any rate, within our period. However, a strong Jewish community did survive in Egypt until well into the Christian era. And during the Greek period Egyptian Judaism, under the leadership of Alexandria, developed a distinctive culture and theology of its own.

3. In Palestine

We do not know for certain what steps the Babylonians took after Gedaliah's murder, though it has been plausibly suggested that there was a further small deportation. It seems that the land was subsequently governed from Samaria. When the Persians took over the Babylonian Empire they certainly regarded Judah as part of the province centred on Samaria.

It looks as if some of Israel's neighbours,

especially the Edomites, infiltrated into her territory at this juncture and took over much of her land. On this subject and the feelings it aroused see below on the book of Obadiah (p. 183). The Jews' intense hatred of the Edomites (later called Idumaeans) dates from this period. One of the things which Herod the Great failed to live down was his Idumaean origin.

The Palestinians continued for a long time as a depressed community, depressed both economically and psychologically. Nevertheless, the picture of them which is presented in some of our biblical sources, notably I and II Chronicles, Ezra, Nehemiah, need not be accepted with unreserved credulity. Not only was the Chronicler biased in favour of the Babylonian exiles, who he thought were the only true and faithful Israel, but virtually all our biblical materials have been edited by men who shared this view. The idea that the Palestinians were at least apathetic and at worst prone to apostasy may not be entirely just. It may merely reflect the exiles' later discovery that the Palestinians had a mind of their own, and that they were less than enthusiastic about having a reform of their religion dictated to them by upstarts returned from Babylon (see II Chron.36.11–21).

The coming of the Persians and the Babylonian defeat

The Babylonian Empire (more properly the Neo-Babylonian Empire) did not last long. Its end is quickly told. Its last ruler was Nabonidus, who seems to have been unpopular. He antagonized the priesthood, possibly by attempting religious reforms. He also spent much of his time away from the capital, and failed to return even for the important New Year Festival, in which the king's rôle was vital.

Cyrus, the conqueror of Babylon, was originally a vassal of the Medes, the ruler of a minor kingdom called Anshan, whose precise location is dubious. He rebelled against his overlord, Astyages, and became master of the Median Empire. He defeated the powerful Croesus of Lydia in 546. He next moved on Babylon. Nabonidus, still absent from his capital, was cut off and defeated by Cyrus' general Gobryas. Cyrus occupied Babylon peacefully in 538, being welcomed by its priesthood and taking the throne as representative of Marduk, Babylon's own god. II Isaiah prophesied this conquest (see Isa.46.1 f.; 47; and 43.14 in RSV translation). But his prophecies were not fulfilled in the manner in which he expected them to be.

Cyrus himself was an outstanding personality, both as a general and as a ruler. A considerable mythology arose around him. Anyone who could be given the title 'messiah' by a Hebrew prophet (Isa.45.1) and at the same time be extolled by a Greek historian (Xenophon) as a paragon of Hellenistic virtue must have been a remarkable man.

As a general his great weapon was unexpectedness. He moved his armies much faster than was common (Isa.41.2 f.), so that his enemies often found him on their doorsteps while they were still thinking of mobilizing. He acknowledged few of the rules of war, and once attacked, for example, after his opponent had called off his campaign for the winter.

As a ruler his policies were enlightened. Before his time the idea of holding an empire was to place garrisons at strategic points and demand the payment of taxes. To 'rebel' meant to refuse payment, and at the death of an emperor his successor usually had to conquer his empire afresh. Cyrus set about seriously the task of governing the lands which he had conquered.

More about the Persian achievement and about Jewish life under their rule will be found on pp. 187 ff. For the present, all that needs to be said is that Cyrus, instead of attempting to crush subject peoples and rob them of their individuality, encouraged their culture and favoured their religions. He fulfilled II Isaiah's expectation that he would allow the exiles to return.

Developments in prophecy

Prophecy was transformed during the period of the exile. Although it had been vindicated by the exile, its day was nearly done. Ezekiel and Deutero-Isaiah are the last really great exponents of it. In their hands it has already changed significantly. It has already become a *literary* phenomenon. Ezekiel (though not II Isaiah) also heralds another change. In him prophecy has become much more pro-cultic. He takes a positive attitude to worship and is interested in the temple ritual. Prophecy also becomes much more optimistic. The pre-exilic prophets whose words have been preserved for us were principally prophets of doom. Ezekiel's pre-exilic oracles were typical doom oracles. After 586, which occurs in the middle of his career, he suddenly becomes a prophet of hope. II Isaiah, whose career was entirely after 586, is optimistic throughout. It is true that these hopeful prophecies were not all very successful ones. Later prophets are less sanguine. When prophecy passed into limbo its mantle fell upon the apocalyptists, and we may detect in Ezekiel the beginnings of an apocalyptic style, in his curious symbolism and imagery.

Prophecy's failure lay in its inability to interpret the continued depression of post-exilic Israel. Now that Israel was reformed and faithful, she ought, according to prophetic theory, to be rewarded by prosperity and independence. The earlier prophets of doom had mostly gone on to predict restoration, salvation after the punishment. The fulfilment of their threats had proved them true prophets. Why, then, were their promises not fulfilled, too ? What, too, of the covenantal promises, especially the promise to David of eternal kingship for his dynasty ? Had Yahweh's word become void ?

These questions were answered by a resort to eschatology. The fulfilment of the prophecies and of the covenantal promises had merely been postponed. And the more depressing the present seemed to be, the more highly coloured were the pictures of the blessed future which the seers envisaged. This turn of ideas is already beginning in II Isaiah. Whether his work contains any genuine eschatology, in the sense of looking to an end of the world and of the cosmic order, may be disputed. What is certainly true is that he paints a romantic, extravagantly poetic picture of the future, and this may well be a response to the disappointments which, on the mundane level, his prophecies met with.

1. Ezekiel

(i) *Selected Passages* (these will be referred to or commented on in the body of the text) chs. 1–5; 8; 11; 12.1–16; 16; 18; 20.1–44; 23; 33.1–20; 37.

(ii) *Critical questions*

How much of the book of Ezekiel is by the prophet himself ? Since the end of the nineteenth century, many radical views have been advanced, but the more radical critics have failed to produce any agreed picture. Now it is common to accept that Ezekiel is responsible for most of the material in the book, though it contains enough problems to suggest that it was collected and edited by another hand, and that the editor possessed much of the material in two forms. It is still common to reject Ezekiel's authorship of the last nine chapters, though the present writer is inclined to accept these, too.

Where did Ezekiel prophesy? The book assumes that he went to Babylon in 597 with the first deportation and did all his prophesying there. This raises difficulties. He seems to be vividly aware of what is going on in Jerusalem (8; 11.1–13). But any alternative theory raises difficulties, too, and the view is taken here that the book is correct in suggesting that Ezekiel did not leave Babylon after 597. Our answer to this question makes little difference to what we think of Ezekiel's ideas. It does make a difference to our estimate of his admittedly extraordinary psychology.

(iii) *Ezekiel's personality*

Ezekiel's book is full of visionary experiences and weird symbolic actions. These help to give us the impression that he was the oddest of the prophets. But is this really so? Perhaps the other prophets had similar experiences, but were less explicit about them. Is Ezekiel's vision in chs. 1–3 different in kind from that in Isa.6, or only more elaborately described? Ezekiel indulges in complicated play-acting of the siege of the city and the captivity of its people (4; 12.1–16). According to Isa.20, a similar performance of Isaiah's lasted three years. Ezekiel's symbolic action in cutting off his hair and dividing it into three portions is quite bizarre (ch. 5). Is it any more so than Jeremiah's dealings with the loincloth (Jer.13.1–11)?

What is really odd about Ezekiel is not that he is a visionary of a very extreme type, but that he is also a rational, even prosaic person. His mystical and rational personalities do not alternate with one another. They seem actually to be combined. Most mystics, if they attempt to describe their visions at all, resort naturally to poetry, to suggestion. Ezekiel resorts to cataloguing. St John the Divine had a vision of the holy city, and he describes it poetically as 'coming down out of heaven like a bride adorned for her husband' (Rev.21.2). Ezekiel, when he saw a vision of the new Jerusalem, took out his tape measure and set down its dimensions (Ezek.40.1 ff.).

Ezekiel is a dual personality in another sense. He is both a prophet and a priest. It is tempting to connect these two functions with his two selves, the visionary and the pedant – tempting but superficial.

(iv) *Ezekiel's message*

Although the first deportation had already taken place before Ezekiel began to prophesy, he still speaks, at first, like a pre-exilic prophet. The catastrophe of 597 had as yet taught the nation nothing. Chapter 8 is a fairly typical catalogue of the prevalent sins. Note that the ones which Ezekiel picks out are primarily cultic, concerned with ritual rather than with morals. Ezekiel's priestly interests are coming out here.

During this phase of his activities no one takes the prophet seriously. He does not expect them to. Then why prophesy at all? He does it, he says, in order to 'deliver his own soul'. He has a moral responsibility to discharge, whether people listen or not (see 3.4–8, 17–21; and 33.1–9). The latter passage contains Ezekiel's famous parable of the Watchman.

Earlier prophets, e.g., Hosea and Jeremiah, interpreted Israel's history as a tragic failure to fulfil the promise of her honeymoon period with Yahweh in the wilderness, her time of faithfulness. Ezekiel denies that there ever was such a period of faithfulness. Chapter 20.1–44 is a prosaic re-interpretation of history to prove his point, and chs.16 and 23 make the same point metaphorically.

After 586 Ezekiel's problem is no longer that people will not take him seriously. They now take him so seriously that they have lost all hope. If, as the prophet says, their fathers have been sinners since the beginning, what is the good of repenting *now*? Good behaviour at this late stage is not going to counterbalance all that huge dead weight of wrongdoing.

The prophet replies with his elaborate discussion of personal responsibility (18; 33.10–20). This is often cited as setting out an uncompromising individualism. But to say so is to miss the main point. Ezekiel's argument is not that each man must stand on his own moral feet, but that each *generation* must stand on its own feet. To this extent Ezekiel is still thinking in corporate and national terms. Put in this uncompromising form, Ezekiel's statement is not theologically acceptable. The generations do suffer for each other's sins. But prophets are not primarily theologians. They are preachers answering people's spiritual needs. In the historical context Ezekiel's argument makes excellent sense.

Ezekiel is convinced, then, of the radical nature of Israel's corruption. She merits (and after 586 has received) radical punishment. If she has any future it can only be through an equally radical intervention of grace. Now his doctrine of grace is the key to Ezekiel's whole thought, even its most unpleasant-sounding

aspects. The miraculous quality of the restoration is well brought out in ch.37, the vision of the valley of dry bones. There is, of course, thought here of individual resurrection or life after death. It is national restoration which is spoken of.

Ezekiel repeatedly says that God will save 'for his name's sake', or 'that his name might not be profaned'. At first sight this seems to mean that Ezekiel's God is a forbidding character who saves Israel not for any love he bears her, but out of concern for his own reputation. In the context of Ezekiel's thinking this can hardly be the correct interpretation. What the prophet is saying is that God saves Israel not because of what *she* is, but because of what *he* is. 'For my name's sake' means, 'Because that's the kind of person I am'. Chapter 16 makes it clear that he does love Israel, worthless as she is.

Israel as she is lacks the capacity to respond to God's affection. God himself must bestow that capacity. Ezekiel takes up an image of Jeremiah's when he speaks of the gift of the new heart (11.14–21).

Whereas the pre-exilic prophets on the whole were critical of the cult, and at best displayed little positive interest in it, Ezekiel's attention is much engaged by it. This is not an accidental consequence of his priesthood. It is bound up with his theology and especially with his doctrine of grace. To the earlier prophets repentance was what mattered, not sacrifices. Their theme is what man must do to put himself right: self-reform. Sacrifice, to them, is an attempt to evade the moral issue. Ezekiel, by contrast, has little faith in Israel's capacity for self-reform. God himself must make up her deficiencies, and the cult is the means by which he does this. Sacrifice, therefore, is not an alternative to repentance, but an expression of it. It is not a means whereby man tries to procure forgiveness, but a means whereby God offers it. Ezekiel therefore plans for the restoration of sacrifice, and all the other ritual which he finds so meaningful. His interpretation of the cultus became normative in the post-exilic period, and was taken up especially by the Priestly writer.

Ezekiel is throughout overcome by the sense of God's reality and holiness. Some of his most bizarre passages are really attempts to express this, the most notable being his call vision in chs. 1–3.

One has the constant impression when reading Ezekiel that here is a man who has not found the appropriate vehicle for the expression of his thought. The Hebrew literary tradition was not well adapted to convey the kind of things which Ezekiel wished to say, and he failed to break through to any new literary forms by which to say them. His message suffers, because he has not mastered his medium. Deutero-Isaiah succeeds exactly where Ezekiel fails.

2. Deutero-Isaiah (Isaiah 40–55)

Deutero-Isaiah (or II Isaiah) is the name given to the unknown author of Isa.40–55, an exilic prophet.

Selected Passages (referred to or commented on below) chs. 40; 41; 42.18–20; 44.21–28; 45.1–13; 47; 51.1–11; 55. The so called Servant Songs, which will be dealt with separately, are 42.1–9; 49.1–6; 50.4–9; 52.13–53.12.

(i) Critical questions

These chapters have been analysed in a number of ways, but there is little doubt that the bulk of the material comes from a single author. Some scholars hold that the Servant Songs are from a different hand, but this is the only possible exception of any substance. It is also clear that unlike most prophetic literature these chapters do not consist of short oracles, but of long poems. How many, and how long they are is disputed.

It seems established that the first part of the work, up to ch.48, was written in Babylon, when Cyrus was already active, but before his capture of Babylon in 538. The prophet speaks much of Cyrus in these chapters, and pins his hopes on him. Chapter 45.1–13 is his longest discussion of Cyrus' work and status (but cf. 41.1–4, 25). He hails Cyrus as messiah (45.1: most versions render the word here as 'anointed'), and says that his success is given him by Yahweh. Yet (45.4) this is not because Cyrus himself is anything to Yahweh. It is for Israel's sake. Cyrus' job is to free Israel (45.13). Verses 9–13 seem to be forestalling possible objections to this theory of Cyrus' messianic status. God is entitled to use his creatures as he sees fit. The imagery suggests that Cyrus is a mere tool in God's hand.

The prophet sees Cyrus as avenging Israel by destroying and humiliating Babylon. Chapter 47 is a lengthy exposition of this theme. These prophecies were unfulfilled. Cyrus was welcomed by Babylon with open arms.

Chapters 49–55 seem to have been written after 538. The prophet is partly disappointed. Cyrus is never mentioned now. The prophet's hope seems to be placed instead in a figure who is called 'the servant of the Lord'. It is possible that ch. 40 was written last of all, as an introduction to the entire corpus. It gathers up the themes from the rest of the work, and seems to be trying to come to terms with the disappointment which otherwise appears only in the second part of the prophecy.

(ii) *The man and his methods*

We do not know Deutero-Isaiah's name. We have no knowledge of his circumstances, or of even one single incident of his life. We have the content of his message, but we do not know how he received it. In all these respects he is as great a contrast with Ezekiel as could be conceived. He also differs from Ezekiel in that he works out dramatically new literary forms to enable him to express his insights. He exploits the capacity of poetic imagery to convey several different ideas at once: to say one thing while recalling or echoing another.

Chapter 51 usually illustrates several features of II Isaiah's use of imagery: vv. 9–11 employ the image of the dividing of the waters. The common Near-Eastern creation myth saw God as having created the world by dividing the waters of chaos. (This still appears in the Priestly account, Gen.1.6–8.) Rahab in Isa.51.9 is one of the names of the personified chaos monster. Yahweh had also saved Israel from Egypt by dividing the waters of the Red Sea. The promised return from exile is constantly spoken of in terms which recall both these events (cf. 43.15 ff.). The return itself involves no dividing of waters, but it does, like the exodus, involve a passage of the wilderness (41.17–20; 43.19 f.; 49.10 f.).

Chapter 51 also illustrates a rarer feature of II Isaiah's imagery, his recalling the paradise myth (51.3) and his use of eschatological language (51.6).

In all this the prophet is not merely playing with words, he is making a theological point. God's saving acts can be understood each in terms of the others. Each can only be fully understood when seen as part of the series. God is always doing 'new things', which only his prophets can predict, yet when they occur they are seen to be in character. II Isaiah thus stresses at the same time God's originality and his consistency. They are not incompatible. And the practical point of all this is that God is to be trusted. He is to be trusted in the particular concrete circumstance of the exile. He who could create the world and bring Israel out of Egypt can surely bring her out of Babylon.

(iii) *Deutero-Isaiah's message*

Babylonian religion was characterized by an elaborate and colourful polytheism, and by very free use of divining, astrology, and other superstitions. II Isaiah's work, correspondingly, is militantly monotheistic and contemptuous of idols, and at the same time is bitingly critical of divination, gleefully contrasting its unreliability with the reliability of Yahweh's prophets. Chapter 41.21–29 illustrates both themes and their interrelation.

Yahweh is the only God, and he is the God who both saves and creates. II Isaiah uses words like 'create', 'make', 'form', 'save', 'redeem', as if they were virtually interchangeable. Theologically they *are* interchangeable, for all express different aspects of the activity of the one God. The unity of God is reflected in the unity of history (which includes creation).

We shall understand II Isaiah better if we remember that as he wrote the Priestly writer was preparing his great work. The Priestly writer combines his own creation account, in which God is said to 'create', with that of the Yahwist, for whom God 'forms' or 'makes' his creatures. And he presents that dual account of creation as the first step in a story of redemption, as part of history.

The Priestly writer and II Isaiah agree in two other respects. First, in their doctrine of the divine word. According to 'P', 'God *said* . . . And it was so.' II Isaiah in ch. 55 explains the Priestly writer's thinking here perfectly. But significantly he draws a practical and limited conclusion. If Yahweh's word is like that, cannot he be trusted to bring us back from Babylon ? Second, they agree in their universalism. The Priestly writer works on a broad canvas. Salvation may be *through* Abraham and Israel, but it is *for* the world. Both the Priestly writer and II Isaiah were in exile thrown into close contact with foreigners and their culture. They could not have been insensitive to them, and could not conceive of God being insensitive to them. In 49.6 f. the prophet is ordained to be a light not only to Israel, but to the nations.

(iv) The servant songs

These are among the most discussed passages in the Old Testament. Some scholars prefer to treat them apart from their context, holding either that they were composed by someone other than II Isaiah, or that they were composed by the prophet as independent poems and inserted into the body of the work later. The chief argument for this view is that the figure of the servant who appears in the songs seems to be different from the servant who is referred to elsewhere. This is true, but it must also be noted that the servant's character also differs from song to song, and further, that the word 'servant' is not used consistently outside the songs either. Outside the songs the servant is usually Israel, and she is called 'servant' because she is God's special obligation (41.8 f.; 44.21). But in 42.18–20, Israel the servant is Israel the inadequate. And in 44.26 the servant is not Israel at all, but the prophet. Within the songs there is the same oscillation between the servant as Israel (49.3) and the servant as an

individual, which he must surely be in the last song, if not in the third.

But within the songs there is development of another kind in the servant's character. The first song (42.1–9) sets out the servant's destiny to be a kind of messiah to the world. There is nothing pessimistic in it (it is the only song to appear in the pre-538 BC half of the work). The second song (49.1–6) emphasizes the servant's preparation by God, but in 49.4 he shows himself conscious of the difficulties of the task. In the third song (50.4–9), he perceives that he must accept suffering as a necessary concomitant of the task to be done. In the final song (52.13–53.12), the suffering is given redemptive value. Perhaps here the acceptance of suffering is no longer a mere consequence of the task. It is the task itself.

In these songs the prophet is trying to come to terms with his experience of suffering and failure, both in his own life and that of the nation. In learning what to do with his own distress he tries to show his people how to regard theirs. That they failed to rise to this destiny goes without saying.

Disputes have raged around the question, Who is the servant ? This is really two questions. It can be taken to mean, Where did the prophet get the idea of the servant ? Put in this form the question can be answered. He clearly has in mind the sufferings of his nation in exile. Very likely he has suffered himself. He is almost certainly influenced by the experiences of his fellow prophets, and especially Jeremiah. The songs might almost be taken as commentary on Jeremiah's career. He may well have in the back of his mind the common Near-Eastern myth of the suffering king, who is ritually abased, only to rise again bringing salvation for his people. He may likewise be affected by the myth of the dying and rising saviour god. He may also have thought of the past heroes of his race who suffered for their people, especially Moses (see Ex.32.32) and possibly even Hezekiah and Jehoiachin. All these, and others, have been at some time identified as the servant. And all these suggestions could be at least partly right.

But the question, Who is the servant ?, can also be interpreted, Who is to fulfil the task of the servant ? Is it for the nation, or a messianic king, or a prophet, or who else ? In this form the question cannot be given a direct answer. Perhaps the prophet himself could not have answered it. II Isaiah is not concerned so much with the person of the servant as with the office. He is writing about servanthood. Whatever the servant's identity, this is what he will have to do and to be. He must give his back to the smiters, and his cheeks to those who pluck out the beard. He must not hide his face from shame and spitting. He must be despised and rejected, and offer himself as an offering for sin. Whoever is willing to do this, whether the nation as a whole, or a group within the nation, a king or a prophet, or any other individual present or to come, will have taken on himself the office and form of the servant.

3. Obadiah

This short work appears to date from the exilic period. It is concerned almost exclusively with Edom (which it often refers to as 'Esau'). The Edomites took advantage of Judah's plight during the exile (vv. 10–14) and the prophet foresees divine punishment for them (vv. 1–9). He looks forward to the day of the Lord (vv. 15–21) when all nations shall be judged and Judah and Israel restored.

HENRY McKEATING

15 The Return

The evidence

1. Biblical references

We are concerned with two complex series of events. These are often confused, so we shall keep them rigorously separate from the start. First, there are the events concerned with the return of some Jews from exile at the end of the sixth century, immediately following Cyrus' conquest of Babylon, and the subsequent rebuilding of the temple.

Our primary sources here are the book of Haggai and chs. 1–8 of Zechariah (the rest of Zechariah is a later composition). The prophets Haggai and Zechariah were intimately concerned with the temple rebuilding and their words are likely to have been written down shortly after the event. They are thus first-hand sources, but not systematic historical accounts.

Our chief secondary source is Ezra 1–6. This does purport to be a systematic historical account. The books we now call I and II Chronicles, Ezra and Nehemiah are parts of a single continuous literary work. Its author is usually referred to as 'The Chronicler'. Up to the end of II Chronicles we can check his account against other sources (e.g., Samuel and Kings) and perceive how freely he treats them. In Ezra we can check him only against Haggai and Zech.1–8. In Nehemiah we cannot check him at all. The value of his account is variable. In Ezra it is certainly confused and self-contradictory, but contains bits which may well be authentic.

We must also reckon with the apocryphal book I Esdras. It contains much material taken direct from Ezra, but sometimes exhibits significant variations.

The second complex of events starts in the middle of the fifth century (about 150 years later) and centres on Ezra's reform and Nehemiah's rebuilding of the walls.

Primary sources: none.

Our secondary sources are Ezra 7–10 and Nehemiah. Ezra 7–10 again shows signs of confusion, but Nehemiah consists largely of a first-person account which may well represent an original Memoirs of Nehemiah. If we could be certain of this it would rank as a primary source.

I Esdras is again relevant.

There is other literature in the Old Testament which dates from this period (see below under *Literature*). Much of it is not the kind that helps with historical reconstruction (e.g., Jonah and Song of Songs) and much that in principle might help (e.g., III Isaiah, or Trito-Isaiah) is so difficult to date precisely that it is historically unusable. But even apart from books specifically mentioned here, most of the Old Testament was put into its present form in this period.

2. Non-biblical literature

Josephus (*Antiquities*, 11.1–5) is usually relying on biblical accounts and is not an independent witness. The background history of Persia is well covered by the Greek historians, Xenophon, Herodotus and Thucydides. Throughout much of our period the Persians were meeting trouble from the Greeks. The epic battles of Plataea and Marathon in 490 BC, and Thermopylae and Salamis in 480, fall about half-way between Zerubbabel's rebuilding of the walls.

3. Archaeological evidence

Many Persian cities have been excavated, providing ample information on Persian history and culture: Susa (cf. Neh.1.1), Ecbatana (Ezra 6.2), Babylon, Erech and Pasargadae among others. From Persepolis the Treasury Tablets give detailed information about Persian financial administration. The accounts of a large business firm called Murashu Sons discovered at Nippur incidentally mention many Jewish names.

The tombs of the Persian kings at Naqsh-i-Rustam are a mine of information. Important among inscriptions is that at Behistun, dramatically placed on a cliff face and recording how Darius I quelled the opposition at the beginning of his reign.

In Palestine, remains from the Persian period have been found on numerous sites. They show that for most of this period the country was neither very prosperous nor well populated. Evidence of the destruction and abandonment of Bethel in the sixth century and of Tell-en-Nasbeh and Megiddo in the fourth shows not only that times were unsettled, but that violent events took place of which our literary sources say nothing.

The Elephantiné papyri are again important, and enable us to fix the date of Nehemiah. Nehemiah's opponent Sanballat is mentioned in them, and elsewhere. Another adversary, Geshem the Arabian, is also mentioned twice in texts from this period.

The Persian achievement

The history of Persia is too complicated to outline here. We need only concern ourselves with the following kings: Cyrus founded the empire, took Babylon in 538 and allowed the Jews to go home. His next successor but one was Darius I (522–486 BC), who usurped the throne and practically had to reconquer his empire, but proved a strong king. In his reign the temple at Jerusalem was rebuilt. Much later we have Artaxerxes II, in the first half of the following century.

The Persians were great imperial administrators. Their organization was initiated by Cyrus but built up by his successors, especially Darius I. It allowed a large measure of local autonomy and encouraged local culture (e.g., local religions). It at least contrived to give the impression that it was governing people for their own good. The administration depended on swift communication. A network of fast roads connected all parts of the Empire, and the imperial postal service could relay messages non-stop and at high speed, through having teams of horses and messengers posted at the ready at intervals of a few miles along all major roads. The Persians established a *lingua franca*, Aramaic, throughout their domains. In Palestine and Syria it quickly became the vernacular. Soon after Ezra's time Hebrew was relegated to the status of a learned tongue. It was not re-established as the vernacular in Palestine until after the Second World War.

The Empire was divided into 'satrapies', each with its Satrap, who was like a powerful minor king. But there were clever checks and balances. Some of the Satrap's most important court officials were not responsible to him but directly to the great king. These included his chief financial officer and the general-in-charge of the garrison in the Satrap's own capital. The Satrap was also subject to inspection by a travelling inquisitor called 'the king's eye'.

Persian religion

Up to the beginning of the Persian period, the religion which held sway in Mesopotamia was for all practical purposes the same polytheistic faith which had been established there by the Sumerians soon after 3000 BC. The Persians, being Indo-Europeans, had a different polytheism of their own, but made no attempt to disturb the existing cults.

Zoroastrianism seems to have originated in the sixth century BC in Persia itself. By the time of Darius I it was the state religion. Its adoption, however, made no difference to official Persian tolerance of other religions.

Early Zoroastrianism may be described either as monotheism with strong tendencies towards dualism, or as dualism with strong tendencies towards monotheism. The good God (called Ahura Mazda or Ormazd) and the evil one (Ahriman) are almost evenly matched. Both have creative power. But the good is destined to win, and the true believer must side firmly with the good.

A simplification and rationalization of the old Persian polytheism lies behind Zoroaster's system, and after his death much of the polytheism came back, albeit in covert form. A rich angelology and demonology developed. Originally Zoroastrianism was purely moralistic. A man stands or falls by the balance between his righteous and unrighteous acts. There is no room for forgiveness or divine grace.

It is generally agreed that later Judaism owes a good deal to Zoroastrianism.

The rebuilding of the temple

We have already distinguished primary and secondary sources, and noted the confusion in the latter. The sensible procedure therefore is to see first what we can learn from our primary sources and then allow the secondary ones to fill out the picture. Where they supply additional facts we may cautiously accept their testimony, but we must not allow them to *correct* the primary sources.

Haggai's carefully dated prophecies are all from 'the second year of Darius' (520 BC), and therefore eighteen years after Cyrus's conquest of Babylon. He graphically pictures the economic depression of the Jerusalem community (1.6; 2.16). The leaders of this community are Zerubbabel (the lay leader) and Joshua (the high priest). The book begins by hinting at discussions about whether to rebuild the temple and the general feeling is that the time is inappropriate (1.2). The common-sense answer evidently was that the community could not afford it. Haggai asserts that their priorities are wrong. If they would put the service of God first, then the economy would sort itself out, with God's help.

There have been convulsions in international politics and Haggai expects more (2.6–9). These were the disturbances at the beginning of Darius's reign, recorded on the Behistun Rock. In this shaking of the Empire Haggai sees Israel's chance of freedom, and even dominion (2.6–9). Zerubbabel (who seems to have been of Davidic ancestry) is given messianic status, and a great future is predicted for him in the age that is about to dawn (2.21–23). Haggai's advice was taken and the work of rebuilding the temple begun (2.18).

Zechariah writes a little later. His first vision

is dated a month earlier than Haggai's last oracle and the rest spread over three years. He confirms Haggai's picture at every point. He reports the same depression (8.10). He, too, is in favour of the rebuilding, which has already begun (4.9 f.), and is convinced that prosperity will result (8.9–13; cf. 1.16 f.). Like Haggai he expects more than mere prosperity (8.1–7). See 2.1–13, where one element in the glorious future is to be the gathering in of the dispersed Jews.

The expected unrest has come to nothing (1.11 f.), but the prophet does not despair, for the future is still assured. The priesthood is to be purified in the person of Joshua (ch. 3). The messiah is to come (3.8). According to ch. 4 it looks as if that messiah is to be Zerubbabel (cf. Hag.2.21 ff.).

We deduce, then, that the foundations of the new temple were laid in 520 BC, by a Jerusalem community which could not well afford the project; that the leaders were Joshua and Zerubbabel, and that they were prompted and supported by Haggai and Zechariah. We also know that their economic and political expectations were sadly disappointed, for other post-exilic literature (e.g., II Isaiah and Malachi) makes this quite clear.

Note the omissions. Nothing is said of any exiles who had returned from Babylon, and there is no suggestion that anyone except the local Palestinian community had a hand in the work. Neither is anything reported of any earlier attempt to rebuild the temple.

What does our secondary source in Ezra 1–6 tell us ? It records that in 538, when Cyrus conquered Babylon, he let the Jews return to Jerusalem and rebuild the temple (Ezra 1.2–4). They returned with enthusiasm (1.5 ff.) under the leadership of Sheshbazzar (1.11). In ch. 3,

suddenly, Sheshbazzar's name is simply dropped from the story. Without introduction Zerubbabel and Joshua appear as leaders. They begin to re-use the temple site (3.1–6) and soon lay the foundations for a new building (3.7 ff.). In ch. 4 they are opposed by some people called 'the adversaries of Judah and Benjamin', who successfully prevent any further progress until the reign of Darius.

In Ezra 5, encouraged by the prophets Haggai and Zechariah, the returned exiles make a fresh start. This brings a renewed attack from the adversaries, who try to stir up trouble with the Persian authorities. In the course of the controversy the history of the project is re-stated. Sheshbazzar is now credited with the earlier attempt (5.14–16) and it is said that since his day the work has never stopped (5.16). The decree of Cyrus is quoted (6.1–5), this time in Aramaic. This convinces the authorities and the work is completed in 518 (6.15).

This agrees with Haggai and Zech.1–8 in stating that the successful rebuilding began in 520; that Joshua and Zerubbabel were the leaders; and that Haggai and Zechariah supported the venture.

It disagrees only in recording an earlier, unsuccessful attempt in the reign of Cyrus. The account of this is suspicious. The Chronicler is in two minds as to who was responsible, Sheshbazzar or Zerubbabel, and contradicts himself about whether the adversaries brought the work to a halt or only slowed it down.

The Chronicler also gives two accounts of Cyrus' decree ordering the return. The Hebrew version (Ezra 1.1–5) gives permission to return but no express permission to rebuild. The Aramaic (Ezra 6.1.–5) gives permission to rebuild but no express leave to return.

In spite of these discrepancies a return under

Cyrus is inherently likely. II Isaiah confidently expects one, and it is in line with what is known of Cyrus' policies. The information that it was led by the otherwise unknown Sheshbazzar may be accepted.

Permission to rebuild the temple is by no means unlikely either. The Aramaic decree is regarded by many as an authentic document. The Elephantiné papyri relating to a Jewish temple in Egypt show that the Persians did interest themselves in such buildings, and in the worship and ritual practices of subject communities. However, if such an attempt was actually made in Cyrus' reign, the Chronicler manifestly knows no facts about it whatever. He has transferred what he knows about Zerubbabel's rebuilding back in Cyrus' reign.

I suggest that if permission to rebuild was given by Cyrus it was never acted on, or that the attempt to act on it was so insignificant that Haggai and Zechariah could ignore it. The Chronicler, is, however, obliged to posit that a serious effort was made. He cannot conceive that his darling returned exiles, in whom the true faith burned, could have done anything other than rebuild the temple as soon as they arrived in Jerusalem. Unfortunately he has to come to terms with the known fact that the existing temple was built by Zerubbabel in the reign of Darius. So he invents reasons why the exiles were unable to carry their project through, and he fails to make those reasons quite consistent.

Comparison with Haggai and Zech.1–8 suggests that the Chronicler has magnified the part played by the exiles. He suggests that they undertook the work alone and rejected offers of local help (4.2 f.). Haggai and Zechariah reflect no knowledge of such tensions within the community, though the accounts of Ezra and Nehemiah show that they did arise later, nearer the Chronicler's own time.

The work of Ezra and Nehemiah

Dates: Ezra and Nehemiah came back to Jerusalem from Babylon at different times. The Chronicler says both came in the reign of 'Artaxerxes', Ezra in the seventh year (Ezra 7.7) and Nehemiah in the twentieth (Neh.1.1; 2.1). Now there were several kings of that name. However, by referring across to the Elephantiné papyri, which give dated references to prominent people mentioned in Nehemiah's memoirs, we can confirm that his activities took place in the reign of Artaxerxes I and that his coming to Jerusalem was in 444 BC.

But there are three principal dates suggested for Ezra. The Chronicler himself clearly thinks that Ezra came before Nehemiah, in the reign of the same king, i.e., in 458. Many scholars believe that the Chronicler is wrong about this, and that Ezra came after Nehemiah in the reign of Artaxerxes II. This gives a date for Ezra's arrival of 398 BC, nearly half a century later than Nehemiah.

A third view is that the Chronicler has, after all, got the right king but the wrong year, and that Ezra arrived in the *thirty*-seventh year of Artaxerxes I: i.e., later than Nehemiah but not much later (428 BC).

The arguments cannot be gone into here. Suffice it is to say that the question remains an open one. The view taken here is the traditional one, that Ezra arrived in 438. On this view the course of events would be as follows:

Ezra, who was a priest and a scribe, came to Jerusalem bringing with him 'the book of the law of Moses' (Neh.8.1). This may have been the entire Pentateuch, or only part of it – the

Priestly writing. This law was the expression of the new religious synthesis which had been worked out in exile. It was Ezra's mission to get the Palestinians to conform to it.

The exact status of Ezra's authority is in doubt. According to Ezra 7.25 f. he was given some political powers, but he was assuredly not made governor. Judah seems still to have been within the province governed from Samaria. Ezra may therefore have lacked the power to carry through the reforms he wished.

But there may have been more personal reasons for failure. Ezra seems to have been a pious but impractical idealist (see his behaviour in the affair of the bodyguard, Ezra 8.21–23). When he met opposition his reaction was to tear his hair (literally) and 'make a scene' (Ezra 9.3). It is interesting to compare Nehemiah's reaction in almost precisely similar circumstances (Neh.13.25).

Acceptance of the traditional dating does involve the conclusion that Ezra's work was a failure. Some of the provisions of his law were successfully resisted. His breaking up of mixed marriages (Ezra 9–10) seems not to have been permanent, for Nehemiah had to tackle the question all over again, in a less high-handed manner (Neh.13.24–27). It is likely that he antagonized the local population; and the authorities in Samaria, who had no wish to see Jerusalem re-established as a political or religious centre, will hardly have been slow to oppose him as they later opposed Nehemiah.

It may be conjectured that this resulted in an attack on Jerusalem of which the Chronicler says nothing. Nehemiah's grief at hearing of the plight of Jerusalem (Neh.1) certainly suggests a *recent* catastrophe. In this attack the walls had again been broken down. When had these walls been rebuilt ? Either they were rebuilt under Zerubbabel or were in process of construction by Ezra himself. Ezra 4.7–23 gives an account of how an attempt to rebuild the walls in the reign of Artaxerxes was frustrated by the local authorities, backed up by a decision of the Persian king.

Nehemiah learns of the failure of Ezra's mission from his brother Hanani (Neh.1). He gets himself appointed governor (see 5.14) and it looks as if at this point Judah is taken out of the jurisdiction of the authorities in Samaria.

Nehemiah rouses the people to repair the walls, and finishes the work in face of ridicule (Neh.4.1–6), threats (4.7–23) and a treacherous offer to come to terms (6.1–5). There were subsequent threats to report the matter to the Persian authorities (6.6–9) and to assassinate Nehemiah himself (6.10–14). This last seems to have been a roundabout attempt to discredit Nehemiah by getting him to seek asylum in the temple, where he had no right to be, for he was doubtless a eunuch. Nehemiah also had to tackle the community's economic troubles (Neh.5).

He was obliged to build up the population of the city by drafting in people from the countryside (Neh.7.4 f.; 11.1 f), because the existing population was inadequate for the city's defence. He brought back the Levites from secular employment to their religious duties, and regulated the payment of tithes (13.10–14; cf. 13.30 f.). He enforced observance of the sabbath (13.15–22). He took active measures against any further contracting of mixed marriages (13.23–27).

Nehemiah after some time returned to Persia, but later came back for a second period of office.

If the traditional dating of Ezra is correct, Ezra must have been in Jerusalem all the time Nehemiah was doing his work, yet the two are rarely mentioned together (only in Neh.8.9; 12.26). In fact, where they do appear together in the account of Ezra's reading of the law (Neh.8.9) the name of Nehemiah is probably an erroneous addition (I Esdras omits it). This eighth chapter quite probably refers to events that took place before Nehemiah's arrival, and is thus out of chronological order. If Ezra had succeeded only in antagonizing people it need not surprise us that he remained in the background and left the work to the more diplomatic Nehemiah.

Nehemiah should in many ways appeal to twentieth-century readers. Though religious, he is not in the bad sense pious. He frequently reports that he prayed, but the prayers are usually brief and practical (2.4; 4.4 f.; 5.19; 6.9,14). He is very much a practical man; an astute politician, good not only at organizing but at handling all kinds of people; he gets things done. But he is no mere pragmatist. He is above all a man of principle. He knows when to be diplomatic, but he also knows when to stand his ground (see Neh.6.3 for a magisterial reply). He gives the impression of great confidence, but it is not self-confidence. It flows from his absolute conviction that he is doing what God has called him to do (Neh.2.20a; 4.19 f.).

All this, however, was accomplished at a cost. Measures were taken against mixed marriages and against foreign elements generally. These foreign elements were in some cases, it seems, just Israelites from further north. We may guess that a number of the undesirables were merely Palestinian Jews who refused to conform to the returned exiles' religious leadership.

It is commonly said that all this, though it looks unpleasant, was necessary in the circumstances, for otherwise religion could not have been kept pure. This comes close to conceding that the end justifies the means. If a religion cannot be kept pure except by such means as these, then the sooner it is adulterated the better. Exclusivism, wherever it is found (cf. Neh.2.20b) and whatever the ostensible reason for it, is always a horrid thing, a very horrid thing.

There was a universalistic movement in the post-exilic age. It was begun by II Isaiah and carried on worthily by III Isaiah, and by the authors of Jonah and Ruth. If this, rather than the Ezra-Nehemiah movement, had prevailed, who is to say that this would have produced religious disaster?

Judaism in the post-exilic age

From Ezra's time onwards Judaism became a religion of law. Piety consisted in the study of it and in obedience to it. The scholar, the interpreter of the law, thus became as important as the priest, and in the long run, more so. Correspondingly the synagogue, where the law was studied, rivalled and eventually replaced the temple. A body of interpretative tradition and comment grew up, and soon came to be regarded as almost as sacred as the written law itself (this is the 'tradition of the elders' mentioned in Matt.15.2 ff. and parallels). The legend developed that at the same time as God delivered the written law to Moses on Sinai he delivered the oral tradition too, and that this had been handed down in unbroken succession.

The written law was of course what stands in the Pentateuch. It consists of high moral precepts (e.g., Lev.19.1–18) and a good deal of cultic prescription, which to our minds seems of far less value (cf. Lev.19.5–8; 19.19). The faithful Jew was expected to know and to keep all these regulations, observing festivals, paying tithes and making other offerings, keeping sabbath and dietary restrictions as punctiliously as he refrained from murder, theft and adultery.

The law prescribed the cult, and it was a cult subtly different from the pre-exilic one. It was more solemn; it took sin more seriously. It allowed expiation by sacrifice and other means, but expiation was only possible for those who had made amends, material amends, for their offences (Lev.6.1–7).

Many of the cultic laws could only be observed in Palestine. The Jews of the diaspora, who were now more numerous than the Palestinians, were expected to fulfil what they could. Palestinian Judaism was still regarded as the norm.

The emphasis on the cult naturally gave the priests a prominent role. But other factors tended in the same direction. The nation, now without a king, and ruled from a foreign centre, had no native head of state but the high priest. Just as, in pre-exilic times, there had been no high priest, for high-priestly functions were fulfilled by the king, so now, lacking a king, many royal attributes and prerogatives were assumed by the high priesthood.

Not everyone accepted this new orthodoxy. Already in the time of Nehemiah a rift with the Samaritan community was widening and the Samaritans developed a religious orthodoxy of their own, which was in some respects quite different from that of the Jews.

The literature

1. *The final shaping of the Pentateuch*

The development of the Pentateuch has been dealt with elsewhere in this volume. It is sufficient to note here that it received its definite shape during the exile or the early post-exilic period, in Babylon, and that it was brought back to the homeland. It seems reasonable to connect the work of Ezra with this bringing of the Pentateuch to Palestine, though whether this means we can boldly equate Ezra's law book with the Pentateuch in its entirety is open to question.

2. *The book of Ruth*

For convenience the book of Ruth is dealt with at this point, though the belief that it was written in the early post-exilic period is not unchallenged.

The heroine, Ruth, is a Moabite woman (Moab being on the opposite side of the Dead Sea from Israel) and the genealogy at the end of the book makes her an ancestress of David. If the book really was written around the time when Ezra and his party were taking such exception to marriage with foreign women this point can hardly have gone unnoticed, though it is now fashionable to doubt whether this was the reason for the book's publication.

Be that as it may, it is certainly not the *only* point of the story. It is a story that begins sadly, but ends with devotion and patience rewarded.

It is set in the period of the judges, when there was no central government. The only security an individual had was in the strength of his family or tribe. A man therefore had a duty to his poorer relatives, however distant. He was expected to avenge them if they were wronged, to support them if they went bankrupt, and marry the widow of his childless relative so that property could be kept in the family and the family name carried on. This protecting kinsman was callsd the 'redeemer'. A woman, especially, was in a difficult and exposed situation if left alone. She needed a husband, and a family to belong to, and children who would look after her when she became old.

When Naomi, living in a foreign country, is bereaved of all her family she does the natural thing, she goes home. But Ruth, in going with her, is hazarding everything. The 'sensible' thing would have been to stay in Moab and find another husband. But she follows Naomi, because Naomi needs her, and because they share a common grief.

In Israel she is an immigrant. Neither she nor Naomi have any livelihood, and Ruth makes what she can by gleaning. The right of the poor to gleaning was part of Israel's rough and ready social security system (cf. Lev.19.9 f.).

Boaz shows his virtue not merely in appreciating Ruth's devotion to Naomi. He accepts his duty as a kinsman to this immigrant who was not strictly a member of his family, but who had come to count herself as one.

The other kinsman (in ch. 4) is willing to accept the advantages of kinship and take up the option on Naomi's old property, but not its obligations – the upkeep and protection of Ruth. We are not to suppose, however, that to Boaz himself the duty of marrying Ruth was an unwelcome one.

The book's universalism is not confined to the genealogy at the end. Ruth is a proselyte (1.16 f.); she accepts Israel's faith and throws in her lot with the chosen people. The book does not merely argue, it *assumes* that she is entitled to all the benefits of membership, even to the point of becoming ancestress to the Messiah. The Magnificat would be as appropriate in the mouth of Ruth as in that of Mary.

In another respect the book of Ruth is universalistic. The Old Testament often gives the impression that Israel's faith is male-centred and male-dominated. It is a wrong impression, and Ruth is one of the books which helps to correct it. Ruth, the very prototype of the gentile who becomes one of the elect, is a woman. This is an interesting foreshadowing of the prominent part played by women both in the proselytizing movement in later Judaism and in the spread of the Christian gospel.

3. *The work of the Chronicler*
(*I and II Chronicles, Ezra and Nehemiah*)

A good deal has already been said about the Chronicler's writings, but looking at them purely as historical sources. As such they have serious deficiencies. But the Chronicler did not intend to write an historical source hook. He intended to write theology, and he wrote it in the way in which Israel's thinkers customarily wrote theology, i.e., by re-telling the history of his race.

His scope is wide. He begins with the creation and ends with the work of Ezra and Nehemiah. His coverage of the period is very uneven. He gets from Adam to the death of Saul in nine chapters, mostly of genealogy. But he spends twenty-eight chapters on the reigns of David and Solomon. He not only misses out a great deal which the earlier literature includes, he also makes significant additions. Many of these additions concern the temple and its worship, and especially the work of the Levites. Every historical event is explained in accordance with a very rigid theory of reward and punishment, and the Chronicler has no qualms about emending the facts to fit his scheme. The wicked king Manasseh had a long reign, so the Chronicler invents a spurious repentance to account for the fact. The good king Josiah was killed in his youth, so a sin has to be invented (and a very curious sin it is) to explain his death away.

God's control of events is direct and detailed. Men have little to do but trust and pray. Nearly all the Chronicler's battles are won by squads of Levites hurling no more lethal missiles than psalms of praise.

The Chronicler's theology, though he often expresses it in crude or naïve ways, is throughout a theology of faith; of confidence in the divine control of history; of conviction that if men would but trust and praise him everything would be all right. Its expression may amuse or infuriate us, but its content should not be despised.

4. *The Song of Songs*

The title means 'the best song of all'. It is unlikely to have any genuine connection with Solomon. In origin it is almost certainly purely secular. It has been analysed in various ways but is most likely a collection of love songs. It owes its place in the canon and its subsequent popularity in both Jewish and Christian circles to the fact that it was interpreted allegorically. Its imagery, though attractive, is rather alien to our western traditions of romantic literature, though we can see why it appealed so strongly to frustrated mediaeval monks.

5. *Trito-Isaiah (Isaiah 56–66)*

These chapters clearly have much in common with II Isaiah, and worthily continue the tradition of the Isaiah school of prophets. The commonest view is that these oracles do not all come from the same hand, or from quite the same period, but that they are mostly later than II Isaiah and reflect conditions in Palestine after the return.

They betray an interest in the cult that II Isaiah does not display; e.g., 56.1–8 appeals for more care in observing the sabbath. Compare ch. 58, which in addition denounces insincerity in worship.

II Isaiah's universalism is, however, taken up, and 56.3–8 anticipates that eunuchs and foreigners will be acceptable in the Lord's temple. Verse 7 finds an important echo in the New Testament (Matt.21.13) as does 61.1 ff. (Luke 4.18 f.). Chapter 60 preaches a less attractive form of universalism but its themes and phrases have been taken up by an extraordinary variety of writings: vv. 19 f. in Revelation, vv. 21 f. as a keyword in the Jewish 'Sayings of the Fathers', vv. 1 f. in Handel's 'Messiah', and v. 5b in the title of a famous work on economics – Adam Smith's *Wealth of Nations*. These, and some other passages, are as fine as anything in prophecy. See, for instance, Isa.57.14–20 on humility, and 58.3–12 on right religion. The latter is very Amos-like in its tone. Chapter 63.1–6 has also resounded down the years, as the test for the 'Battle Hymn of the Republic'. It is perhaps better appreciated for its sonority than for its sentiments.

6. *The book of Joel*

Joel is a problematical book. It is usually taken to date from the post-exilic period, though the arguments are not entirely conclusive and some eminent scholars prefer an earlier date. It is also difficult to say what *kind* of writing it is, and to specify the setting and purpose for which it was intended.

It appears to consist of prophecies delivered on the occasion of a devastating plague of locusts. The prophet sees the plague as God's judgment and calls for demonstrations of penitence (1.13 f.; 2.12–17). However, he seems to see even more in it than this, for he represents the locusts as God's army, and sees in their attack a foretaste of the day of the Lord (1.6; 2.2–11). He promises salvation (2.20–27), but then, from 2.28 onwards, he reverts to eschatology and the day of judgment.

It has been suggested that a prophecy originally delivered for the particular occasion of a locust plague has been adapted as a liturgical document, i.e. for use in worship on subsequent occasions, and given an eschatological significance, perhaps by the addition of 2.28–3.21. Chapter 2.28–32 is, of course, a famous passage, which the New Testament writers see as fulfilled at Pentecost.

7. The book of Jonah

The book of Jonah is pure fiction. It is perhaps the only book in the Bible which is actually meant to be funny, though it is humorous with a deadly serious purpose. It destroys racism and nationalism and exclusivism by poking fun at it. Its technique is that of the *reductio ad absurdum*. The racist and religious exclusivist is forced by the logic of his own position (and such people are often as strong on their own kind of logic as they are short on humour) to set himself above God. Jonah, in the name of his religion, rejects God's call. And if you grant his religious premises he is doing the logical thing. He does so because he, Jonah, personally disapproves of God's offering of salvation to foreigners. He is the only man in the Bible who *accuses* God of being merciful (4.1 f.). The author is realistic enough to present Jonah as remaining unconvinced to the end.

We cannot be very precise about the date at which the book was written, but the religious background against which it must be placed is only too obvious.

8. Haggai and Zechariah 1–8

The value of these books as historical evidence has been sufficiently dealt with above. Their religious outlook, however, requires further comment.

We see in them very clearly the new, positive attitude which post-exilic prophecy takes towards the cult. To get one's worship right is the first priority; all else will be put right in consequence. This is a fine sentiment, and not to be despised as a superficial concentration on the externals of religion. It does, however, raise acute problems. The builders of our mediaeval cathedrals would have agreed wholeheartedly with Haggai's priorities. Can we, in the age of cost-benefit analysis, do the same? Granted that we ought to worship God in the best possible way, is it an acceptable expression of this aim to erect splendid buildings which strain the economic resources of the religious community?

Even if we concede that Haggai's priorities are right, is he appealing to unworthy motives in suggesting that the rebuilding of the temple will pay off in economic terms (2.18 f.)?

I do not think that the answers to any of these questions are self-evident.

Zechariah 1–8 calls for another comment. Chapters 1–6 consist of a series of visions. We have not space to deal here with the interpretation of these, but their method of putting across the prophetic message is noteworthy. The visions are of fantastic and dreamlike type, and in some of them an angel appears as interpreter. They are not a completely new phenomenon in prophecy. Ezekiel, at least, had already produced something like them, but they are very close to the methods of apocalyptic. A glance at Daniel 8 and 10 will confirm this.

9. *The book of Malachi*

This book comes from another unnamed prophet. 'Malachi' means simply 'my messenger'. It certainly falls within our period, though in spite of its position in the canon it is by no means the last of the Old Testament books to be written.

In common with the most post-exilic prophecy it is very concerned about the cult. The sins it condemns are priestly negligence (1.6–2.9) and the bringing of inadequate tithes and sacrifices (3.8–12, cf. 1.8 and 1.13 f.).

It is also very much on the defensive. It is clear that the community is not prosperous. Earlier prophetic promises of glory, or even comfort, have gone unfulfilled. In 2.17–3.5 the prophet asserts, in the face of doubters, that notwithstanding the delay, the day of judgment and salvation really is near (cf. 4.1–6).

Unique to the prophet is his condemnation of divorce (2.13–16). In the New Testament, 3.1 and 4.5 f. are taken as prophecies of the coming of John the Baptist.

HENRY McKEATING

16 The Seleucids and the Maccabees

This section describes Jewish history from 312 to 63 BC. This was a period when the Palestinian Jews attempted to establish their own independent state and live according to their own religious conscience, and the Jews abroad were forced to work out for themselves how they should live and how they should express their faith in order to bear clear witness in their faith in the alien and often cultured world about them. It is these issues that matter, not the details of the battles of the Maccabees.

The evidence

1. Biblical references

The book of Daniel was written about 164 BC and reflects the struggle against the Seleucids. The stories told about Daniel, however, are set in Babylon in the time of Nebuchadnezzar (605–562 BC). The device of setting stories in an earlier age was sometimes adopted by writers in times of danger or when they had something unpopular to say, though for a different explanation see under *The Book of Daniel* below (pp. 205 f.).

2. Extra-biblical references

The Apocrypha is a selection of writings which did not find a place in the Jewish canon of scripture. Of the writings included in the Apocrypha, the most important is I Maccabees, which gives a reliable and factual history of the period. II Maccabees is history interpreted from a particular religious standpoint and is much less reliable.

The coming of the Seleucid rulers

The Seleucids take their name from Seleucus, one of the officers of Alexander the Great. In 312 BC, Seleucus established himself as ruler over the eastern part of Alexander's empire; in 301 BC he gained most of what is now Turkey, and for better control of his new empire founded Antioch in Syria as his capital, naming it after his father, and Seleucia as its port (cf. Acts 11.19; 13.4). Seleucus' rival, Ptolemy, who on Alexander's death had seized Egypt, had meanwhile annexed Palestine, thus starting the struggle between 'the kings of the north' and 'the kings of the south', described in Daniel 11. For nearly a century Palestine was the battleground of these opposing forces and was frequently conquered and reconquered. The struggle ended in 198 BC when the Seleucid Antiochus III took all Palestine and sealed a treaty by betrothing his daughter Cleopatra to Ptolemy V (Dan.11.15–17).

The Greek way of life: 'Hellenization'

Palestine now belonged to the Seleucids, but Ptolemaic rule had left its legacy to the Jews. There had been Jews in Egypt since Jeremiah's day (Jer.43.5 ff.), and in 312 BC, Ptolemy I had settled captives from Jerusalem, Judaea and Samaria in Alexandria, where they were greatly affected by the Greek way of life. According to the Letter of Aristeas, a document probably written by a Hellenistic Jew c.150–100 BC, Ptolemy II had the Hebrew Scriptures translated into Greek at Alexandria for the benefit of the new library; in fact, the translation was probably made for the benefit of the new Greek-speaking Jews of the city. Here, too, the philosopher Aristobulus (second century BC), the author of the Wisdom of Solomon (first century BC), and the Jewish philosopher Philo (first century AD) all made different attempts to show that Greek and Jewish ways of thought could be used to illuminate each other.

Judaea itself was also affected by the Hellenistic way of life, which was founded on the Greek *polis* (city), with its urban civilization and its emphasis on the training of young men in athletic and literary prowess. The Jews were surrounded by the Hellenistic cities of Egypt, of Nabataea, Transjordan, Phoenicia and Philistia, and there were Greek colonies at Acre (called Ptolemais), Bethshan (called Scythopolis), and Samaria (later called Sebaste). There was a Greek colony in southern Judaea itself, at Marisa. From official Egyptian correspondence we hear of one Tobiah (probably descended from Tobiah the Ammonite of Nehemiah's day, Neh.2.10) in charge of an Egyptian military colony in Transjordan. His son Joseph, nephew of the high priest Onias II, succeeded in becoming the official Egyptian tax-collector in Palestine. Joseph's son Hyrcanus succeeded to the business by bribing Ptolemy, though he thereby alienated his father and the high priest Simon II, and had to retire to the family estates in Transjordan. It was leading families such as these who by their contact with the ruling classes of Judaea's neighbours mediated Hellenism to the Jews, and it was a high priest, Jason, who introduced the gymnasium and the Greek games to Jerusalem (II Macc.4.12 ff.).

However, reaction to this trend came early, as we can see from works like Tobit and Ecclesiasticus (see below, pp. 207 f.), which preached a distinctive Jewish piety. But the Seleucids in 198 BC took over a country which was neither unaware of nor altogether hostile to the possibilities afforded by Hellenism. Nor was Antiochus III hostile to the Jews and their religion; when he annexed Judaea he promised to restore the damaged Jerusalem, provide materials for temple sacrifices, allow self-government, and make some generous tax concessions. We are told that he used Jews (whom he called 'guardians of our interests' and allowed to keep their own laws) as occupying troops holding Lydia and Phrygia for him.

Antiochus III died in 187 BC, leaving Seleucus IV to mend the finances shattered by Antiochus's unsuccessful attempts at empire-building in Asia Minor and Greece and by the fines imposed by the Romans (cf. Dan.11.18). One expedient was the tax-gathering mission of Heliodorus and his attempt to raid the temple treasury at Jerusalem (II Macc.3; Dan.11.20). Meanwhile Rome had supported the Ptolemies against the Seleucids, playing one off against the other; Armenia and Parthia were breaking away from the Seleucid empire; and in 175 BC the throne was seized by Antiochus, the son of Antiochus III. Antiochus had learned Western ways from his early exile as a hostage in Rome and from his freedom in Athens where, though a stranger, he had actually been elected chief magistrate; and on reaching the Syrian throne his policy was to unify Greek and oriental in one empire and one culture. Thus he encouraged immigration from Hellenistic cities to cities of his own empire; he conferred the Greek title and honour of 'city' on oriental towns such as Babylon and Hamath; and he tried to forge a common religious bond for his empire by equating the Greek Zeus with the Syrian Baal-Hadad and eventually by claiming that he as king would not bother Greeks – Alexander had made similar claims – but was blasphemy to Jews, and to them this policy was the more outrageous because associated with the king's support of ungodly and unlawful high priests.

In 175 BC Jason (the name is a Greek form of the Hebrew Joshua), brother of the legitimate high priest Onias III, offered Antiochus 440 talents for the high priesthood, and 150 more for the right 'to establish a gymnasium and a body of youth for it, and to enrol the men of Jerusalem as citizens of Antioch' (II Macc.4.9). Perhaps, ambition apart, Jason was promoting a policy of integrating the Jews into the Hellenistic empire of Antiochus on the same terms as 'the Gentiles round about us' (I Macc.1.11) and of making Jerusalem a privileged Hellenistic city of Antiochus' empire. From Antiochus' viewpoint, a Hellenized Jerusalem, integrated into his empire, was an important buffer state against Egypt and Antiochus visited Jerusalem with this in mind, was magnificently received, and perhaps reassured (II Macc.4.21 f.).

In 171 BC, however, Menelaus outbid Jason for the high priest's office, and took his place. He did not belong to the legitimate high priestly family, and so to secure his position he had the legitimate high priest Onias III, who was in exile near Antioch, murdered (Dan.9.26; II Macc.4.23 ff.). In 169 BC, Antiochus IV campaigned in Egypt; on his return Menelaus let him plunder the temple (I Macc.1.20 ff.; Dan.11.25 ff.). The next year Jason attacked Jerusalem in an attempt to remove Menelaus, and Antiochus, ejected from Egypt by the Romans ('the ships of Kittim', Dan.11.30), supposing that Judaea was in revolt, took Jerusalem, profaning temple and fortress

(Dan.11.30 f.), slaughtering large numbers of people, and leaving a governor, 'Philip, by birth a Phrygian and in character more barbarous than the man who appointed him' (II Macc.5.22). Then Apollonius was sent (167 BC), who sacked Jerusalem, pulled down its walls, and established a garrison (I Macc.1.29–40; II Macc.5.24–26), which in spite of all attempts, military and diplomatic, to oust it remained there till 142 BC (I Macc.14.36).

Antiochus now decreed (I Macc.1.44 ff.) that 'all should be one people, and that each should give up his customs', and he wrote to the Jews directing them, on pain of death,

to follow customs strange to the land, to forbid burnt offerings and sacrifices and drink offerings in the sanctuary, to profane sabbaths and feasts, to defile the sanctuary and the priests, to build altars and sacred precincts and shrines for idols, to sacrifice swine and unclean animals, and to leave their sons uncircumcised.

II Macc.6.1 f. says that 'the king sent an Athenian senator to compel the Jews to forsake the laws of their fathers and cease to live by the laws of God, and also to pollute the temple in Jerusalem and call it the temple of the Olympian Zeus'. In December 167 BC the temple was desecrated by the erection of a 'desolating sacrilege upon the altar of burnt offering' (I Macc.1.54; Dan.11.31 ff.) – probably the erection of a heathen altar is meant. The miseries that some Jews suffered out of loyalty to the Law are vividly described in I Macc.1 and II Macc.6.7 ff. It seems that in the interests of peace and unity in his empire, Antiochus was trying to abolish Jewish nationalism. He probably underestimated Jewish feeling, supposing that their attitude to religion was much the same as that of the Greeks, and over-estimated

Jewish support for his attempt to introduce Hellenistic culture, perhaps here being misled by Menelaus.

Jewish resistance to Hellenization

It is important to realize that there were different reactions among the Jews to Hellenization. Not all opposed it. There were *Hellenists* even among the priests (II Macc.4.13 ff.), who supported Antiochus from policy or perhaps from weak-mindedness. The high priests Jason, Menelaus, and Alcimus were men of the world, ready to compromise. Secondly, there were the *Hasidim*, 'the pious', who in contrast to those who 'abandoned the holy covenant' for a covenant with the Gentiles were 'mighty warriors of Israel' and 'chose to die rather than profane the holy covenant' (I Macc.1.63). The *Hasidim* at first took to passive resistance, but many of them joined the more militant Maccabees until religious liberty was regained. From the *Hasidim* developed in different directions the *Pharisees*, who fostered a lay spirituality for the whole nation, thus ensuring Israel's continuity after the destruction of Jerusalem by the Romans in AD, and the *Essenes* and the related *Qumran community*, who broke away from the official orthodoxy of the temple and priesthood in the belief that the future lay with the elect, separated from the pollutions of the world.

The fiercest reaction to Antiochus' policy came from Mattathias of Modein and his sons and their followers, known as the *Maccabees* after the third son Judas, who soon took the lead and acquired the nick-name 'Maccabee' from a Hebrew word meaning 'hammer'. When in 166 BC the people of Modein, twenty miles north-west of Jerusalem, were required to offer pagan sacrifices, Mattathias killed a Jew who was prepared to do this, killed the king's officer, tore down the altar, and fled to the hills with his sons and 'many who were seeking righteousness and justice'. A group of them were attacked on the sabbath and died rather than break the law by defending themselves; but it was then decided that self-defence on the sabbath was allowable in the circumstances. More people, including some of the *Hasidim*, joined the Maccabees, who organized an army, destroyed altars, forcibly circumcised babies, and campaigned against Hellenizing Jews and persecuting Gentiles alike (I Macc.2.1–48).

Mattathias soon died, and Judas took his place. The first aim was the regaining of freedom to obey the Jewish law, and the recovery and purification of the temple. This was achieved by two seasons' fighting in the years 166 and 165 BC (I Macc.3.10–4.35). Exactly three years after pagan sacrifice had first been offered on the old altar, a new altar was dedicated and a new annual Feast of Dedication appointed (December 164 BC). The Maccabees fortified the temple area and garrisoned it, and did the same for the town of Bethzur to the south (I Macc.4.36–61).

In 163 BC Judas campaigned to help Jews resident among the surrounding Gentiles (I Macc.5). The Syrians counter-attacked successfully, but the death of Antiochus forced the Syrians to offer terms to the Jews, allowing them to 'live by their laws as they did before' (I Macc.6.59). The death of Menelaus, and the accession to the high priesthood of Alcimus (a Greek form of the Hebrew Eliakim), who was at least a member of the priestly house of Aaron, meant victory to people like the *Hasidim*. The Maccabees, however, opposed the Hellenizing Alcimus, and defeated the Syrian army sent to support him at Adasa on March 17, 160 BC; the day was thereafter kept as a festival (I Macc.7; II Macc.15). II Maccabees ends with this victory, clearly regarding it as the climax of the war. But two months later the Syrians killed Judas in battle and re-occupied Judaea (I Macc.9). The Maccabees fled to the wilderness to regroup under Jonathan, Judas' youngest brother. In 159 BC Alcimus died, leaving the high priesthood vacant, and the Syrians departed. 'The land of Judah had rest for two years' (I Macc.9.57).

It was a peace of exhaustion which satisfied no one. The Maccabees now wanted nothing less than political freedom; and the *Hasidim*, who would have been happy with religious freedom, had been disillusioned when Alcimus began his high priesthood by murdering sixty of their number (I Macc.7.12 ff.). This disillusionment may have led to the withdrawal about this time of a group of *Hasidim* to settle in a closed community at Qumran. The Hellenists did not feel secure while the Maccabees were free to harry them from the wilderness. They asked the Syrian general Bacchides to capture Jonathan (157 BC), but Bacchides was beaten and made a final peace with Jonathan, who settled at Michmash, a stronghold north-east of Jerusalem (I Macc.9.73), and like the judges of old 'began to judge the people, and he destroyed the ungodly out of Israel'. The Maccabees had won.

Independence

From now until the arrival of the Romans in 63 BC, Judaea was virtually independent. The Seleucid empire was weakening as to the east the Parthians became more powerful and at home rivals contended for the throne. In 142

BC 'the yoke of the Gentiles was removed from Israel, and the people began to write in their documents and contracts, "In the first year of Simon the great high priest and commander and leader of the Jews"' (I Macc.13.41 f.). It was seen as the first year of a new era.

In 134 BC Simon and his sons Judas and Mattathias were killed near Jericho by Simon's ambitious son-in-law Ptolemy. However, Simon's son John, in command of the army near Gezer, heard the news in time to reach Jerusalem before Ptolemy, and was welcomed as high priest and ruler (I Macc.16.11–22). The Seleucid king successfully attacked Jerusalem, but in 128 BC was killed by the Parthians, and thereafter the internal struggles of the Seleucid empire preserved the Jews from further molestation.

It was the people in Jerusalem, not the king in Antioch, who made John Hyrcanus ruler and high priest: but the precedent for such an appointment lay in the use the Seleucid rulers had made of the high-priestly office, and it is hardly surprising that Hyrcanus and his successors ruled like Seleucids. Hyrcanus used mercenary troops to capture territory in southern Judaea, Moab and Samaria; he destroyed the Samaritan temple on Mount Gerizim and forcibly circumcised the Idumaeans into the Jewish faith. Naturally the Pharisees – descendants of the *Hasidim* – objected to his political rather than his spiritual aims, and to the combination of priestly and civil rule in one person (particularly in one of neither Davidic nor Aaronic descent). Hyrcanus therefore supported the Sadducean party.

In 104-103 BC Aristobulus I ruled briefly as high priest, starving his mother to death, killing his brother Antigonus, and adding Galilee and Ituraea to the Jewish state. In 103 BC his widow made his brother Alexander Jannaeus king and high priest, and married him. (Jannaeus was probably the first of his family to take the official title of 'king'.) He seized parts of Transjordan and Samaria, deliberately judaizing all the conquered Hellenistic cities. But his behaviour as high priest alienated the Pharisees; civil war broke out which Jannaeus finally won in spite of the entry of Demetrius III of Syria on the Parisees' side. Jannaeus killed 6000 rebels, and strengthened his position by building the forts of Alexandrium, Machaerus and Masada. Meanwhile the Nabataeans of Petra under Aretas were becoming powerful; they defeated Jannaeus near Lydda, forcing him to come to terms with them. Their main interest was in the trade route across southern Judaea.

In 76 BC, Jannaeus' widow Alexandra Salome inherited the throne. Following Jannaeus' advice to make peace with the Pharisees, she appointed her son Hyrcanus II as high priest. His brother Aristobulus led the Sadducees, who had military control of the land. When Salome died in 67 BC, Aristobulus defeated Hyrcanus and became king and high priest. Hyrcanus gained the not entirely disinterested support of Antipater of Idumaea and Aretas of Nabataea, defeated Aristobulus and besieged him in Jerusalem. At this point the Roman general Pompey the Great, fresh from his conquest of Pontus and Armenia, arrived in Syria. Pompey took Jerusalem and removed Aristobulus to Rome, leaving Hyrcanus as high priest. It was Antipater, however, who gained most, for the Romans at first relied on him for stable government and later gave him the official title of procurator of Judaea. This family, under the Romans, ruled Palestine; Antipater's son was Herod the Great, and among his grandsons was Herod Antipas, tetrach of Galilee in the time of Jesus. Once again, religious and political authority had become separated; and it is noticeable that even in the independent Jewish state the combination of religious and political authority in one man was not always popular. Church and State have always been uneasy partners; this Jewish attempt to combine the two is of abiding interest.

The literature

The issues and events outlined above are all reflected in the literature of the time, especially in the book of Daniel and in the Apocrypha.

1. *The book of Daniel*

This was written about 164 BC at the height of the Maccabaean struggle. Chapter 11 describes the history of the Seleucids up to Antiochus IV, the details of whose death are wrongly given. The author was probably writing just before Antiochus died; description of events changes to prediction at this point. But why did the author use the figure of Daniel, a wise man of old (see Ezek.14.14,20; 28.3), and set the narrative in the time of Nebuchadnezzar (605–562 BC)? Why did he later, from ch. 8, pretend to be Daniel himself? A righteous figure Daniel is known as far back as the fourteenth century BC. It is often said that this device of 'pseudonymity' was used for safety in difficult times, and that while the Jews would recognize Antiochus in the figure of Nebuchadnezzar, the Seleucid officials would not. But this motive is unconvincing; Daniel was hardly 'published' like a modern work – it was meant only for the eyes of the faithful few – and even if it were, why should not the author simply remain anonymous ? The answer is that Daniel belongs to 'apocalyptic' literature. Apocalyptic books claim to be revelations (*apokalupto* is Greek for 'I reveal') of divine secrets made to famous figures of the past – such as Enoch, Abraham, Ezra, and Daniel – who subsequently wrote down the revelation in secret books (see II Esdras 14). Thus the book is ascribed to Daniel because it belonged to the apocalyptic tradition which was traced back to Daniel, in much the same way as wisdom literature was ascribed to Solomon and psalms to David. Apocalyptic writers believed that in view of the approaching end, the revelations made must now at last be divulged to the faithful. Divulged, they describe past, present and near future events in enigmatic and symbolic terms (cf. Mark 13.14. 'let him that readeth understand'). Such terms, however, were not designed to conceal the message from foreign eyes (though they would have that effect), but to convey the mystery of God's dealings. The symbolism had its roots in Old Testament tradition and ancient Near Eastern mythology. The message of these writers is that in spite of present troubles men must remain faithful, for God's purpose will soon triumph. These books were clearly relevant to the Jews under their Seleucid and Roman masters; many survive, others are lost, and some previously unknown examples have appeared among the literature found at Qumran.

The writer of Daniel, then, wrote with a message for the Maccabaean age. Thus ch. 1 encourages the Jews to keep their food laws, showing Daniel and his friends on a restricted diet to be wiser than the well-fed youths of the king's court;

Chapter 2 shows Nebuchadnezzar's dream of a mountain boulder crushing an image of gold, silver, brass, iron and clay, which Daniel interprets to mean that the kingdom of God will suddenly crush the kingdoms of the Ptolemies and Seleucids and their predecessors;

Chapter 3, telling the story of Shadrach, Meshach, Abednego and the fiery furnace, ridicules image-worship and shows the ultimate triumph of those tortured for their faith;

Chapter 4, in which Nebuchadnezzar is reduced to eating grass like an ox, reminds the Jews that even men like Antiochus are subject to the rule of God, for 'those who walk in pride he is able to abase' (v. 37);

Chapter 5 shows the doom of Belshazzar and his empire for its idolatry (v. 23), a message of hope to Jews suffering Antiochus' idolatry;

Chapter 6 praises Daniel's obedience to the Law in defiance of an edict reminiscent of Antiochus' edict; Daniel's deliverance and his accusers' fate in the lions' jaws conveyed an obvious message;

Chapter 7 is a vision showing how the four beasts, symbolizing the kingdoms of the world (the 'little horn' of the fourth beast being Antiochus' kingdom), lose their authority, while the 'son of man', symbolizing, in contrast to the beasts, the people of Israel (for its heavenly representatives), is invested with an eternal kingdom;

Chapter 8 describes Daniel's vision of the ram (the Persian empire), the goat (Alexander the Great), from whose four horns (the empires which followed Alexander's death) came a little horn (Antiochus IV), 'a king of fierce countenance' who will do God's people great harm but will be destroyed (vv. 23–25);

Chapter 9 contains a long national 'general confession' put into Daniel's mouth, followed by Gabriel's reassurance that in these final years the persecuting prince will suffer the wrath of

God;

Chapters 10–12 contain Daniel's last vision, which describes the Seleucid empire (11.2–20) and especially Antiochus' career and persecution of the Jews (11.21–40), predicts his death (11.41–45), and encourages the *Hasidim* who have suffered for their faith by promising deliverance for God's people and a resurrection to shame or glory for 'many of them that sleep' (probably those who have died on either side in the recent struggles), 'the wise' and 'they that turn many to righteousness' (? the *Hasidim*) being especially singled out for glory. The beginning and end of the vision (10.1–11.1; 12.5–13) set these events in the context of a heavenly war between the kingdom of God and the powers of evil, represented by the guardian angels of different countries (cf. 10.13).

It can now be seen that Daniel, ridiculing idolatry, encouraging faithfulness, promising the end of worldly empires, was supremely relevant to its time (see I Macc.2.60, where Mattathias himself quotes Daniel as an example to be followed). Daniel is a book produced out of the struggle between two rival ways of life, one seeking to impose itself on the other in order to destroy the independent spirit of a small nation. Such a situation has its parallels today; what sort of modern parallels are there to the book of Daniel ?

2. The Apocrypha

Apocrypha means 'hidden away', and these books were so named because they were thought either too profound or not orthodox enough for the general reader. The Apocrypha contains those books included in the Greek translation of the Jewish Bible made at Alexandria but not found in the Hebrew Bible. The more interesting and important passages are asterisked. All the books express in their different ways Jewish reactions to the issues and events of these centuries.

Of immediate importance as historical records are *I and II Maccabees*. *I Maccabees*, originally written in Hebrew in Hyrcanus' time (134–104 BC), uses eye-witness accounts and official documents to give a reliable and factual history sympathizing with the Maccabees rather than the *Hasidim*. The author describes the sufferings of persecution or the glory of battle in simple, factual sentences; but the result is vivid and moving. Read, e.g., 1.41–64,* 6.28–47. *II Maccabees*, summarizing the late second-century BC work of Jason of Cyrene, is Greek both in language and approach. (Read 2.19–32,* the original introduction.) II Maccabees sympathizes with the *Hasidim* against the Maccabees, emphasizing martyrdom and the resurrection hope (see ch.7*), sabbath-keeping, and festivals of Dedication (1.18 f.; 10.1 ff.) and Nicanor's Day (15.36). II Maccabees is interested in the lessons to be learned from history rather than in the events themselves; L.H. Brockington describes the work as 'caricature with a great deal of truth in it'.

Ecclesiasticus is teaching; Ben Sira (*c*. 180 BC) instructs his pupils how to live according to the Law, which he equates with wisdom. Ben Sira's attitude is well seen in 37.16–39.11*, where of all wise men he that 'meditateth in the law of the Most High' is the wisest. His shining example was the high priest Simon II (see ch. 50). *Judith* is a story, told to encourage Jews to resist invaders who threaten to profane the sanctuary (4.12) – perhaps Holofernes was originally the Persian Orofernes, a general of Artaxerxes III (358–338 BC). But the emphasis on prayer, sabbath-keeping, festivals, circumcision, ceremonial cleanliness even in time of war would all have been relevant to the Maccabees. From a much later period, the end of the first century AD, comes *Baruch*, which probably reflects the Jewish War of AD 66–70 (see 4.5–5.9), and II *Esdras*, of which chs. 3–14 are an apocalypse apparently relating to 586 BC, but in fact dealing with the events of the first century BC. The legend of ch. 14 tries to put apocalyptic tradition on a par with the Law as Scripture, assigning it to secret traditions given by God to Moses on Mount Sinai. This may reflect the problem that arose after the destruction of Jerusalem of deciding which books were to be received as true guardians of Jewish tradition and belief.

These books were most probably written in Palestine; but some apocryphal books show the reaction of Jews abroad to Hellenistic and other influences around them. The story of *Tobit* underlined for such Jews the importance of traditional practices such as giving alms, paying tithes and dues, keeping the feasts, supporting widows and orphans, refraining from Gentile foods, washing before eating, marrying within one's kin, and generally keeping the Mosaic law. 'The Letter of Jeremiah' (*Baruch* 6) is an attack on idol-worship by a fourth or third century Babylonian Jew – an attack repeated more humorously by *Bel and the Dragon**, one of

the Greek Bible's additions to the book of Daniel. Other additions are *Susanna**, perhaps just a didactic story from the first century BC; the *Prayer of Azariah*, which, mentioning the loss of prince, prophet, leader and sacrifice, may be from Maccabaean times; the *Song of the Three Young Men*, perhaps an old hymn, with no intrinsic relevance to the fate of the three young men. The *Book of Esther*, too, received additions when it was translated into Greek in the first century BC. Clearly, Alexandria in Egypt, where the Greek Bible was translated, was the scene of much Jewish literary activity.

The greatest example of Jewish writing from Alexandria is the *Wisdom of Solomon*. Addressed to rulers who are going astray (highly placed Jews affected by Hellenism?) the book combines both Greek and Jewish beliefs (e.g., the immortality of the soul and the resurrection of the body, 3.1,7*), and describes the Jewish figure of 'wisdom', God's helper at creation and the revealer of God's mysteries (cf. Prov.8), in terms of the Greek *pneuma* (divine spirit) or *logos* (word or thought linking the divine being and the world; see 7.21 ff.*; 9.1,17; 16.12; 18.15 f.). The book is in part an attack on the attitudes of Ecclesiastes (see, e.g., Wisd.2), a book also attributed to Solomon (Eccles.1.1).

J.R. BARTLETT

FOR FURTHER READING

A The authority of the Bible

Barr, James, *The Bible in the Modern World,* SCM Press 1973

Dodd, C.H., *The Authority of the Bible*, Fontana Books 1960

Grollenberg, Lucas, *A Bible for our Time*, SCM Press 1979

Nineham, D.E., *The Use and Abuse of the Bible*, SPCK 1978

B Some reference books

Black, M., and Rowley, H.H., eds. *Peake's Commentary on the Bible*, Nelson 1962

Brown, Raymond, Fitzmyer, Joseph and Murphy, Roland E., eds., *The Jerome Biblical Commentary*, Geoffrey Chapman 1969

Hastings, J., ed., *Dictionary of the Bible*, revised by F.C. Grant and H.H. Rowley, T. & T. Clark 1963

The Interpreter's Dictionary of the Bible, four volumes, Abingdon Press 1962

Laymon, Charles M., ed., *The Interpreter's One-Volume Commentary on the Bible*, Collins 1973

May, H.G., *Oxford Bible Atlas*, Oxford University Press 1974

Richardson, Alan, ed., *A Theological Wordbook of the Bible*, SCM Press 1950

C On the Bible as a whole

Grollenberg, Lucas, *Rediscovering the Bible*, SCM Press 1978

Hayes, John H., *Introduction to the Bible*, SPCK 1971

Sandmel, Samuel, *The Enjoyment of Scripture*, Oxford University Press 1972

D The Old Testament: general

Anderson, B.W., *The Living World of the Old Testament*, Longmans 1969

Anderson, G.W., *The History and Religion of Israel*, Oxford University Press 1966

Beyerlin, Walter, ed., *Near Eastern Religious Texts relating to the Old Testament*, SCM Press 1978

Bright, John, *A History of Israel*, SCM Press 1970

Dale, Alan T., *Winding Quest*, Oxford University Press 1972

Herrmann, S., *A History of Israel in Old Testament Times*, SCM Press 1975

Kenyon, Kathleen M., *Archaeology in the Holy Land*, Benn 1979

Magnusson, Magnus, *BC: The Archaeology of the Bible Lands*, The Bodley Head/BBC 1977

Miller, J. Maxwell, *The Old Testament and the Historian*, SPCK 1976

Noth, Martin, *The History of Israel*, A. & C. Black 1960

Noth, Martin, *The Old Testament World*, A. & C. Black 1966

Smith, George Adam, *The Historical Geography of the Holy Land*, Fontana Books 1966

Soggin, J.A., *Introduction to the Old Testament*, SCM Press 1976

Thomas, D. Winton, ed., *Archaeology and Old Testament Study*, Oxford University Press 1967

Vaux, R. de, *Ancient Israel*, Darton, Longman and Todd 1961

For Further Reading

Wiseman, D.J., ed., *Peoples of Old Testament Times*, Oxford University Press 1973

E From the patriarchs to the exile

Clements, R.E., *God and Temple*, Blackwell 1965

Heaton, E.W., *The Hebrew Kingdoms*, Oxford University Press 1968

Heaton, E.W., *Solomon's New Men*, Thames & Hudson 1974

Herrmann, S., *Israel in Egypt*, SCM Press 1973

Mayes, A.D.H., *Israel in the Period of the Judges*, SCM Press 1974

Rad, G. von, *Old Testament Theology*, Vol.1, SCM Press 1975

Vaux, R. de, *The Early History of Israel*, two volumes, Darton, Longman and Todd 1978

F Prophecy, worship and wisdom in Israel

Carroll, R.P., *When Prophecy Failed*, SCM Press 1979

Clements, R.E., *Prophecy and Tradition*, Blackwell 1975

Fohrer, Georg, *History of Israelite Religion*, SPCK 1973

Heaton, E.W., *The Old Testament Prophets*, Darton, Longman and Todd 1977

Lindblom, J., *Prophecy in Ancient Israel*, Blackwell 1962

McKane, W., *Proverbs: a New Approach*, SCM Press 1970

Rad, G. von, *The Message of the Prophets*, SCM Press 1968

Rad, G. von, *Wisdom in Israel*, SCM Press 1972

Zimmerli, W., *The Law and the Prophets*, Blackwell 1965

G The exile and after

Ackroyd, P.R., *Exile and Restoration*, SCM Press 1968

Ackroyd, P.R., *Israel under Babylon and Persia*, Oxford University Press 1970

Bruce, F.F., *Israel and the Nations*, Paternoster Press 1963

Coggins, R.J., *Samaritans and Jews*, Blackwell 1975

Hengel, Martin, *Jews, Greeks and Barbarians*, SCM Press 1980

Hengel, Martin, *Victory over Violence*, SPCK 1973

Russell, D.S., *Apocalyptic Ancient and Modern*, SCM Press 1978

Russell, D.S., *Between the Testaments*, SCM Press 1964

Russell, D.S., *The Jews from Alexander to Herod*, Oxford University Press 1967

INDEX OF BIBLICAL REFERENCES

OLD TESTAMENT

Genesis
1.2–4	43, 54, 60, 61 f., 82
1–11	49, 60 ff., 71
1.6–8	181
1.14–19	55, 62
1.26 ff.	55, 62, 65
2.2	55, 60, 62, 138
2.4 ff.	43, 47, 62, 66
2.10	148
2.18	47
3	47, 50, 60, 63, 66
4	47, 63, 64
5	64
6	64, 65
6–8	60
6.18	68
8.20 f.	55
9.1 ff.	54, 55, 65, 66, 73
10	66
10.9	160
11	47, 63
11.7	62
11.10 ff.	54, 66
11.31	31, 71
12	47, 48, 71
12–50	47, 69, 70, 71
12.6 f.	73
12.10 ff.	48, 69, 71
13	49
13.3 ff.	48
13.10 ff.	34, 71
13.18	46, 70
14.5 ff.	32, 69
14.18–20	134
14.22	70, 74
15	65, 81
15.3	69
15.4–7	71, 72
15.13 ff.	73
16.7 ff.	73
17.1 ff.	55, 71, 72, 73

18.1 ff.	46, 49, 73
18.11 ff.	72
18.18	71
19.1 ff.	73
20	69, 71
20.3	50
21.13 ff.	73
22	72, 141
22.5 ff.	73
24	48
25.8 ff.	54, 55
25.19–33	68
25.21 ff.	48, 70
25.26	71
26	48, 68, 71
26.1–11	69, 71
26.4	72
27.1 ff.	48, 68
27.32 f.	70, 71
28	49, 71, 72
28.2	32
28.10 ff.	48, 50, 73
28.19–21	70
29 ff.	48
31.13	74
31.19 ff.	69
31.38 ff.	38, 65, 70, 74
32.4 ff.	73
32.24 ff.	70, 73
32.32	33
33.18–20	70
35.2,4	50
35.7	74
35.11 f.	71
36.1–30	54, 69
37	43, 46, 49, 54, 68, 70, 71
38	49
38.15	68
39–50	68, 70
45.5	72
48.15 f.	71
48.20	49
49.8 ff.	46

49.24	74
49.29 ff.	55
50	72

Exodus
1.11	77, 78
2 ff.	50
2.10 ff.	77, 78
3	49, 50, 79
3.6,7,16, 17	78
3.12 ff.	79
4	78
6	54
6.2 f.	78
7–10	50, 76
12	55, 137
12.11	81
12.13	76
12.21–27	81
13.21	79
14.19 ff.	79, 80
15	80, 81
15.25	151
16–17	76
17.1–7	151
18.10 ff.	79
19–20	80, 81
20.1	72
20.2	80, 82
20.22–23.33	76
21–23	37, 91
21.1–11	83, 119
22.29 f.	92
23.14 ff.	76, 81, 92
24.3 f.	140
24.4–8	82
24.10–18	81
24.16	56
25–30	55
29.44 ff.	56
32.21	50
32.32	183

33	79
34	81.82
34.18	81
34.22–24	76
34.27	82
35–46	55
40.34	56

Leviticus

1–16	55
6.1–7	193
8	55
16	56
16.20–22	141
16.22	37
17.11–14	65
17.26	55, 76
18	56
19	192
19.9 f.	194
23	76
23.34	61
23.42 f.	81
25.23	38
25.29–34	126

Numbers

1	76
1–9	56
10.35	79, 94, 148
11.25 ff.	50
12.1–8	76
12.7 f.	50
14	48
15.22–31	147
20.1 ff.	151,178
21.20 ff.	33
21.25	38
22–24	116
22.5	31
26	76
34.11	34
35.19,24	37

Deuteronomy

1–4	52
4.15 ff.	83
4.32 ff.	53
5–26	51, 52
5.6 ff.	72, 80, 82
6.4	53

6.6–9	175
6.11	36
6.20 ff.	53, 80
7–9	53
11.14	36
11.18–20	175
12	53
12–26	52, 76
12.23	65
14	76
15–21	53
16.1,3	81
16.13	61, 81
18.9–22	76, 117
22.8	16
22.10	38
23.4	31
23.9 ff.	53
26.5–10	45, 77
27	52, 142
28	51, 52, 142
29–34	52
31.9 ff.	52, 93, 94
32.51	181
34.1 ff.	33, 77

Joshua

1–9	86, 88
2.6	39
3 f.	141
5.11	141
6	141
6–8	88
6.17–21	94
8	78
9	87
10	86, 88
10.31 ff.	78, 86, 88
11	78, 86, 88
11.5,7	34
13–21	86
13.9	33
15.32	38
20.8	33
24	89 f., 141
24.2 ff.	37, 77, 89
24.16–18	90
24.19–22	83
24.30	88

Judges

1	44, 52, 86, 87, 88
2.6–3.6	86
3	90
5	93
5.19,21	35
6–8	90
7.1	34, 35
7.22	94
8.18	34
8.29 f.	87
9	87
9.45	32
9.46	39, 87
10.1–5	93
11–12	90
11.12 ff.	33
12.8–15	93
13 ff.	36, 90
19.1 ff.	35
20.31 f.	35
21.19	35, 38, 87

Ruth

1.16 f.	194
4	194
4.1	38

I Samuel

1	35
1–2	142
3.14	143
4–6	143
4.1–10	97
4.4,6–8	94
6	143
7.2	148
7.7–14	97
8 ff.	52, 97
9.1–10.25	97
9.13 ff.	38, 116
10.5–13	117
10.11 f.	160
10.17–24, 27	97
11.1–15	97
13	97, 98
14	98
14.31 ff.	36, 98
15.10–35	98

16.1–13	116
16.14	98
17	36
18.3	65
18.6–9	98
19.20–24	117, 160
20 ff.	35, 98
22.2	99
22.5	116
23–31	99
24	116
25	99
31.10	100

II Samuel

1–2	35
1.2	116
1.10–14	116
2	99
4.7	34
5	99, 100
6	100, 148
7	100, 103, 117, 118, 123
8.1	99
8.16–18	156
8.17	157
8.18	102
9–20	104
10.15–19	99
11	102
12.1–15	116, 118
12.26–31	99
14.17	102
15–20	102, 156
15.2	38
16.5–8	102
16.23	157
17	157
18.6 ff.	33
18.23	34
20.23–25	156
20.25	157
21.1	146

I Kings

1,2	104
2	103
2.26 f.	127
3	104
4.1–7	157
4.5	156
4.7–19,22	35 f., 103
4.29 ff.	39,104
5.13–18	103
6.1	78
7.1–12	39
7.13 ff.	104
8.13	128
9.10 ff.	103
9.26	34, 39
10.1–10	104
10.2,13, 26 ff.	103
11	103
12.1–20	107
13.1–10	118
14.25 f.	108
15.18–21	108
18.20–30	117
19.5	36
20	108
20.11	160
20.34	39
21.3	38
22	108
22.5–28	126
22.39	106

II Kings

1.1	106
3.4 ff.	38, 106
4.10	39
5–7	108
8.26	110
8.28 f.	108
9–10	109, 121
10.18–27	109
10.32 f.	108
11.1–3	110
11.4–20	110
12.4–16	157
12.17 f.	108, 110
13	108
14.25,28	108, 110
15	111
15.37	108
16.5 ff.	108,111
16.10 ff.	112
16.29 ff.	108

16.31	109
17	125
17.4 ff.	111
17.6	31
18.4	52, 112
18.7	112
18.11	31
18.13–16	112
18.18	157
18.22	52
18.31	36
20.20	106
21	109, 112
22–23	43, 113
22.3 ff.	157
23.8	36
23.15–18	118
23.25	112
23.29 ff.	35
23.30–35	113
24.1	113
24.14,16	174
25	114, 172

I Chronicles

10–29	96
15–16	143
20	143
27.32–34	156

II Chronicles

1–9	96
3.1	116
10–36	106
26.6–15	110
36.11–21	176

Ezra

1–6	186, 189
1.1–5	189
4.7–23	191
6.2	187
7–10	186
7.7	190
8.21–23	191
9–10	191

Nehemiah

1.1	187, 190, 191
2.1	190

2.4	192	18	153	124	26
2.10	201	18.20–25	145	124.1–5	144
2.20	192	21	153	126–8	152
4.1 ff.	191, 192	22	153	130	147
5–6	191, 192	22.12	38	132	123, 134, 143,
7.4 f.	191	24	150		148
7.25 f.	190	29	150	132.11 ff.	123, 128
8.1	190	33	150	136	145
8.9	192	44	26	136.10 ff.	80
11.1 f.	191	46	125, 149, 153	144	153
13	191	46.7	119	145–150	150
		47	150 f.		
Job		48	125, 135, 149,	*Proverbs*	
3	164, 168		153	1–9	159
4.12 f.	162	48.2	33, 123	10.5	161
5.17 f.	163	50	151	13.4,7	161
6.1 f.	164	50.2	123	16.26	161
7.11 f.	164	50.3	140	20.4	161
8.5–7	161	51	147	22.17–24.22	
9.32 f.	164	65	152		159
10	164	66.6	80	24.27	161
11.7 f.	163	67–72	123	26.13,15,27	
11.13–19	161	68.15 f.	33		161
13.4	163	71.22	78	27.7	161
13.21–23	164	72	153	31.1–9	159
14.1 f.	164	74.12–17	149	31.10–31	160
16.12	164	75	151		
17.1 f.	164	76	125, 149	*Ecclesiastes*	
18.14–19	163	77.19 f.	80	1–3	167
19.6–9	165	78	123	3.17	169
19.14 f.	163	78.11 ff.	80	3.19–22	168
21.19	163	81	151	4.1–3	168
22.21–30	161	82	151	5.18 f.	167
23	165	84	145 f.	6.3–6	168
27.2–5	165	85.7–13	145	7	168
28	164	87	147	7.18	169
29.7	38	89	145, 153	8.5	169
30–31	163	89.12	33	8.10 f.	168
32–37	161	89.19–37	123	8.12 f.	169
35.12 f.	162	93	150	9.4 f	168
36.5 f.	162	93.4	144, 149	11.9	169
36.26	165	93.5	148, 151	12	168
38–41	161	95	151	12.12–14	169
40.15 f.	166	96–100	150		
42	161	100	26	*Isaiah*	
		101	145, 153	1–39	15
Psalms		103–4	150	1.2–20	131
2	153	104.7–9	149	1.4	78, 123
2.7	102	110	153	1.12–23	111
8	62	114.1 f.	144	2.2–4	126
15	146, 150	122	145	3.16 f.	110

5.8–12	110, 126
5.9,24	78
6	78, 123, 178
7	158
7.1–17	111, 124
8.5–8	124
9.1	35
9.2–7	126
10.5 f.	124
10.7–19	125
10.9	31
10.12	125
10.33 f.	125
11.1–9	126
14.13 ff.	33
14.24–26	125
17.12–14	125
27.8	36
28.1–8	110
29.5–8	125
29.13–16	111
31.4 f.	125
32.9–14	110
32.18	16
36–37	125
36.1	112
36.3	157
40–55	15, 173, 180 ff.
40.12 f.	164
41.2 f.	176, 180
41.8 f.	182
41.17–20	181
42.1–9	182
43.1 f.	176
43.15 ff.	181
44.6–8	84
44.21,26	182
45.1	84
45.1–13	176
46.1 f.	176
47	176, 180
49.1–6	182
49.3	182
50.4–9	182
51	181
52.13–53.12	182
55	182
56–66	15, 195
56.1–8	195
57.14–20	195
58	195
65.1–6	195

Jeremiah

1	78
1.4–10	127
1.5	132
1.11–16	127
2.1 ff.	128, 131
3.1–5	128
4.5–8	127
5.24	36
6.22 f.	127
7.1–20	128
11.21–23	168
12.1–6	128
12.5	34
13.1–11	178
14.11 f.	128
15	128
17.12–18	128
18.18–23	128
22.10–19	129
22.15 f.	113
24	173, 174
26–30	127, 128
26.16	120
26.18	127
27–28	129
29	173, 174
30–31	130
31–45	127
31.29	160
34.18 f.	72
35.6 ff.	37
36–39	158
36.11 f.	157
37.15 f.	157
38	130
38.6	36
39–44	173
40.1–12	130
42.1–17	130
43.5 ff.	200
43.8–13	130
44	175
49.19	34
52.28 ff.	174

Lamentations

2.5,7	130
4.20	130

Ezekiel

1–3	178
3–5	178
8	178
8.1	174
11.1–13	178
11.14–21	179
12.1–6	178
12.22	160
14.1	174
14.4,20	205
16	179
16.44	160
18	179
18.2	160
20.1–44	179
23	179
28.3	205
28.14,16	33
30.1 ff.	174
33.1–9	178
33.10–20	179
40–48	54 f., 175
40.1 ff.	178
43.8	39

Daniel

1–7	206
8	197, 206, 206
9	206 f.
10	197, 207
11	200, 207
11.15–17	200
11.25 ff.	202

Hosea

1–3	120
1.1	120
1.3–11	121
1.4	109
2	37, 50, 121, 131
2.2,7	120, 131
2.8	121
2.14 ff.	122
3.1 ff.	120, 122
4.1 ff.	50, 121, 122
5.1 ff.	121, 123
6.6	122
6.8 ff.	121 ff.

7.4	121
7.14 ff.	122
8.4	123
8.12	121
9.1,10	121
9.6	121, 122
10.3,7,15	123
10.5	107, 122
11.1 ff.	80, 122
12.4	71
13.1	121
13.2	107, 122
13.10 f.	123

Joel
1.6	196
1.13 f.	195
2.2–11	196
2.12–17	195
2.20 ff.	196

Amos
1.1	118, 119
2.6–8	110, 119
2.10	80
3.2	120
3.9	119

4.1–3	110, 118, 122
4.12	131
5.2	118
5.4 f.	119
5.10–13	119
5.18–20	120
5.21–24	111, 119, 120
6.7 f.	118
7.1–6	119
7.7–9	118, 119
7.8	121
7.10–17	118, 120, 121
8.1	121
8.1–3	119
8.2	118
9.1–4	119

Obadiah
1–21	183

Jonah
4.1 f.	196
4.8	36

Micah
1–3	126
2	110, 126
2.2	38

3.5–8	126
3.9–12	111, 127
4.1–4	126
6.1–5	131
6.6–8	146

Haggai
1.2	188
1.6	188
1.11 ff.	189
2.1–13	189
2.6–9	188
2.18	188, 196
2.21–23	188, 189
3–4	189
8.9–13	189

Zechariah
1–8	186, 189, 190, 196
7.1 f.	147
14.16 f.	137

Malachi
1.6 ff.	136, 197
2.5–7	146
2.13–4.6	197

APOCRYPHA

II Esdras
3–14	208

Judith
4.12	207

Wisdom
2–3	208
7.21 ff.	208
9.1,17	208
16.12	208
18.18 f.	208

Ecclesiasticus
37.16–39.11	207
50	143, 207

Baruch
4–6	208

I Maccabees
1.11	202
1.44 ff.	202, 207
1.54	202
1.63	202
2.1–48	203
2.60	207
3.10–4.35	203
5	203
6.5	203
6.28–47	207
7	204
9	204
11.67	34
13.41 f.	204

14.36	202
16.11–22	204

II Maccabees
1.18 f.	207
2.19–32	207
3	201
4.9	202
4.12 ff.	201, 203
4.21 ff.	202
5.22 ff.	202
6.1 ff.	202
7	207
10.1 ff.	207
15	204
15.36	207